Houston, Tx 77079

# Mummies of the Pharaohs

The Present Work is a translation from the French:

"Les Momies des Pharaons et la Médecine. Ramsès II à Paris
Le Pharaon et Moïse"
Librairie Séguier, Paris, 1987
by Alastair D. Pannell and the Author

The French edition won a 1988 History Prize from the Académie
Française

## By the Same Author

*The Bible, the Qur'an and Science*

FRENCH EDITION:
Seghers, Paris
Fourteenth Edition, 1989
Golden Book Award, 1986

ENGLISH EDITION:
Seghers, Paris, Sixth Edition, 1989

OTHER EDITIONS available in:
Arabic, Turkish, Serbo-Croatian, Indonesian, Urdu, Persian,
German, Gujarati, Bengali

*What Is the Origin of Man?*
*The Answers of Science and the Holy Scriptures*

FRENCH EDITION:
Seghers, Paris
Third Edition, 1989

ENGLISH EDITION:
Seghers, Paris, Fourth Edition, 1988

OTHER EDITIONS available in:
Arabic, Turkish, Indonesian

# MUMMIES
## *of the*
# PHARAOHS

---

*Modern Medical Investigations*

Dr. Maurice Bucaille

Translated from the French by

Alastair D. Pannell
and
the Author

St. Martin's Press

New York

*Production Editor: David Stanford Burr*

*Design by Susan Hood*

**Library of Congress Cataloging-in-Publication Data**

Bucaille, Maurice.
   Mummies of the Pharaohs : modern medical investigations / by Maurice Bucaille.
      p.    cm.
   ISBN 0-312-05131-X
    1. Mummies—Egypt. 2. Diseases—Egypt—History. 3. Pharaohs.
I. Title.
DT62.M7B78   1990
932—dc20                               90-37420
                                                        CIP

First Edition: December 1990

10 9 8 7 6 5 4 3 2 1

# Contents

# CONTENTS

Photographs appear between pages 140 and 141.

# Introduction

On September 26, 1976, the mummy of the pharaoh Ramesses II arrived at Le Bourget Airport in France. It had been transported by the French air force from Cairo to Paris and received full military honors upon its arrival. The solemn character of the reception marked the unique journey, for it was indeed the first time that a royal mummy had ever left Egypt—and, more important, Ramesses II was its magnificent pharaoh.

The event aroused international interest. A few months earlier, the Paris opening of an exhibition on Ramesses II had already reawakened the keen French public interest in Egyptology. This time, however, it was the mummified remains of the pharaoh himself. The intention was not, as had once been the plan, to put the mummy on display. The purpose was to allow the remains of the pharaoh, who had wanted his body to be preserved by mummification, to be examined through the advantages of modern science.

From the beginning, it was understood that this examination was the purpose of Ramesses II's stay in Paris, where the mummy was "hospitalized" in a laboratory at the Museum of Anthropology (Musée de l'Homme). "Operation Ramesses" lasted almost eight months and was directed by Christiane Desroches-Noblecourt, curator of Egyptian Antiquities at the Louvre, and by Professor Lionel Balout, Director of the Museum of Anthropology. There appears to be no other example of an enterprise involving so many specialized disciplines and mounted on such a vast scale in a museum. Not a single university professor of Egyptology participated in it. This immediately leads one to ask why the Egyptian authorities chose France. There were clearly other countries with eminent well-equipped specialists and with considerable financial resources that would not have hesitated to include experts in such an operation, an operation that was bound to bring recognition to the nation organizing it. Moreover, the first journey of a pharaoh outside Egypt—Ramesses II, the most famous of all—was regarded as a signal honor bestowed on France.

Enterprises of this nature are brought about by factors that history only partially reveals—if at all. It occasionally happens that those who originate a project are taken by surprise when their initial actions come to fruition. This, I think, is more or less what happened with Operation Ramesses. When I went to Egypt for the first time, there was not a single harbinger that might have helped me foresee the developments that were to follow.

It all began roughly two years before the mummy of Ramesses II arrived in Paris. I had journeyed to Egypt during the second half of 1974 in search of various archeological and medical data concerning certain pharaohs. In particular, I was after documents pertaining to the Exodus. My intention was to compare certain passages in the Bible and in the Qur'an with the information provided by Egyptian archeology. (This general study has now appeared in my book *The Bible, the Qur'an and Science*. Seghers, Paris, 1988.)

As far as the pharaonic mummies were concerned, I was particularly interested in the mummy of Merneptah, son and successor of Ramesses II. My studies indicate that he was the pharaoh of the Exodus who lost his life during the pursuit of the fleeing Hebrews.

At first, I was of course fascinated by the outward appearance of both pharaohs when I entered the Mummies Room of the Egyptian Museum in Cairo in 1974. In those days, the Mummies Room was open to visitors—but by 1979 it was closed to the public: The Paris rescue operation had failed and the remains of Ramesses II could no longer be put on display. This event was subsequently followed by the removal of all the royal mummies from public exhibition. (There is now hope, however, that they will again go on display, thanks to the current Getty Conservation Institute project.)

The only parts of the body of Ramesses II visible to visitors in 1974 were the head and the left hand, the rest being draped with coarse linen not unlike burlap. The mummy was lying supine in an open coffin (see Fig. 3), visible through the glass sides of a rectangular display case with a removable glass cover.

My guide told me that in his opinion these conditions of preservation were excellent, for they allowed the glass cover to be slid upward so that the mummy could be sprayed with insecticide. This process was considered the best for preserving the mummies and avoiding contamination. I later had occasion to witness the procedure, which involved the use of an antiquated spray gun of a type I remember being used some sixty years earlier. Witnessing the scene brought to mind Ramesses II and the other pharaohs, who in their day enjoyed the scents of the "sacred" fragrances. These were reserved exclusively for the pharaoh-god and were ceremoniously wafted through the air by servants. I then thought of the same pharaohs being subjected to a cloud of chemical spray usually reserved for flies. How the mighty had fallen!

Remains of wrappings could be seen on Ramesses' left hand and fingers. The nails appeared very long, most likely due to the phenomenon of continued growth after death. The nails had in all probability been colored with henna. The sight of the hand, a symbol of power and force, led me to imagine Ramesses II as a young sovereign and warrior during the first twenty years of his long reign of just over sixty-seven years. I remembered a picture I had seen of the famous bas-relief in the temple of Abu Simbel. The carving shows the young king riding his horse-drawn chariot while holding a spear in his hand and doing battle with the Hittites.

My thoughts then turned to more peaceful scenes and most of my attention was devoted to the head (see Fig. 3). I noticed that the pharaoh's forehead was studded with small brownish tumors (which dermatologists later diagnosed as senile comedones), but what struck me most were the mummy's closed eyelids, indicating that embalmers had removed the eyes. Those eyes had enabled one of antiquity's greatest sovereigns to see one of the greatest figures of religious history—Moses. Moses was one of the very rare people to have received directly from God a communication concerning orders for all of humanity, a teaching that is found in the sacred doctrines of Jews, Christians, and Muslims alike. Having looked at those closed eyelids, I was certain beyond the shadow of a doubt that Ramesses II knew Moses personally. For at that time both Moses and the pharaoh were young men, and Moses resided at the Egyptian king's court, where he was raised as an Egyptian prince. There came a time, however, when Ramesses II learned that Moses had suddenly vanished from the country. The Bible tells us that Moses went to live in the land of Midian, and that after a long reign, Pharaoh died while Moses was still living in Midian. In the presence of the remains of one who had in all likelihood participated in one of the great events of ancient history, how could one not be deeply moved?

In piecing together the history of Moses, I examined the mummy of Ramesses II's thirteenth son and successor, Merneptah. Because of their difference in age, I am reasonably certain that

Merneptah could not have known Moses before he went to Midian. Most likely, Merneptah met Moses when he returned to Egypt and requested permission for his enslaved brethren to leave the country, and having turned down Moses' request, Merneptah probably was the pharaoh on whom the plagues described in the Holy Scriptures were inflicted. When Moses subsequently led the flight of the Hebrews from Egypt in the Exodus, it was undoubtedly Merneptah who pursued them at the head of his army and lost his life.

In order to gain more knowledge about Ramesses II's family, I visited the mummy of Sethos I (see Fig. 31), the father of Ramesses II, which lay nearby. The black color of the mummy is due to the resin used for mummification. In 1974, I was under the impression that Sethos I, the grandfather of the pharaoh of the Exodus (Merneptah), could not have known the young Moses either. Today, however, recent excavations at the site of the Northern capital city built for Ramesses II have indicated that the building of the city was begun near the end of Sethos I's reign, at a time when Ramesses II held the monarchic regency. Since the Bible states that Moses was born at the time the enslaved Hebrews were building the city, it is possible that Sethos I may have known Moses while he was still a child, in the early thirteenth century B.C.

It was an impressive sight to see the twenty-seven royal mummies several millennia after their death, preserved to this day despite the very poor conditions of conservation. Several kinds of studies had already been devoted to the mummies. I knew for example that Marc A. Ruffer had carried out extremely useful research in Egypt at the beginning of the twentieth century, involving the microscopic examination of mummified tissues. In addition, many radiologists from all over the world had collected extremely interesting findings, and many prints of their X rays are displayed to the public on the walls of the Royal Mummies Room in the Egyptian Museum in Cairo. The purpose of my own project was to examine the possibilities of making new discoveries and to extend the research to branches of medicine that had not yet been included. The research was to focus on the remains of pharaohs who may have reigned while Moses was alive (up to the end of the thirteenth century B.C.) and in particular on the mummies of two pharaohs: Merneptah, who died in pursuit of the Hebrews (research in the field of forensic medicine was to prove of great value in determining the cause of his death); and Ramesses II, thought by many Biblical scholars to have been the pharaoh of the Exodus. It seemed to me that the experts' arguments were weak in terms of factual evidence and that precise data on the condition of the pharaoh at the end of his life could cast light on the matter, providing indisputable evidence.

During my first visit to the Royal Mummies Room, I wondered whether or not my plans for this research would lead to positive findings, and whether I would be able to effectively justify the confidence the Egyptian authorities had placed in my project. My access to the Egyptian Museum in Cairo, where the study was to be carried out, was due to President Sadat, who had given orders that I was to be allowed to perform any type of research I wanted, providing of course that no damage was done to any of the mummified bodies. In my own country, I was not officially entitled to carry out such research, nor was any endorsement given to me by the French government or a university. My presence at the museum, where I was very kindly granted every possible facility for research, was uniquely the result of personally contacting certain people. My initial contact was Mrs. Sadat, whom I knew through my medical practice. Her family had greatly honored me with its confidence after the successful treatment (in collaboration with fellow practitioners in Paris) of a family member.

I took the opportunity of informing Mrs. Sadat of my conclusions regarding the likelihood that a particular pharaoh may have taken part in the Exodus. At that time, however, my theories were supported merely by data drawn from my study of history, archeology, and hieroglyphic texts. On my first visit to the Royal Mummies Room, I remembered my talks in Paris with Egypt's First Lady, and her kind attention to them. Once again, she honored me with her confidence by agreeing to present a request to President Sadat. With extreme gratitude, I later paid a visit to the President himself. Today, as in 1974, I still cannot adequately express the great debt I owe Mrs. Sadat and the late president.

Following my first visit to the Royal Mummies Room, I moved quickly to establish the best possible conditions for the research project. During a subsequent stay in Cairo, in order to perform special medical investigations, I was accompanied by Professor Michel Durigon, a French colleague and specialist in forensic medicine invited by the Egyptian government at my request. During my first visit in 1974, however, I relied on the help of fellow practitioners who were to be recruited in Cairo. Of these, the radiologist and the endoscopist (a specialist in the visual examination of the inside of bodies) were of particular importance. Thanks to the kind assistance of Professor K. Kassem and the general at the Navy Medical Corps—Al Chiaty—doctor in chief at the Al Maadiy Hospital in Cairo, I was put in touch with Professors R. El Meligiy and Mustapha Manialawiy. Both professors immediately agreed to collaborate with me on the research project. Without their kind contribution, the first and basic research could not have been carried out as quickly as was needed. Finally, I am greatly indebted to all of my collaborators, from both Egypt and France, for the success of that venture.

In all, there were ten doctors and dentists engaged in the primary investigations. An expanded field of study led by such experts allowed us to make certain discoveries that cast new light on a variety of old questions pertaining to Pharaoh Merneptah, in particular the visible lacuna in his skull. Also included in our study was the mummy of Ramesses II.

The general findings of these studies are well known within the medical profession, and the final reports were read before various scholarly and professional societies, of which the most important was the French National Academy of Medicine on February 17, 1976. Also included were the French Society of Radiology and the French Society of Forensic Medicine. The medical profession was perfectly well informed and up-to-date concerning the work that had been carried out in Egypt during 1974 and 1975. The mummy of Ramesses II arrived in Paris in September 1976 and when it entered the Museum of Anthropology in 1976 those concerned knew perfectly well that its trip to Paris was the direct result of the work carried out by French and Egyptian doctors.

I cannot overemphasize the important part played by those who resolved major problems in arranging the date and conditions of transportation to Paris of the pharaoh. It is nevertheless very clear from Egyptian documents that most of the important work had already been done, and all that remained for others, if I may so phrase it, was to jump on the bandwagon that had been initiated earlier by those responsible for the initial medical work in Egypt.

Our earlier studies had already shown that the mummy of Ramesses II, and likewise other pharaonic mummies, had suffered serious damage before the bodies of numerous kings were discovered in the necropolis at Thebes nearly a century ago. In the case of Ramesses II, the damage was twofold: first structural, the extent of which had already been determined by X rays; and secondly biological, the causes of which had already been discovered as well.

The Egyptian authorities were informed of these two factors the moment the observations were first made. I discussed these problems several times during my talks with President Sadat and those around him. On January 23, 1976, in a declaration made to the Cairo newspaper *Al Ahram*, Sadat noted how he had described to President Giscard d'Estaing, during his visit to Egypt a few weeks earlier, the work I had carried out with my collaborators on the mummy of the pharaohs in the Cairo Museum. It was at that time that President Sadat announced his decision to entrust the mummy of Ramesses II to France. He asked me personally to announce the measures that needed to be taken to rescue the other deteriorating mummies after Ramsesses' stay in Paris.

The Franco-Egyptian studies I was involved in were strictly of a medical nature. No specialist from a French museum, no museum authority or head of department, was at any time actively involved in them. This is why those who were later to take over Operation Ramesses II in Paris were so interested in our studies. Christiane Desroches-Noblecourt invited me to give her a detailed account of our studies before the Department of Egyptian Antiquities at the Louvre in autumn of 1975. Professor Balout suggested that I present my findings in May 1976 in two lectures given at the Institute of Human Paleontology of which he was then head. These museum specialists wanted, not unnaturally, to know the results of our various investigations carried out on several royal mummies: it simply wasn't their expertise. In the case of Ramesses II, they were desperate, because of his fame, to find out our medical diagnosis.

I was dismayed to hear subsequent interpretations of certain investigations carried out on Ramesses II at the Museum of Anthropology that do not appear to be correct. I shall not at this time go into the copious and varied information, which was to me of a whimsical nature, that was once bandied about, but I shall try to confine myself only to what appeared in print. One published account claimed, for example, that through the use of X rays it was possible to ascertain that the heart of Ramesses II, which many believed had been removed, was indeed present in the thoracic cavity, and that the presence of tobacco in the mummy's abdomen was proof that this plant was used by the ancient Egyptians. The latter was in fact a contradiction to the theories held before the traces of tobacco were found in Ramesses II.

The main conclusions of the documents were published in French and foreign journals and reviews of various learned societies before they were brought to the attention of many people in the medical profession. These documents later became the subject of various lectures given in several countries.

To make it easier to understand the problems we shall be dealing with later, I will explore in the chapters that follow certain general points concerning mummification—first, the preservation of the bodies, and second, their insulation in tombs—and what became of certain bodies, including the processes involved in the modern discovery of mummies, such as the tragedy, perhaps, from the point of view of conservation, of unwrapping and displaying the bodies without appropriate precautions, particularly in the case of Tutankhamun. Such precautions might have prevented the bodies from becoming contaminated. I will then turn to the medical studies of the mummies. A doctor's inspection of them can tell us about the diseases or wounds the subject suffered during life through the application of modern medical techniques such as microscopic examination of mummified tissues; X-ray studies; and endoscopic exploration, a method permitting the investigator to examine and photograph the interior of certain cavities inside the body.

One medical phenomenon will be treated in particular depth: the cranial lacunae found in certain mummies, and how their examination sheds light on the cause of death of Pharaoh Merneptah, who is thought to be the king who perished during the Exodus of the Bible.

Finally, I shall return to Operation Ramesses to provide more details on the points mentioned earlier, to which I take exception, and to stress how very regrettable it is that certain, perfectly feasible, precautions had not been undertaken.

Throughout the research carried out in Cairo, my personal relations with the Egyptian authorities were consistently marked by a spirit of warm and friendly collaboration. In particular, I would like to express my sincere gratitude to Dr. Gamal Mokhtar, President of Egyptian Antiquities at the time of the studies. Thanks to him, the task of the French and Egyptian doctors was made considerably easier. He encouraged us in our research and even asked us to carry out additional investigations that were not included in the project—to wit, the examination of the mummy of Ramesses II.

I owe a great debt to all the specialists and to the dentists who collaborated with me. Our research involved a number of different disciplines and required the participation of many people. The first I called upon were my Egyptian colleagues: radiologists and endoscopists who eagerly carried out the investigations I assigned to them. I also enlisted the help of various specialists from Paris. It is the excellence of the contributions made by every one of them that enables me to present a highly documented study.

This study also illustrates what can happen when one begins a research study with a definite object in mind but discovers, as one goes along, that one has quite unintentionally stumbled on some completely unforeseen path. This is exactly what happened to me. As I mentioned earlier, when I commenced studying the mummy of Merneptah in 1974, my objective was confined to seeking data that would cast new light on some of the historical questions surrounding the Exodus. I was trying to situate the Exodus in relation to the pharaoh mentioned in the narrations of the Holy Scriptures. This material was to be included in a chapter of my book *The Bible, the Qur'an and Science*. At that point, I had absolutely no intention of carrying out research on the mummies on any wider scale. Furthermore there was nothing to indicate the bearing that this enterprise would have on the mummy of Ramesses II. However, the study of Merneptah's mummy led to that of Ramesses II's, chiefly as a result of a request made to me by Dr. Gamal Mokhtar, President of Egyptian Antiquities. He wanted me to repeat for Ramesses II the work my collaborators and I had carried out on Merneptah. Dr. Mokhtar explained that he had received a request from Christiane Desroches-Noblecourt, Director of the Department of Egyptian Antiquities at the Louvre, who was organizing an exhibition in Paris the following year on the "Era of Ramesses II." Desroches-Noblecourt wished to have the pharaoh's mummy transported to France for display along with other objects from the Egyptian Museum in Cairo. But because there had been no detailed scientific study performed on the state of the mummy, Dr. Mokhtar felt one would have to be made before her request could be considered.

With the help of three Egyptian colleagues, whose aid I enlisted, I set to work on investigations identical to those carried out on the mummy of Merneptah. I employed the use of X rays and endoscopic explorations in particular. When we had finished our examination and it came time to inform the Egyptian authorities of our conclusions, we placed particular emphasis on the serious deterioration of the mummy. It was then and only then that the Egyptians began acting on these discoveries.

Throughout the long winter months of 1975–1976 in Paris, it was generally expected that the mummy of the pharaoh would be part of the exhibition due to open at the Grand Palais in May. A few weeks before the exhibition opened, however, President Giscard d'Estaing finally decided to abandon his request that Egypt send Ramesses II's mummy.

When Ramesses II finally *was* transported in September 1976, it was not to go to Paris to be put on display. He went there for treatment as part of the rescue operation, which was based on the guidelines established in my earlier medical investigations that Egyptian authorities held in high regard. In contrast, the results of what was undertaken in Paris by the museum specialists were very poorly received when the mummy arrived back in Cairo: The Egyptians were unable to display the mummy because of the conditions in which it had been transported back to Cairo by Professor Balout, supervised by Desroches-Noblecourt.

Some of the data that surround the investigations dealt with in this book are no doubt complex. I hope that I have been able to present them in as clear and simple a manner as possible. My aim in describing them is to inform the general public how, after several thousand years, modern investigations finally allow us to cast an extremely impressive light on our past.

The French edition of the present work was published in November 1987. It was ten years in the making—ten years during which the original investigations performed in 1974–1975 have gradually been completed by further information gathered from the execution and far-reaching results of Operation Ramesses II in Paris. My wish has been to set forth these findings with the distance appropriate to an objective study on a controversial subject, especially because from one year to the next, the failure of the operation has become increasingly clear.

Since I also wished to have the findings brought to the attention of a wide readership, it seemed useful to also produce an English version of the work. Having translated two of my previous works, Mr. Alastair D. Pannell has during all these years collaborated with me on the production of a text that on several occasions has been enriched with new information. I would like to express my warmest appreciation and thanks for his patient and meticulous work.

In 1985 a book entitled *La Momie de Ramsès II (The Mummy of Ramesses II)* was published in France under the supervision of museum specialists who attached little importance to medical data. On examining the work, I thought it necessary to delve more deeply into what actually had become of the mummy of the pharaoh and expose the obvious untruths proclaimed in the book. Hence the decision to turn my notes into a finished work, which resulted in the publication of a French edition of the present volume.

For the English version I was hoping to publish, it would have been impossible to find more far-sighted and considerate champions for my cause than Mr. and Mrs. Gerard Hamon, to whom I wish to express my most profound gratitude. To Mrs. Lana Hamon, I would like to convey my particular thanks for the perseverence, thoughtfulness, and deft touch she brought to the task of locating a publisher.

Through Mrs. Hamon, I was able to find in Mr. Jim Fitzgerald, senior editor at St. Martin's Press, a person who impressed me from the moment we first met. I realized that he had immediately grasped the medical, historical, and religious significance of the subjects examined. I want to express my great indebtedness to Miss Kara J. Leverte who edited this book.

I would like to express my thanks to the Department of Egyptian Antiquities and the Egyptian Museum in Cairo, for their special permission to take photographs, as well as to the Griffith Institute at Oxford University, Professor R. G. Harrison in Liverpool, and the late F. Filce Leek, for their kind authorization to publish several documents.

Unless otherwise stated, the photographs and X rays were taken by the author or his collaborators. Those taken by Elliot Smith are reproduced from his book of 1912, *The Royal Mummies*, in the general catalogue of the Egyptian Museum in Cairo.

*Part I*

—

# FROM
# EMBALMER
# TO
# EGYPTOLOGIST

# 1. Mummification

The ancient Egyptians held certain beliefs about the afterlife that led them to take every precaution to ensure that the deceased's appearance resembled (as closely as possible) his appearance during life. This was the *sine qua non* condition for eternal life. They also felt obliged to provide him with the various objects he needed during his earthly life. Thus the tombs contained a plethora of objects as reminders of life on earth.

It is thought to be at about the time of the Fourth Dynasty (around 2600 B.C.) that the Egyptians began to embalm and mummify. It was not until much later, however, during the New Kingdom (after 1580 B.C.), that mummification attained its highest degree of perfection. The records of formal embalmment rituals, with precise descriptions of the various stages of the operations, date from this later period. It was a long and delicate process, performed by remarkably skilled experts.

There exist a number of bodies found in a state of preservation that is quite impressive, considering the number of years that have elapsed since the ancient Egyptians. The most complete and oldest mummy known at present would appear to be that of Merenre I, from the Sixth Dynasty. I photographed it in 1975 at the Egyptian Museum in Cairo (Fig. 1). The mummy unfortunately had been preserved in such appalling conditions that it was already in a state of decomposition. I have good reason to believe that this decomposing persists today, and that it has not been treated and therefore the mummy is likely to deteriorate even further.

Whereas mummification was a very crude art during the early dynasties, the New Kingdom saw the arrival of a highly accomplished technical process. The largest number of best-preserved mummies date from this period.

The places where embalmment took place were attached to necropolises which, in the case of the kings, were raised to the rank of temples. Explorations in these areas have revealed sophisticated equipment, among which we find operating tables made of wood or stone, with grooves to drain off liquids. They were specially designed for the extraction of viscera, in particular the entrails and the brain of the deceased. There were also other special tables, such as royal ceremonial beds, exclusively used for the winding of the wrappings.

To be successful, embalmment had to be performed very soon after death. The organs that tended to putrefy early had to be removed from the body first, especially those contained in the abdomen, thorax, and cranial cavity. The operations involved in the removal of the viscera, or internal organs, were generally performed through an orifice made in the left side of the lower abdomen. Great skill and adroitness were required to remove all the abdominal and thoracic viscera through the incision made in the abdominal wall (Fig. 2). Procedures gradually changed, however: the bladder might or might not be left in place, whereas the kidneys often were. To gain access to the thorax, the embalmers passed through the diaphragm, which separates the abdominal and thoracic cavities. In doing this they were able to reach as far as the neck to remove the lungs and the esophagus. The heart was either left in place or removed and placed in a canopic jar, or removed and replaced in the thorax after treatment with embalmment resins.

The technique the embalmers used for the brain was extraordinarily skillful for the time. It was removed through the nose, leaving the deceased's face totally unharmed. For example, no damage was done to Ramesses II (Fig. 3) by the removal of the brain, nor is there any sign of injury whatsoever to the face of the mummy. I found embalmment instruments (Fig. 4) on display at the Egyptian Museum, many of which were hooks, scalpels, or scoops, used by the embalmers to break up the brain and extract it piece by piece. A high-pressure irrigation system was employed to force the shredded pieces of brain out of the cranial cavity. What is remarkable is that the embalmers performed their operations by sheer trial and error. They did not have our contemporary knowledge of anatomy, but they were nevertheless able to find the passage of least resistance for penetrating the skull without harming the face: they went through the weakest point in the floor of the cranial cavity, which is the ceiling of the nasal cavities. Modern anatomy labels this the lamina cribriformis of the ethmoid bone. In 1975 we were able to perform the first of many other endoscopic investigations on the skull of the mummy of Ramesses V. By introducing an endoscope into the skull, it was possible to examine and photograph this orifice (Fig. 5).

Other routes may have also been used to gain access to the cranial cavity. Because the subject's eyes were also removed (occasionally replaced by delicately painted artificial ones), it was also possible to remove parts of the brain by pushing in the ceiling of the eye socket. There are also instances where removal of the brain was performed by decapitation or by perforating the cranial vault. The latter may have been used by the embalmers to provide an additional orifice, enabling them to perfect their process of embalmment. This is probably the case for Ramesses V, whose body exhibits both the customary ethmoid orifice and the additional perforation of the cranial vault (figure 6).

This technique of removal, which was probably reserved for the mummification of persons of great rank, was completed by the cleansing of the cranial cavity and the introduction of a resinous liquid into the space formerly occupied by the brain. This liquid would subsequently solidify. In the case of several pharaonic mummies—Ramesses II, for example (Fig. 7)—X rays of the skull show the presence of this resinous material. For Ramesses V, the cranial cavity was stuffed with a strip of cloth, approximately one-and-one-half inches wide and ten yards long. (It was extracted from the skull when the wrappings of the mummy were removed.)

After all the surgical procedures had been performed, the body was carefully washed. Palm wine was frequently used in this process: it had a high alcohol content, of about fourteen percent and might therefore have had a mildly antiseptic effect. Next, the hollow organs of the digestive tract were emptied of their contents, carefully washed, then dehydrated by use of natron salts. Once the body had been relieved of its other putrescible viscera, it too underwent a dehydration process. It was buried under a pile of natron salts, which absorbed the water from the tissues. The mixture of the natron salts and the water drawn from the tissue, which flowed out of the body, was drained by the sloping bed on which the corpse lay. This dehydration process is thought to have lasted forty days.

The salt used in this process was extremely precious and was extracted from deposits left by the dried lakes in the Natron Valley (known in Arabic as *Wadi Natroun*). The salt itself was a mixture of various salts, with a predominance of carbonate, bicarbonate, chloride, and sodium sulfate. The carbonate would literally pump the water out of the body and in the process remove the fats from the tissues. The salts also caused skin burns. The epidermis, or outer layer of skin, is generally absent from mummified skin for this reason. This was shown by an initial microscopic examination and was again evident when checked by our team of collaborators. However, the epidermis may possibly have been detached from the body when the wrappings were removed.

While the body lay on a bed of dry natron, bags of natron salts were introduced into the trunk to absorb liquids and fats. Sawdust was also added, along with various elements of vegetation, such as lichens. Microscopic traces of these vegetable elements were found on fragments from the inside of the body of the subject. This was the case for Ramesses IV.

This dehydration process of forty days is a period of time mentioned in the Bible. Jacob, father of Joseph, most probably came to Egypt in the seventeeth century B.C. and subsequently died there. He was embalmed in Egypt and, as we read in the Revised Standard Version of the Bible (Genesis 50: 1–3): "Then Joseph fell on his father's face, and wept over him, and kissed him. And Joseph commanded his servants the physicians to embalm his father. So the physicians embalmed Israel; forty days were required for it, for so many are required for embalming. And the Egyptians wept for him seventy days." Furthermore, because the Bible mentions that physicians were expected to perform this task, one may suppose, therefore, that at the time they could very easily have become the *ad hoc* embalmers. Israel is the name given to Jacob by God after his struggle with the Angel. The descendants of Jacob-Israel kept the second name in memory of their great ancestor.

I may be right in assuming that out of the seventy days used in the mummification rite, according to Egyptian texts, the last thirty were devoted to all types of practices and ceremonies subsequent to dehydration. Before describing this process, however, I shall return for a moment to the viscera.

Once the viscera had been dehydrated with the natron salts, they were either stored in funeral jars or replaced, partially or totally, in the subject's body. They were coated with a perfumed oil, after renewed cleansing, and then covered in a melted resinous substance. Great emphasis was given, during the ritual of embalmment, to the treatment of the viscera. They had to be carefully wrapped and placed in containers. There usually were four of them, called canopic jars. Each lid represented the head of one of the sons of Horus, the deity who protected the entrails. It is said that each of them had a specific function for the respective organ they protected; the intestines, liver, stomach, and lungs were thus under the protection of their appropriate deity. During the Middle Kingdom period, the jars were placed in a funeral box, separate from the sarcophagus. For the poor, the jars were made of clay, but for the pharaohs they were made mostly of alabaster and decorated with gold and precious stones. Those belonging to Tutankhamun are very well known. For over three thousand years a statue of Anubis, the god of mummification, watched over them.

When the mummified organs that had been protected in this manner were discovered and placed in the hands of the experts, they became the subject of extremely interesting research studies. Marc A. Ruffer, a scientist working in Alexandria before World War I, when examining mummified tissues under his microscope, recognized and identified extremely clear features of these visceral organs—even to the degree of recognizing certain illnesses. Drawings made at the time (color photography had been invented by then, but Ruffer did not have it at his disposal) show the perfect preservation of these organs. Along with certain other details seen through his microscope, the results are very similar to what may be found today on a freshly taken sample of tissue. I shall later describe the remarkable results obtained in Paris by my collaborators who were specialists in this field and examined the mummified tissues that I brought back from Egypt in 1974 and 1975.

Although the embalmers in some cases replaced the viscera in the body, they did so without any regard to their correct anatomical location. An abdominal organ might well have been resituated in the thorax. The organs, nevertheless, were always very carefully wrapped, sometimes with votive statuettes, as Ruffer exhibited in his drawings of a mummified liver.

Once the body cavities had been emptied of their organs, they were washed with palm wine and stuffed with cloth and various substances to fill the vacuum left by the viscera. I mentioned earlier that resin was placed in the cranial cavity and then it was sometimes stuffed with cloth. In the case of the trunk however, apart from the organs that may have been replaced in it, many different materials such as sawdust, sand, natron salts, myrrh, various resins, and spices, onions, lichens, and other forms of vegetation were used. The trunks of the mummies we have examined today are either wholly or partially filled in this way. Precious objects such as amulets adorned with gems were also left inside the body. Ancient tomb robbers and modern treasure seekers have removed most of the contents of the trunk. The abdomen of Ramesses II is today completely empty of the various objects originally placed there. The thorax, however, still contains the organs and various materials used for stuffing. It is impossible to gain access to the thorax because a solid wall of resin blocks the entrance to it through the abdomen.

Abdominal orifices, which allowed the embalmers to remove the viscera, were in some cases sewn up, and in others, blocked with a plug made of cloth soaked in resinous paste and wax. It was covered with a plaque fashioned in wax or precious metal and sometimes engraved with an effigy of the eye of Horus. Unfortunately, in the vast majority of mummies, the hand of man (whether ancient or modern) has not left them untouched. Where a plug of gold should have been there is often nothing left but a gaping hole. This is the case with Ramesses II (Fig. 2). For him, the Eye of Horus was unable to ward off tomb robbers.

Before enveloping the body in wrappings, embalmers performed various operations on it. Eyes were dried with natron salts or removed. In their place we found either painted false eyes or a simple plug of material soaked in wax and resin. The eyelids and the area where the eyebrows had been were painted. There is little doubt that the faces of Ramesses V and Merneptah were treated in this way. The same holds true for both the fingernails and toenails, which were painted with henna. The external genital organs in the male were sometimes removed completely (Ramesses II) or partially, as in the case of Merneptah (Fig. 8), the son of Ramesses II. Only a segment of the penis of Merneptah has been preserved. For women, the procedure was to remove the internal genital organs.

The embalmers were careful to reconstitute cavities that had subsided such as those of the mouth and nose. They wanted to make the subject look as natural as possible. This was done by stuffing them with cloth, wax, or resin. Resin was inserted while still hot to plug up winding or sinuous parts. The resin was extracted from a type of wood called *ash*, found in Syria. Years later, embalmers used bitumen. It seems that it is from this word that the term mummy was derived, for the Persian word for bitumen is *mummia*.

The skin color of the mummies varies according to whether or not the paint used to adorn the body is still present. It also depends on the coat of resin applied to the corpse before it was enveloped in wrappings. Tuthmosis II appears totally black, although this was not the natural color of the skin. It is also possible to observe on the same mummy spotted variations in color: in one place the skin covered in a thin coating of transparent resin retains its normal shade; in another it is darker, for the skin has in fact disappeared and what we are looking at is bare muscle. The mummy thought to be that of Queen Twosret (Fig. 9), a daughter of Ramesses II, provides an example of this peculiarity.

At a later period, embalmers were so eager to make the deceased's exterior form look as much like it had been during his life that they refined their techniques to such an extent that various substances were inserted under the skin, including cloth, sand, and sawdust. The method used to insert these materials was to make appropriate incisions keeping the body looking as aesthetically acceptable as possible. What amazed all of us was the consummate skill of the embalmers in the way in which they succeeded in slipping their hand through the evisceration orifice in the left flank made to remove viscera up as far as the neck and down as far as the lower limbs and knees. This enabled them, with the aid of instruments, to stuff the thighs. With the feet and upper limbs however, they were still obliged to make incisions.

The posture of the mummy was of great importance. First, the deceased's arms were laid alongside his body. During the Eighteenth Dynasty, they were crossed over the chest or thorax, with the hands at varying distances from the shoulders. This is the posture in which we find the most famous mummies of the New Kingdom, from those named Amenophis to those called Ramesses. Later on, the customs changed several times according to the period.

The final stage in the long operation designed to preserve the body was its envelopment in wrappings. These varied in quality: those of the finest quality were made of linen and were actually in contact with the body itself. Wrappings made of coarser linen were placed over these. In the case of the pharaohs, items of jewelery, rings, necklaces, bracelets, earrings, plaques, and all kinds of amulets were included within the wrappings. The mummy of Tutankhamun contained 143 such items. The wrappings were soaked in liquid resin or gum to ensure complete insulation. The wrappings were of such a degree of completeness that observers such as Aidan Cockburn have noticed a change in the color of the mummified body within twenty-four to forty-eight hours after removal of the wrappings. This is mere testimony to the perfection of the technique. In certain instances, the wrappings bore inscriptions that proved to be extremely useful for identification purposes, and in all cases they were wound with exemplary regularity. The total length of the numerous strips of cloth used could run at times as high as several hundred yards. It was possible to measure the cloths while carrying out autopsies on various mummies that have been discovered intact; but unfortunately, many others, among them those of the most famous pharaohs, were ripped open by tomb robbers in the necropolis in Thebes. The tombs were ransacked in spite of all the precautions taken, usually soon after the mummies were placed in their tombs. The mummified bodies were often moved to several different sepulchers, so that by the time they were discovered in modern times, they had lost the beautifully neat appearance of their system of protection. This was not the case with Tutankhamun, whose sepulcher had remained intact and untouched by plunderers. In the case of Sethos I, however, the body had been decapitated by robbers. The priests of the Twenty-first Dynasty were obliged to remummify it, but the techniques they used were clumsy and crude when compared with the work of their predecessors.

The rites that accompanied mummification involved various rituals concerning the body: the famous ceremony of the simulated opening of the deceased's mouth before he was completely covered in wrappings, the sprinkling of lustral ablutions on the corpse to purify it, the rites for the bereaved, the procession from the place of embalmment to the tomb, among them. All of these ceremonies differed according to the rank of the deceased and the historical period, and where the kings themselves were concerned, not only the rites but also the techniques used on them changed over time.

It seems that at the time of the early dynasties, the embalmers simply removed the organs and swathed the body in wrappings soaked with resin. Nevertheless a royal mummy dating from the Sixth Dynasty exists today: that of Merenre I. This mummy is roughly forty-three centuries old and has survived for over four millennia in this state. I mentioned this mummy earlier, having examined and photographed it very carefully with my colleague

Michel Durigon in Cairo in 1975, because it may well be the oldest and most complete of the royal mummies we possess at present. I question whether the unfavorable conditions under which this mummy is presently being preserved are not damaging it more seriously than the forty-three centuries spent in its sepulcher. In 1975 nothing had been done about the fact that it was in an obvious state of decomposition.

It was during the New Kingdom that the art of mummification attained its highest degree of perfection. The famous mummies on display at the Egyptian Museum in Cairo are modern examples of this achievement. Even though the art of mummification declined in precision later on, it continued to be practiced for an astonishingly long time. Mummification was still being performed during Roman times and even after the advent of Christianity. During the first centuries A.D., corpses were still embalmed, and mummies have been discovered in Christian catacombs. The Alexandria Museum contains examples that are perfectly preserved.

Today, the processes then used are no longer secrets, at least as far as the essentials are concerned. The mystery of mummification has disappeared. Experimental studies have shown that it is perfectly possible in modern times to use a similar outline for successful mummification, as far as embalmment is concerned, although it is perhaps not possible to reconstitute a mummy with wrappings impregnated with resin or gum. (Zaky Iskander, a collaborator of the famous Egyptologist Lucas, embalmed ducks forty years ago. During one of my trips to Cairo, he showed them to me and they were in a perfect state of preservation. It remains to be seen whether, like Ramesses II, Zaky Iskander's ducks will survive for at least another three thousand years.)

From a medical point of view, the most prodigiously impressive aspect of mummification is the perfect preservation of tissues. The high point of the tissue-preserving technique was achieved during the New Kingdom, from the beginning of the sixteenth century B.C., to that of the eleventh century B.C. Even though bodies were often damaged by tomb robbers, carted from one tomb to another, or spent decades in unfavorable conditions at the Egyptian Museum (apart from the mummy of Tutankhamun, which has remained in its tomb), specialists who have examined the tissue under a microscope have clearly shown that human tissues and organs preserved in this way can still be identified today. We shall see later how a modern technique applied to mummified tissues has clearly been able to show cells, with their nuclei, and help identify different tissues—even blood cells—which are known to be extremely fragile. This was achieved by Aidan Cockburn's team of researchers in the United States, and in Paris by Professors Jacques Mignot and Michel Durigon, using mummified tissues provided by me for microscopic examination. Nothing better exemplifies the perfection of the preservation technique used during the New Kingdom.

# 2. The Sepulchers

## From the Ancient Necropolises to the Egyptian Museum, Cairo

It is not just the high degree of perfection attained in mummification that accounts for the fact that human bodies were able to survive for hundreds, indeed thousands, of years without any apparent change. Certain factors concerning the sepulcher itself were also responsible for their preservation. This is true of all the mummies, but particularly of those of pharaohs: the deified king, or king-god, who especially benefited from being placed in a special sepulcher. For now, we shall examine the unique advantages of such a sepulcher from the point of view of insulation.

Regardless of the period, a king was always protected by the most elaborate methods imaginable. The pyramids constructed during the Old Kingdom are a case in point, the most famous being those of the Giza plateau (Fig. 10). The coffin itself was lined with wood placed inside a stone sarcophagus—made of granite, basalt, limestone, or alabaster—with a matching lid.

15

Such sarcophagi afforded genuine protection. They can be found in tombs dating from various periods: from the Old Kingdom (the sarcophagus of Cheops, in the famous pyramid bearing his name, can still be seen in the king's chamber) as well as the New Kingdom. Of note is the stone sarcophagus and the richly ornamented gilt-covered lid of the coffin of Tutankhamun in which the pharaoh lay when he entered his tomb in the Valley of the Kings (Fig. 11). From the discoveries made in this particular sepulcher in 1922, which was practically intact, we know that the mummified body was placed in a sarcophagus and in a series of gilt "shrines." These gilt shrines were the famous gold-plated casings placed one inside the other; these casings were constructed in the sepulcher in the small mortuary room, which was designed to receive the royal remains. The fact that there were so many different casings around the body ensured a remarkable degree of insulation.

The chambers built to house the royal remains were integrated into the vast tomb complex itself. During the Old Kingdom the complexes were of gigantic proportions, for the pyramids of Lower Egypt were built at this time. They were designed to provide their royal occupant with effective protection from all unwanted intrusion. The mummified body was remarkably isolated within its mortuary chamber in the middle of the pyramid. Plunderers, nevertheless, managed to get into these gigantic constructions. In most cases the mummified bodies have been found in fragmented condition. There is one exception, however: the body of Merenre I, whose mummy is today in the Egyptian Museum in Cairo (Fig. 1).

Most of the royal mummies I have studied date back to the New Kingdom. It was then that the kings of Egypt chose Thebes, on the other side of the Nile opposite Luxor in Upper Egypt, for the site of their burial place. The valley today is known as the Valley of the Kings. In this desert landscape, the pharaohs had tombs built at varying depths in the cliff. Access to them was through galleries of varying lengths, some very long, others very short. The nearby tomb of Queen Hatshepsut, of the Eighteenth Dynasty, was at least two hundred yards long. These sepulchers were ransacked and plundered as well. The bodies were probably removed from the more vulnerable tombs to be placed in areas that were apparently easier to guard. The bodies of Ramesses II and several others were transferred to a hiding place near the Valley of the Kings, the famous cache of Deir El Bahari. There they remained for nearly three thousand years until they were discovered in 1881 and transported to Lower Egypt. They have all been kept here, with the exception of Ramesses II, whose eight-month stay in Paris (1976–1977) disturbed his peaceful repose on the banks of the Nile.

A second group of mummies, discovered in 1898 in the tomb of Amenophis II, was also transferred to Lower Egypt, with the exception of Amenophis himself, who remained in his tomb in the Valley of the Kings until 1934.

In 1974, when I first became interested in these subjects, all the royal mummies (with the exception of Tutankhamun) had been collected in the Royal Mummies Room of the Egyptian Museum in Cairo. Their conditions of preservation had radically changed since the end of the nineteenth century. The hand of man had removed the protection of the mummies and, without taking the appropriate steps, unfortunate consequences ensued.

Cairo and its surrounding regions received two successive influxes of mummies; one in 1881 and the other in 1898. They included the great kings of Egypt, mostly dating from the New Kingdom, accompanied by a few queens from the same period, the Twenty-first Dynasty. In all there was a total of thirty mummies. What Egyptologist of the time would not have removed the wrappings from the mummies to examine the royal body? One can easily imagine the emotion Gaston Maspero and M. Fouquet must have felt on June 1, 1886, when they first unwrapped the mummy of Ramesses II. This ceremony was performed in the presence of the Khedive of Egypt, high-ranking authorities of the Department of Antiquities, other famous Egyptologists, as well as prominent members of society invited to witness the scene. All the wrappings were removed with the exception of those from the shoulders to the hands, which surrounded the upper limbs. The mummy was then replaced in its wooden sarcophagus. The same procedure was carried out on the other mummies. These Egyptologists had absolutely no idea what terrible damage they had done to the mummies' future preservation. We shall see later how, thirty years after the event, Gaston Maspero sensed the danger threatening the mummies whose wrappings had been removed.

The various transfers from place to place that some mummies underwent, among them Ramesses II, and the careless way they were carried out is another factor that led to deterioration. At one time the body of Ramesses II was displayed standing up. Thus unprotected, the mummy fell prey to pollution, and a host of foreign bodies could attack it, whether at surface level or through the hole in the abdomen where the viscera had been removed. When the announcement that a great discovery had been made in Paris in the late 1970s—that remains of tobacco had been discovered in the abdominal cavity of the mummy—everyone overlooked the peregrinations to which the mummy was subjected after its discovery. The fact that it was no longer protected from exterior conditions exposed it to the risk of accidental contamination. I shall return to this later.

To measure the extent of the changes in the conditions of preservation of the mummified bodies as a result of their removal from the tombs, their transfer to Lower Egypt and their unwrapping, we should first consider the environmental conditions that prevailed for thousands of years in their sepulchers and compare them with the situation today in the Egyptian Museum in Cairo.

Some of the old descriptions of the climatic conditions within the tombs in the Valley of the Kings dating from the New Kingdom seem to be highly exaggerated. The generalizations made using such data create a false impression as to the true state of affairs. I have good reason to believe, having visited a number of such sepulchers, that the mummies in their tombs enjoyed an ambient temperature and a hygrometric level that was infinitely more constant than those to which they are presently being subjected in the Egyptian Museum in Cairo. Their present climatic conditions are extremely detrimental to their preservation. The excellent state of preservation of the wall paintings found in many tombs bear witness to the effectiveness of the protection afforded by the sepulchers. Those paintings in the tomb of Ramesses VI (Fig. 12), and the objects at least three thousand years old found in 1922 surrounding the body of Tutankhamun are in an excellent preserved state.

In his book *Mummies*, Ange P. Leca quotes the observations made by a member of Napoleon's expedition to Egypt. His name was Jomard and his findings were reported in the voluminous book *Description of Egypt*. Jomard's exploration of the necropolis in Thebes led him to visit the tombs in the Valley of the Kings. A suffocating heat is said to have prevailed in them. Ange P. Leca considers this to corroborate the readings taken by Lucas in 1924 in some of the tombs. They both claimed that the tombs were very humid or extremely hot—in some of them the temperature is said to have reached 30° C. I certainly do not doubt the readings taken by Lucas, but I nevertheless consider it wrong to make sweeping generalizations. In general, the differences in temperature and humidity were decidedly less in an intact tomb than they were in the Royal Mummies Room of the Egyptian Museum in Cairo.

The room in which the mummies were kept is located on the second floor of the museum. To the detriment of its occupants the hall undergoes great variations in both temperature and hygrometric level. Each mummified body is covered by protective glass which is *not* hermetically sealed. The body is in no way insulated from the atmosphere of the vast hall. The grouping of the mummies side by side also promotes contamination. From an epidemiological point of view, the conditions are appalling. It would hardly be surprising to find out that biological agents have invaded the various mummies kept in this fashion.

I also believe that it is detrimental for the royal mummies to be displayed in full sunlight. It is a known fact that ultraviolet rays encourage certain biological processes. The mummies were much better off in their tombs, where they were protected from light.

The question regarding deterioration was first raised by Gaston Maspero in 1916. He forsaw the dangers caused by the absence of insulation. He wrote at that time that the mummified bodies "have been severely damaged since their discovery, whatever care may have been taken to surround them with preserving substances, most of them have been attacked by insects. The day may be foretold when they will disappear as a result of such assaults." This observation was made by the man who had, with his own hands, removed the protective wrappings from Ramesses II thirty years earlier.

The lesson here concerns the harm caused by certain human initiatives. However well-intentioned, they are equally as detrimental. Occasional sprayings of insecticide around the mummies also do not seem to have alleviated the present problem. Judging by the work of the original embalmer and that of Egyptologists working around the turn of the century, it seems that the royal mummies have hardly benefited from modern methods. Not, at least, until the studies carried out in 1975.

As sometimes happens in such circumstances, an impetus coming from outside the normal field is required for things to change. A new fact may be discovered by a person who approaches the problem from a different angle. When the problem was seen through the eyes of medical specialists, the question was viewed somewhat differently from the way it appeared to those who were confronted with it daily.

I alerted the Egyptian public authorities to the very bad condition of the Royal Mummies. In the course of several talks, President Anwar Sadat and his wife were kind enough to devote their full attention to the account I laid before them concerning this disastrous predicament. Since these meetings there has been much talk about the creation of several new museums to relieve the Egyptian Museum in Cairo. It is overburdened with the wealth of antiquities it contains. The overall idea is to transfer the mummies to better conditions of preservation, since the royal remains are gradually deteriorating as time goes on. It was hoped that what was achieved in terms of museum conservation for Ramesses II in Paris would serve as a lesson, and that the Royal mummies in Cairo, at present, could also be saved from further destruction and deterioration.

*Part II*

—

# THE MEDICAL EXAMINATION OF MUMMIES

# 3. Which Royal Mummies Have Come Down To Us So Far?

In his book, *Mummies* (*Les Momies*), Ange P. Leca provides interesting information concerning the mummified bodies of what are thought to be several Old Kingdom pharaohs. I shall be drawing from his work in the following chapter concerning this period.

The founder of the Third Dynasty was Zoser, whose reign was around 2700 B.C. Zoser commissioned Imhotep, an architectural genius, to build a funerary complex on the Sakkara plateau near Cairo. The largest building in the complex is the Step Pyramid (Fig. 13). It was designed to protect Zoser's tomb, the latter being sunk to a depth of thirty yards and situated more or less at the center of the monument. The pyramid was probably 60 yards high and had a base measurement of over 100 to 120 yards. It is even older than the regularly shaped pyramids on the Giza plateau. Despite the colossal pile of stones surrounding the king's chamber, it had been ransacked several times. In 1932, the French Egyptologist Jean P. Lauer, found fragments of ribs and of sternum in the tomb, as well as a left foot wrapped in linen soaked in resin. Six years earlier, part of a spinal column and

ɔ discovered in the same chamber. More than a
other remains are said to have been found in an
corridor of the tomb, but unfortunately were lost.

When Dedkere Isesi, the second to last king of the Sixth Dynasty (around 2400 B.C.), was found in the funerary chamber of his pyramid in Sakkara, all that remained was the left side of his body and wrapped viscera. The canopic jars that had once contained the viscera had been smashed. The pyramid of Unas, dating from the same dynasty and also located at Sakkara, had likewise been plundered. When the mortuary chamber was uncovered, only fragments of the king were to be found: a forearm, a hand, and a few pieces of skull.

In his works, Ange P. Leca does not mention any other discoveries of mummies dating from the Old Kingdom. I believe that I am right, however, in thinking that the mummy of Merenre I is the oldest and most complete mummy known at present. This king lived in the Sixth Dynasty and reigned around 2300 B.C. Previously I had been unable to find any mention of his mummy, but came across one quite by accident one day in the Egyptian Museum in Cairo. I had asked permission to check the state of preservation of those mummies that were not being kept in the Royal Mummies Room. While I was being shown these reserves, where every available inch of space was occupied, I lifted a covering lid and found a mummy lying on its pedestal in the well of a staircase. It was seriously damaged. Several fragments of the thoracic wall and the lower half of the face in particular had deteriorated. I consulted the museum inventory to identify the mummy, and Michel Durigon and I figured out that we were in the presence of a Sixth Dynasty mummy, namely that of Merenre I.

I shall always remember the pleasure we had in being guided to this mummy. I am also unlikely to forget the indescribable stench of putrefaction coming from it. The woman from the museum who had accompanied us implored us to finish photographing as quickly as we could, because the air was becoming quite unbearable. Before the cover was replaced on the sepulcher, the mummy was sprayed with a cloud of goodness knows what from an extremely ancient-looking can.

It leads one to wonder just what state the mummy will be in the next time someone examines it.

From the Sixth Dynasty to the New Kingdom, which began around 1580 B.C., the remains of only a single king have survived: Sekenenre, who reigned in the Seventeenth Dynasty, seventeenth century B.C. The knowledge of certain details concerning this mummy, in which the loss of cranial matter has been established, was extremely useful when it came to making comparisons with other similar cases. Sekenenre died in the course of a battle against the Hyksos and was probably embalmed under highly unfavorable conditions. Although the mummy has been badly damaged, the multiple wounds he received are far from negligible.

The vast majority of pharaonic mummies that we have today date from the New Kingdom. Along with Sekenenre, they are to be found in the Egyptian Museum in Cairo, with the exception of Tutankhamun. There are almost thirty of them ranging from Ahmosis to Ramesses IX. Many of them are the mummies of the most famous kings of Egypt: Tuthmosis II, Amenophis II, Sethos I, Ramesses II, and Merneptah. They were discovered, as I stated earlier, in three places: the necropolis in Thebes, the hiding place at Deir El Bahari, discovered in 1881, and the tomb of Amenophis II, discovered in 1898. It is worth recalling the circumstances surrounding their discoveries.

The Theban necropolis is situated on the left bank of the Nile, opposite present-day Luxor. This area was not one of traditional pyramids that housed the mummies, but rather one of the tombs carved out of the side of the mountain (Fig. 14). This process began during the New Kingdom, or the Eighteenth Dynasty to be exact. In the nineteenth century A.D., the site must still have looked as it does today—namely, valleys surrounded by high rocky cliffs. Today, ruins are scattered here and there, along with ancient villages, but above all, there are the temples, such as the imposing construction at Deir El Bahari. Nearby, there are villages that are still inhabited today. The police were continuously informed as to the activities of certain villagers who were suspected of selling relics that they had unearthed at sites yet unknown to the department of antiquities.

From 1875 to today, the inhabitants of Sheikh El Gournah, a local village, began to traffic objects found as a result of clandestine excavations in areas known to contain ancient tombs. These tombs were discovered at the beginning of the nineteenth century, but were found empty. One inhabitant of Sheikh El Gournah was arrested in 1881 and his famous hiding place, where he had been storing his artifacts, was discovered near the temple of Deir El Bahari. Numerous coffins and funerary objects were found piled in this gallery, which was located about ten yards below ground. It was constructed at the time of the Twenty-first Dynasty, to guard the precious articles from tomb robbers. Over the course of time plunderers had succeeded in locating and violating many sepulchers in the nearby Valley of the Kings. Gaston Maspero, a French archeologist, played a crucial role in the discovery and subsequent removal of a number of mummies from this hiding place. Those uncovered were Ramesses II and his father, Sethos I; the bodies of several other kings from the two preceding dynasties (Seventeenth and Eighteenth); and the bodies of several queens from the New Kingdom. Their remains were transported to Lower Egypt.

Another discovery was made in 1898 by French archeologist Victor Loret in the Valley of the Kings. The tomb of Amenophis II, uncovered with nine other royal mummies dating from the New Kingdom, had likewise been transferred. Among those transferred was Merneptah, the successor of Ramesses II. The bodies were all transferred to Lower Egypt, with the exception of Amenophis II, who remained in his personal tomb until 1934, when he too was taken to Cairo.

28

The discovery of Tutankhamun's tomb in November 1922 by Howard Carter and Lord Carnarvon was particularly interesting, for the tomb had been only slightly pillaged. It is estimated that the pillaging had occurred some time during the Twentieth Dynasty, in the twelfth century B.C. The sepulcher is considered to have survived almost intact. In the case of Tutankhamun the mummy was also intact along with the canopic jars that had been placed beside it and contained some of the viscera of the king, who had died at a very young age due to causes as yet unknown. The wrappings were removed from Tutankhamun's mummy after the discovery of the sepulcher and the body was left lying inside one of its coffins in the tomb. It is still there today. I have not seen it uncovered, but my guess is that a simple examination would probably not be of very great interest. I have many regrets concerning what could have been done to preserve the mummy but appears not to have been.

# 4. The Mummy of Tutankhamun: Destruction and Lost Opportunities

I have heard Christiane Desroches-Noblecourt speak admiringly of certain studies carried out on the mummy of Tutankhamun. Her observations provide further evidence in support of her theory that Semenkhare was Tutankhamun's brother. The similarity of the anthropometric statistics and the fact that they had the same blood type are what led her to this conclusion. Though these two factors did not, in fact, constitute a decisive argument in favor of the hypothesis advanced, the fact remains that this medical and biological fact is useful to the Egyptologist. The mere possibility of determining blood type by taking only a tiny quantity of mummified tissue from the body of a pharaoh who lived more than thirty-three centuries ago is indeed of great interest and a very big step forward (R. G. Harrison and R. C. Connolly).

Despite these advances in the understanding of mummies, many great opportunities have been lost as a result of the many tomb robbers that disturbed many mummies of the New Kingdom. Such research would have been especially interesting in ascertaining the causes of his death. Tutankhamun's death, something Egyptologists know little about, is said to have occurred between the ages of sixteen and twenty-two.

The mummy was discovered absolutely intact in its tomb, protected by several coffins, one inside the other. In 1925, it was decided to proceed with the removal of the wrappings to extract the precious objects placed with the body inside the covering itself. It was known at the time that such items were present with many other royal mummies dating from the New Kingdom. Until 1925 the sepulcher of Tutankhamun had remained untouched, in contrast to those of the other pharaohs. It was hoped and believed that many valuable pieces would therefore be found.

This unwrapping operation probably took place in the tomb itself, making it impossible, at the time, to install or utilize X-ray equipment, which would have helped locate the objects beforehand. The X rays would have provided information as to the objects' sizes and forms, and subsequently facilitated their removal, and required less handling of the mummy, reducing the risk of injury. From a medical point of view, it would have been worthwhile to have made an X-ray examination before using the procedures required to remove the objects, which subsequently seriously damaged the mummified body. For this to have been done right, however, it would have been necessary to transport the mummy, lying in the last of its coffins, to an X-ray clinic. Other investigations could have been performed as well, such as a microscopic study. This would not have required the transfer of the body and would have been extremely useful. To my knowledge, this was not carried out either.

Howard Carter, in collaboration with several others, including Dr. Douglas E. Derry, unwrapped the mummy. In so doing, they removed an impressive number of gold items, which today form part of the Treasure of Tutankhamun.

These items rightly arouse the admiration of the many visitors to the Egyptian Museum in Cairo and of those who visit exhibitions organized outside Egypt, such as the one in Paris twenty years ago.

What is not generally known is that the price paid for these treasures was the definitive destruction of the mummy. Contradictory accounts of this disaster were given in the book *The Tomb of Tutankhamun* by Howard Carter (Cassel and Co., Publishers, London, 1933), and in the book *The Human Remains from the Tomb of Tutankhamun* by Filce Leek (Oxford University Press, 1972). The latter text is supported by photographs that show a dismembered body and the multiple fragments of mummified tissue. These tissues form the pieces of a jigsaw puzzle, which having been reassembled, now form (for better or worse) the mummy that was once intact under the protection of its wrappings and multiple coffins. A gold cover now prevents the remains of the pharaoh from being seen by visitors to his ancient tomb in the Valley of the Kings, where he is now located.

Due to the research performed for scientific purposes, man has added to the damage already done. In an article published in the *Journal of Egyptian Archaeology* (63, pp. 112–115, 1977), F. Filce Leek recalls how, in 1925, Dr. Douglas E. Derry, wishing to examine the calcification of the mummy's teeth, performed an overall exploration, in which he incised and deflected downward the floor of the mummy's mouth to gain access to its teeth. Having done so, Derry found that the wisdom teeth had grown to a height that was half of the second molar. This indicated to him that the king had died at eighteen years of age. He then repaired his incisions by gluing them back together with resin. The traces were found by Filce Leek in 1968. At that time, Leek collaborated with R. G. Harrison on a new general medical examination of the mummy. In the course of their studies they were able to use portable equipment to take X rays of the human remains in the tomb.

From 1925 onward, the dismemberment of the mummified body by Egyptologists in search of precious objects enabled doctors to gain substantial visual access to the mummy's now exposed joints. They were able to examine the state of the shoulder, elbow, wrist, hip, knee, and ankle joints from both sides. This type of examination, which is rarely allowed to be performed on such a grand scale with a mummy (even those violated by tomb robbers), concentrated on areas of the body where there are epiphyseal ends, that is, deep inside the long bones. These are the areas where the bones develop lengthwise. As a person grows older, so do the epiphyseal lines, and they gradually ossify. Little by little, they disappear as a result of this ossification process, which finally leads to a soldering of the bone. In the case of Tutankhamun, the evolution of bone development was made visible in many places by fractured joints. Derry noted (vol. 11, pp. 143–161 of the above mentioned work by Carter) that none of the bone cartilages that usually unite around the age of twenty were present in the mummy. The bones were united in those places where such fusion normally occurs much earlier on. Knowing as we do that the fusion of bones occurred at an earlier age in ancient Egypt, Leek suggests that the pharaoh is more likely to have died at age seventeen or perhaps even sixteen.

As we shall see later on, an X-ray examination of the teeth would also have been of great help in estimating the pharaoh's age. We do not, however, today possess these documents or X rays. I know of an X ray of the skull, taken by R. G. Harrison in 1968 and reproduced in Filce Leek's book, but unfortunately, the quality of the picture does not allow me to draw any conclusions concerning the teeth. This is in no way meant to be a criticism of those who carried out the medical exploration, I simply have good reason to believe that the battered state of the mummy prevented them from taking satisfactory X rays. Figure 11 shows the present position of the coffin in which the body lies, surrounded by its limestone casing.

In an article published in 1977, Filce Leek explains how he was refused permission to take panoramic X rays of the teeth by introducing, with the aid of a fine needle, a radioactive isotope of iodine. This operation would hardly have damaged the mummy further, considering all it had undergone in 1925.

There remains one problem—namely, that of the pharaoh's

viscera, which were found mummified in the ritual canopic jars. Microscopic research could and should have been carried out on them. Specialists in forensic medicine would have found then, and even more so today, material and data for further types of investigation and analysis, and perhaps further information might have been gathered with respect to the young king's death, which still remains an enigma. What has become of the viscera? I searched in vain in Egypt for something that might have provided an answer. Perhaps my inquiries were incomplete. Whatever the case may be, we in the medical community lament not only the sad state of the remains of Tutankhamun, but the absence of certain research that could have been carried out on the remaining parts of the mummified body. These research studies would have increased our knowledge concerning this famous pharaoh.

# 5. The Camouflage of the Dismemberment of Tutankhamun's Mummy and the Problem of the Curse of Tutankhamun

"Nowhere is the temptation to write a romance instead of an historical study more compelling than here and it is for that reason that the greatest care has to be taken in the use of all these documents." Walther Wolf quoted at the beginning of *Tutankhamen* by Christiane Desroches-Noblecourt, New York Graphic Society, Boston, 1963 (11th printing, 1978).

"By providing his mummy with the elaborate and costly outfit which he thought essential to its dignity, the king was himself compassing its destruction." When Howard Carter made this remark, he was thinking of the other pharaohs buried in the Valley of the Kings who had suffered from tomb robbers. He was not referring to Tutankhamun, whose sepulcher had been discovered very late—Tutankhamun therefore benefited from being "intact in its golden shrine." Unfortunately, the truth of the pharaoh's condition was quite different. Tutankhamun's mummy is today in many pieces.

Howard Carter and his collaborators discovered the tomb in 1922. In October 1925, they decided to investigate the body of the pharaoh itself. It has been stated that an account of the facts is given in Carter's book of 1933, *The Tomb of Tutankhamun* by Howard Carter and A. C. Mace (Cassel, Pub., London, 1933). There is, however, a much more interesting account in his private diary, which remained unpublished until 1972, when Filce Leek included the description in his book *The Human Remains from the Tomb of Tutankhamun* (Griffith Institute, Oxford University Press). Filce Leek also quotes the report and certain notes by Dr. Douglas Derry, then a professor of anatomy at the University of Cairo. Together with Carter and Dr. Saleh Bey Hamdi, Derry proceeded to extract the mummy piece by piece from its solid gold coffin so that the objets d'art could be removed.

As Leek remarked, Carter showed little interest in the human remains. He did, however, note certain precise details, which can be usefully compared with Derry's report. The data derived from each source must be placed side by side, for Carter completely ignores important points reported by Derry, and vice versa. For example, Carter says nothing about the dismemberment of the mummy, whereas Derry reports that after removal of the entire pelvis and lower limbs, followed by the upper trunk and limbs, the head was left inside the gold mask.

The sequence of events was as follows: The sepulchral chamber of the tomb contained four gilt shrines; these were concentric and had doors that opened one into the other. The final gilt shrine contained a stone sarcophagus in which a first coffin lay. It was covered in gold plaques and encrusted with semiprecious stones of various colors. Inside the first coffin, there was a second coffin, of similar worksmanship, which in turn enclosed a third and last of solid gold. Carter was able to remove the lids of the three coffins to gain access to the mummy, but was unsuccessful in freeing the third coffin from the second, because a resin or pitchlike substance cemented them together. The mummy was intact under its perfectly wound wrappings (Fig. 50) and its upper part was covered by the famous gold mask. Both mummy and mask were stuck together and cemented to the bottom of the third coffin. This same pitchlike substance partially coated the mummy's wrappings. Carter writes that it was probably semi-liquid at first, but had subsequently solidified by "carbonizing" the outermost wrappings. This was a pity, since the substance was later found to be soluble in acetone.

At this point, it seems that Carter, instead of proceeding slowly and taking samples of this substance to establish what it was and how soluble it might have been in various liquids, decided to forge ahead and use techniques that were, in fact, highly damaging to the mummified tissues. The first method employed was heat treatment.

On October 31, 1925, Carter had the mummy and two coffins removed from the tomb and exposed outside. On that day, the temperature reached 65°C in the sun, but the glue did not melt. There can be no doubt that serious damage was caused to the mummy by subjecting it to such intense heat, as was seen when the wrappings were removed. It is now a well-known fact that heat causes mummified tissues to burst.

Carter asked Derry to come from Cairo, and on November 11, 1925, Derry and his Egyptian colleague arrived in the Valley of the Kings, where Derry opened the mummy without delay.

It must be stressed here that in addition to the damage caused by heat and exposure to the sun, the cuts made by Derry's instruments constituted the first trauma the mummy had undergone since its three-thousand-year rest in the tomb protecting it. I have heard people maintain, without any proof whatsoever, that the deterioration in Tutankhamun's mummy had occurred before either Carter or his collaborators had laid a finger on it. It is claimed that the mummification had been bungled. These are indeed strange statements in view of the fact that all the other pharaonic mummies from this period indicate the supreme degree of perfection attained in the mummification process by this time. There is every reason to believe, therefore, that the mummified body beneath the wrappings was in excellent condition before the damage caused to it—first by exposure to intense heat, and second by human handling of it. We shall see in fact how such handling resulted in the division of the body into three main parts:

1. the pelvis and lower limbs
2. the upper part of the trunk and upper limbs
3. the head and neck.

Each of these sections was removed in the order indicated from the mummified body as it lay in its coffin. The first was withdrawn in order to facilitate the freeing of the second, and the second to disengage the third.

Carter's book, mentioned above, does not expand on the dismemberment of the body. It simply notes the presence of dislocated limbs, without making any reference to the real cause of the damage. Derry's report and Carter's diary do record, however, the deliberate destruction caused by the retrieval of precious objects. Derry's report reads as follow:

> "As it was found impossible to continue the work of removing the numerous objects still covering the thorax and upper part of [the] abdominal wall, it was decided to remove the limbs and finally to cut through the trunk above the iliac crests as the latter was firmly glued to the bottom of the coffin. This was done and the lower part of [the] trunk removed."

Filce Leek adds the following comment: "That the trunk was in fact cut through is confirmed by a photograph taken at the time, and may also be seen from the X-ray."

Elsewhere, Derry notes that after freeing the trunk, work was possible from beneath, and then "it was decided to withdraw the mummy from the mask. This was finally accomplished. . ."

The fact that the trunk was severed by Derry is registered on the X rays taken by R. G. Harrison in 1968 (Fig. 51). Here we see the transversal cut, which passes through the third lumbar vertebra, along with numerous defects in the skeleton of the thorax.

In order to disengage the upper part of the trunk from the mask covering it both in front and behind, "hot knives" were used to free the glued surfaces. Alas, the head remained under the mask when the trunk was lowered. Plate XII of Filce Leek's book shows the upper part of the headless trunk. Thus it was then possible to remove the famous vulture's-head pendant without damaging it. This, along with other items of jewelry on the chest, forms part of the Treasure of Tutankhamun, exhibited worldwide.

The head, which had remained imprisoned under the mask, was also freed with the help of "hot knives." Filce Leek's book contains several photographs of the head in isolation, resting upright on the seventh cervical vertebra, or more probably, the first dorsal vertebra. It is held in place by a support stay (Fig. 52). The nape of the neck has been destroyed. The cervical vertebrae are bare, and half of the outer tissues of the anterior of the neck are missing.

Many bracelets were found on the two forearms. The joint of the wrist was dislocated and broken at the lower extremity of the ulna. Meanwhile, the lower end of the radius "came away easily from the shaft, bringing the entire hand with it," (Douglas Derry quoted in Filce Leek's work, op. cit., p. 13).

The feet were ornamented with sandals that had gold soles and were kept in place by a band of metal encircling the ankles. One of the photographs in Filce Leek's book reproduced here (Fig. 53), shows the gold sandals on the still-intact mummy. Another (Fig. 54) indicates that, once they had been removed the joint of the left ankle had been left gaping open; the soft tissues covering the metatarsal bones had been destroyed, and the bones laid bare.

Photographs were also taken by Harry Burton, the photographer employed on Carter's expedition. Like the others cited above, they are to be found in the archives of the Griffith Institute at the Ashmolean Museum in Oxford, England. They, too, show the crevices present in the pelvis and the gaping joints of the lower limbs (Fig. 55).

As stated earlier, Carter makes no mention in his book of the deliberate destruction described here. In fact, in a note taken on November 18, 1925, he affirms that "after photographic records are made of the King's remains, these will be reverently rewrapped and returned to the sarcophagus." (Filce Leek, op. cit. p. 8). However, there is a photographic document, taken by the Carter expedition (Fig. 56), that shows how the fragments of the mummy were laid out on a bed of sand, then assembled in such a way as to reconstitute a rough semblance of a human being. The fragments have remained in a state of dislocation to this day. This damage was clearly observed by F. Filce Leek during the British expedition in 1968, at which time access to the mummy was still permitted (Fig. 57).

These data are beyond dispute and may well astound those who have read certain well-known books on the subject, such as *Tutankhamen* by Christiane Desroches-Noblecourt, that describe the tomb and the discovery of the mummy, but fail to mention the damage that the mummy suffered at the hands of Carter and Derry. There is no mention of its exposure to intense heat, nor of the division of the mummy into three sections, which enabled Carter and Derry to remove the precious objects in the wrappings without damaging the trinkets and items of jewelry. We know this action to be the cause of the mummy's deterioration. Nevertheless, of the seventy-seven references in Desroches-Noblecourt's book to documentation, both written and photographic, preserved at the Griffith Institute in Oxford, none mention these acts.

In the acknowledgments of the 1977 French edition of her work, Desroches-Noblecourt writes the following: "I should like to express my warm thanks to the team of experts at the Griffith Institute–Ashmolean Museum, Oxford, for their generously given assistance allowing me to consult the archives of the discovery together with Carter's journals and notes." In her text one may search in vain, however, for a description of the mummy that corresponds to the documents at the Griffith Institute. Desroches-Noblecourt speaks of

> a mummy almost burned away by excessive use of unguents. (p. 74). . . . Too many of these were lavished on Tutankhamen, burning away nearly all the tissues and attacking the bones. Only the parts protected by gold were preserved: the face covered by the mask and the hands and feet guarded by finger stalls. The larger bandages of the outer wrappings were also impregnated with unguents (p. 222). . . . The mummy, in a very bad state of deterioration, was treated—and that is indeed the right word—by Dr. Derry (p. 76).

It is difficult to imagine a narration of the events that is more distant from what we read in the personal notes kept by the two who dismembered the mummy, and from what is to be seen in the photographs taken by the Carter expedition. Those readers interested in finding out more about the so-called "parts protected by gold" should consult the numerous reproductions of photographic documents in Filce Leek's book. They will undoubtedly be convinced of the illusory nature of this "protection." It has been established that the precious objects surrounding the mummy did, in fact, provoke the frantic desire to retrieve them, leading to its dislocation.

As for the diligent "treatment" that the mummy is supposed to have received, one may again search in vain for traces of it in the documentary evidence. Once Derry had finished his observations as to the state of growth of the limb bones, made possible by the fact that the body had been laid bare and cut into sections, he promptly withdrew from the Valley of the Kings, on November 19, 1925, exactly eight days after he had arrived.

Earlier we mentioned that Dr. Derry had dismembered the mummy in order to observe how the cartilage and bone had soldered together, at the extremities of the long bones, as well as in the other parts of the body. The results of these findings are shown in the photographic documents provided by the Griffith Institute in Oxford. The findings were made possible through the perfect preservation of the osseous structure, a fact that is in total contradiction to the supposed "excessive use of unguents" purported to have burned "away nearly all the tissues."

It has been established that these allegedly harmful substances were indeed used to cement together the coffins in which the pharaoh was placed, and that when the coffins were opened, garlands of natural flowers appeared under the lids, as shown in figures 39 and 40 of *Tutankhamen* by Desroches-Noblecourt. Can we seriously imagine, however, that the close proximity of these supposedly harmful substances could have been totally harmless to the flowers (confined in a tightly closed space for over thirty-three centuries), while possessing the power to destroy human tissues and bones?

More than the inaccuracies in the texts, spread widely all over the world, the photograph of the mummified head of Tutankhamun, as in figure 134 in Desroches-Noblecourt's book (Fig. 58, *above* ), leads the reader to imagine that the pharaoh was not decapitated. This document, presented by her as having been provided by Oxford University, has in fact been altered.

A comparison of the original and the altered photograph (Fig. 52 and Fig. 58, *below* ) shows that all that existed in the lower part of the original, below a horizontal line marking the lower limits of the soft tissues of the neck, has been cropped. Consequently the remains of two or three vertebrae and the plinth on which the head is vertically positioned are not visible. What is more, the strut supporting the decapitated head has simply disappeared.

An extract from Howard Carter's diary is indicative of the untruths recorded in official documents at the time of the dismemberment of the mummy. On November 8, 1925, Carter wrote in his diary, "After photographic records are made of the

King's remains, these will be reverently rewrapped and returned to the sarcophagus. M. Lacau, who was present during the whole of this examination, left today for Cairo, taking with him a final archaeological bulletin as well as the two doctors Derry and Saleh Bey." This text, kept at the Griffith Institute, Oxford University, is reproduced by F. Filce Leek in his book *The Human Remains from the Tomb of Tutankhamun.* p. 8. M. P. Lacau, a French Egyptologist, was Director of Egyptian Antiquities in 1925.

## Why has the truth been hidden?

One may imagine that Howard Carter, facing multiple administrative difficulties, was in a hurry to finish collecting all of the mummy's treasure. When the fabulous wealth possibly contained in the wrappings became evident after the opening of the third coffin, revealing the famous golden mask, the English Egyptologist decided to cut open the mummy, no matter what the damage to the pharaoh's corpse. Today's evidence makes it clear that the damage was considerable, and we now understand why Carter decided not to draw attention in his notes and works to the dismemberment of the mummy. Since he obviously supposed that the separation of the mummy into parts would sooner or later be discovered, he exaggerated the damage to the outermost wrappings by asserting in all his writings that the wrappings and, by a false extension, the mummy itself, had spontaneously suffered from the attack of fatty acids supposedly contained in ointments poured onto the wrappings, as clearly repeated in his book *The Tomb of Tutankhamun.* Carter's false thesis was also resumed in a spectacular manner by Desroches-Noblecourt.

Carter lied blatantly on this point, as on many others. In the same book he asserted that simple exposure to heat made it possible to relatively easily remove the mask that was stuck to the bottom of the third coffin. Both Carter and Desroches-Noblecourt should have foreseen that, eventually, the photographic documents at the Griffith Institute would by themselves allow anyone who objectively looked at the plates to see that the mummy had been separated into several main sections. We must remember that this separation procedure was required to free the mummy and the mask from the bottom of the third coffin; the mask at this stage contained the upper extremity of the corpse (head and upper part of the neck). There is absolutely no doubt that Desroches-Noblecourt was aware that Carter had blatantly lied, since she had seen at least the photographic archives, and perhaps other documents as well.

One then wonders what the purpose of Desroches-Noblecourt's verbatim repetition of Carter's thesis was, since she writes in her book that she was perfectly well informed by the documents she had received from the Griffith Institute–Ashmolean Museum in Oxford. In her book she warmly thanks the team of experts at the institute "for their generously given assistance" since she was "allowed to consult the archives of the discovery" of the mummy. We must note that the most revealing and unflattering extracts from these archives concerning the mummy itself were published in the book written by the late F. Filce Leek in 1972. Inevitably, the day had to come when Desroches-Noblecourt's account would appear untenable. The reproduction of the head of the pharaoh, carefully faked in her book, was bound to be exposed as a fraud when compared with the authentic documents supplied by Oxford University.

Moreover, it is difficult to explain why the former director of the Metropolitan Museum of Art in New York City, Thomas Hoving, in his excellent book on the untold story behind the discovery of the tomb, would have chosen to omit the same facts gleaned from an examination of the Griffith Institute documents. In 1978, Hoving published at Simon and Schuster *Tutankha-*

*mun, the Untold Story.* This book devotes fewer than two pages to the mummy itself. On page 367, the author writes about Carter:

> "Most of his notes, catalogue cards and drawings today are preserved in the Griffith Institute at Oxford University. Five studies have emerged in the years that have elapsed since the discovery and ten more are in preparation. But there is little money to publish the rest of the material and, apparently, few opportunities to raise funds and provide the absolutely obligatory scholarly studies."

By 1972 the Griffith Institute had already published *Tutankhamun's Tomb Series,* Oxford University Press (General Editor: J. R. Harris). Five books were published in 1972, the last one written by F. Filce Leek and entitled *The Human Remains from the Tomb of Tutankhamun.* It provides essential data included in this work and can be assumed to be the same study referred to by Hoving as containing five volumes.

Hoving was aware of the wealth of documents supplied by the Griffith Institute. The captions of many illustrations published in his book mention this source. His account, while denouncing other of Carter's untruths, nevertheless repeats Carter's narrative concerning the mummy and attributes the damage to the pharaoh's corpse to the profusion of oils, ointments, and natron salts, which were used during the allegedly bungled mummification. He says nothing about the slicing of the mummy into three main parts by Dr. Derry.

Of course, Thomas Hoving does not write, as Desroches-Noblecourt does, that Derry "treated" the mummy, nor had he faked any Griffith Institute documents. Nevertheless, when one knows how the head, deliberately detached from the trunk, was extracted from inside the mask that enclosed it, the following account by Thomas Hoving concerning Carter's reaction is difficult to take seriously:

"The removal of the last linen obscuring the face of the king needed the most exacting care. With fine sable brushes the last few fragments of decayed fabric were brushed aside. The face of Tutankhamun himself was finally revealed. To Howard Carter, the royal visage was placid, the features well formed. The king must have been handsome beyond belief. As he held the head in his hands, Carter. . . was profoundly shaken by the experience" (p. 362).

The perpetrators of the dismemberment are almost depicted as having seen the pharaoh thanking them and were touched by his gratitude.

In actual fact, they had broken up the mortal remains of a human being into separate pieces, and he was not merely a museum object. The pharaoh had once wanted his anatomic integrity kept as complete as possible—every Egyptologist knows perfectly well that this integrity was in ancient Egypt considered essential for eternal salvation.

One may suppose that the desecration of a mummified body, preserved for almost thirty-three centuries, would have taken place in secret, in the deepness of a burial chamber bored under a rocky hill in a desert area. This is not at all what happened, however. The last draft of the treaty preceding this expedition, drawn up between the Egyptian government and the group assembled by Carter for the winter 1925–1926 excavations, stipulated even more rigorous controls by the Egyptian authorities, particularly by the Department of the Egyptian Antiquities. At the time, the department was directed by the French specialist in Egyptology, Pierre Lacau, who was no more ignorant of the dismemberment of the mummy—since he was present at the time—than other Egyptologists of worldwide repute who also were then in Egypt. None of them dared open their mouths.

Almost half a century was to pass before the most significant part of the written archives on this subject was published by Oxford University Press at the initiative of Professor W. Brian

Emery. Nevertheless, it must be noted that before 1972 the photographs of Carnarvon's and Carter's expedition could be obtained from the Griffith Institute–Ashmolean Museum by investigators who requested them and who could consequently discover, if they looked carefully, that the mummified corpse had been sliced into sections. With the exception of the late Filce Leek, no one else in Egyptological circles has said a word about the dismemberment.

I visited the tomb of Tutankhamun in the Valley of the Kings in November 1974 with a very competent Egyptian official guide. When I asked him about the condition of the mummy, his reply was that it was bad, due to defective mummification. I then asked for references of studies on the subject, not only during my visit to the necropolis in Thebes but also from the chief librarian at the Egyptian Museum in Cairo. The reference unanimously cited was Christiane Desroches-Noblecourt. When, later, I made the acquaintance of F. Filce Leek and looked at the details contained in his previously published book, I clearly understood that a distinction was to be made between the romantic tales, widespread throughout Egypt and the rest of the world concerning this mummy, and the authentic well-founded data, soberly preserved by reliable and scholarly British specialists.

Unfortunately, we live in a period in which it is impossible to have absolute trust in the assertions of persons possessing titles of authority. Yet, when academics brilliantly put forward rash hypotheses, their persuasive talent—which throws reservation to the wind—becomes a trap into which most people fall.

Alain Decaux, a member of the Académie Française, presented an episode entitled "Tutankhamun-Treasure-Curse" on January 14, 1987, on his monthly French television program. Rational discussion of the "curse" would obviously have meant taking human factors into account. In order to consider the problem of the curse, the point was to inform viewers about the exact reason for it. Was the offense to be punished by this so-called curse limited simply to the opening of the tomb; or was it the more serious offense of opening the coffins and their surroundings, which had constituted protection; or was it the attacking of the mortal remains?

Alain Decaux merely said at the end of his program that "The mummy of Tutankhamun is not at the Cairo Museum. This mummy is the only one that has been left in its sarcophagus in the Valley of the Kings. I think we should be clear on this, though the main reason the mummy is there is the deplorable condition it is in."

Alain Decaux made no other comment concerning the mummy.

Was he being as clear as he claimed to be? For assistance, he called on the collaboration of a single person, Christiane Desroches-Noblecourt. In less than two minutes, she justified the enthusiasm over the objects in the treasure, without, however, saying a word about the human aspects of the opening of the tomb. Thus, while millions of television viewers were eager to learn from Alain Decaux, "the professor of history with the largest audience in France," they were given an absolutely incomplete view of the matter, since the crucial question was the following: Did the Egyptologists concerned have the right to desecrate the perfectly preserved human remains of the pharaoh, effectively protected by the wrappings (see Fig. 50), in order to add objects possibly included in the wrappings to the multitude of treasures already collected outside the sarcophagus?

Alain Decaux has praised the high quality of Thomas Hoving's book, with which he is obviously very familiar. Since Alain Decaux is recognized as an excellent historical investigator, he could have gone beyond the enthusiastic proclamations of Desroches-Noblecourt. He could indeed have remembered what Thomas Hoving wrote in his book on past studies and the wealth of the documents kept by the Griffith Institute.

Luckily Alain Decaux avoided saying anything that would have appeared ridiculous to experts on the subject, nor did he quote Desroches-Noblecourt's assertion that "The mummy, very much damaged, was treated—and that is indeed the right word—by Dr. Derry," even though at first sight this statement would have been an even more spectacular conclusion.

In fact, the photographs in the Harry Burton collection at the Griffith Institute are enough to disprove the curse of Tutankhamun—no other proof is needed. Alain Decaux could have easily discovered this and presented it as the most significant piece of evidence. If such a curse had existed, its first target would have been the person who committed the utterly sacrilegious offense. Since the question was thought to haunt the minds of many television viewers, it would have been more meaningful, at the end of the program, to state that the person who sliced the pharaoh into sections, Dr. Derry, died in 1961 at the ripe old age of eighty-seven—more than thirty-five years after the infamous deed he committed in 1925.

It appears that the chronology of the mummy of Tutankhamun may be summarized as follows:

—thirty-three centuries for the sleep of the dead
—a week of dismembering
—a quarter of a century of misleading narratives.

The renowned Egyptologist, Professor Hans Goedicke of the Johns Hopkins University, in 1966 published a critique of the American edition of *Tutankhamen* by Desroches-Noblecourt. The complete text of the critique, which originally appeared in the *Journal of the American Research Center in Egypt*, vol. V, 1966, p. 127, reads as follows:

Tutankhamen; Life and Death of a Pharaoh, by Christiane Desroches-Noblecourt. Pp. 223, 132 illus., 32 color plates. Doubleday & Co., Inc.

The shelves of the bookstores are well stacked these days with expensive books on art and archaeology, but little is available in a modest price range. It is to the merit of the publishing house, Doubleday and Company, to have made an attempt to provide a book from its expensive price list in an inexpensive edition. Despite the smaller format and lower price, the illustrations and especially the color plates are of good quality and should give a wide range of readers a vivid impression of the splendor of the objects found in Tutankhamen's burial treasure.

While one can only praise the intentions of the publisher, it is unfortunate that the text of this volume does not merit the publisher's efforts. No doubt Mme Desroches-Noblecourt's statements will meet the fancy of the uncritical public, and Egyptologists for years to come will have to battle with the fantasies and misconceptions instigated by this book. Aside from the account of the discovery, which of course relies heavily on Carter, the reviewer had difficulty in deciding between the two alternatives: either it was intended as fiction, in which case Waltari's *Sinuhe the Egyptian* is certainly a more captivating narrative, or it is intended as a scientific account, in which case one can only wonder where the author got her information. To go critically into all details would mean rewriting the book. Only two points will be picked out, one for its general concern, the second for its curiosity.

The first concerns the rendering of Aten by "globe" as the latter denotes a spherical body, it is as such not applicable to Aten, the sun *disk*.

The second concerns Semenkhare's appointment as co-regent of Akhenaten. According to the author, "this position may confirm Akhenaten's efforts to transfer to Semenkhare the mystical role of Nefertiti as half of the royal couple," with the implication of an unnatural relationship between the two kings.

While the illustrations could make this book a valuable tool in teaching, the accompanying text is such that one can only warn against its use.

# The "Curse" of Tutankhamun

For over fifty years now, journalists looking for something sensational to write about have found plenty to keep them busy in the events surrounding the discovery and exploration of Tutankhamun's tomb. A curse is supposed to have descended on all those who were the promoters, principal actors, collaborators, or even simple spectators of the "rape" of the sepulcher.

Let us recall some facts, however: Lord Carnarvon, the patron of the expedition, had hurriedly returned to Egypt from England to be the first with Carter to enter the tomb on November 25, 1922; a few months later, he died at the age of fifty-seven. Some say he died of an insect bite, but the exact cause of death is unknown. Lord Carnarvon's death in Cairo was accompanied by the death of his dog in England and also a power failure. Nothing further was needed for the cry to be raised that the pharaoh-god was punishing him for the sacrilege he had committed. People claimed there was an inscription in the tomb warning the reader that "death would strike whoever disturbed the Pharaoh." Both the death of Lord Carnarvon's brother and that of Carter's secretary were ascribed to the curse. The same applied to many visitors to the tomb, whenever they had the misfortune to die shortly after their visit, or even some time after it.

Now let us examine the objections to this curse raised by the Egyptologists. Not one of them takes it seriously, and they insist that the existence of the curse is untenable for the following reasons. First, as Desroches-Noblecourt noted in an article published in the review *Atlas*, the inscription threatening the intruder with punishment is the product of pure invention. Her second argument is that

"the tomb has not been visited by tomb robbers, who would have ransacked the coffins to melt down their golden coverings

51

or remove the encrustations of agate and lapis lazuli. Quite the contrary, the objects have been carefully reinforced and restored, and have been transferred to the Egyptian capital. Thanks to the foresight and insistence of Pierre Lacau, at that time the Senior Head of Egyptian Antiquities, the objects were not dispersed. Instead, they were assembled at the Egyptian Museum in Cairo, where millions of visitors came to admire them—and still do."

Unfortunately, the third argument put forward suggests that the young king was given "preferential treatment," as it were. It is therefore stressed that he is "probably the only mummy of a Pharaoh to remain in the center of the tomb made for him, *in his original surroundings.*"

One could in fact say the exact opposite, for we should remember that many pharaonic mummies, either shortly after they were installed in their sepulchers, or even in modern times, were visited by tomb robbers who damaged the mummies by removing items of jewelry of great value; but the mummy of Tutankhamun undoubtedly remained untouched for nearly thirty-three centuries. It is today's treasure seekers who have carved Tutankhamun into pieces in order to retrieve precious objects. Can we honestly say that the fact that they did not share with the tomb robbers the sole motive of material gain excuses them for having profaned the pharaoh's mortal remains? If a curse really did exist, surely it would have first and foremost struck those responsible for the dismemberment of the mummy.

It is worth inquiring into what became of each of the two who performed the dismemberment. We know today that they both ended their days in the most natural way. Howard Carter was forty-nine when he entered Tutankhamun's tomb in 1922. He died in 1939, at age sixty-six. The pharaoh does not appear to have wrought vengeance on him during the seventeen years following the discovery of the tomb.

Douglas E. Derry had used cutting instruments to carve the

body into sections, and caused far more damage to the mummified body than Carter, who had merely limited himself to opening the doors and extracting precious objects. Yet Derry lived much longer than Carter. Filce Leek reports that he died on February 29, 1961, at the age of eighty-seven, nearly thirty-six years after he had dismembered the mummy.

What further evidence is needed to disprove fifty years of romantic tales about the so-called curse of Tutankhamun?

# 6. Data Observed at the Examination of Other Mummies

The fact that doctors have recognized the value of closely examining mummified bodies is hardly news today. The data revealed is very useful to medical science, especially that from examinations made by Egyptologists who were either doctors themselves or called upon doctors to assist in their investigations.

The data that has been drawn from the latter types of examinations is less well-known. Even less well-known is the fact that medical examinations are sometimes compared, which helps diagnose the state of decay of mummified bodies. This fact has surfaced only recently and has attracted much attention from those responsible for the royal mummies at the Egyptian Museum in Cairo as well as foreign Egyptologists, particularly the French. I was amazed to find in Egyptological circles that the things that immediately caught my eye as being self-evident had hardly been of any great relevance to them until then.

With regard to the illnesses that might have affected the subjects while alive, all the books dealing with pathology in ancient Egypt mention the fact that the mummy of Ramesses V showed, in spite of the shrinkage due to mummification, an extremely large scrotum. This indicates to the physician that the pharaoh was suffering from an inguinal hernia of considerable size, which simply confirms that the malady has been suffered throughout the ages.

What is certainly of greater interest in the history of diseases is the examination of the lower limbs belonging to the mummy of Merneptah-Siptah (Fig. 15), who reigned around 1200 B.C. To all those who looked at the uncovered body it appeared that the left foot was in fact a club foot. This simple diagnosis was subsequently added to, when it was considered that club foot was the result of infantile paralysis with atrophy and thus caused the considerable shortening of the left leg. Professor Amin Rida, an orthopedic surgeon working in Alexandria, published a highly documented study of these facts in 1964. In this study he mentions other relevant material concerning the same disease (e.g., the stele of the Syrian goddess Astarte in Copenhagen) showing that poliomyelitis already existed in Egypt in the fourteenth to fifteenth centuries B.C.

Several of the pharaohs suffered from skin diseases. Some of these afflictions were not of much importance other than their persistence in spite of mummification. In the other cases, however, comparisons between mummies showing the same diseases proved to be fairly important with regard to hypotheses made from a genealogical or historical point of view.

We shall only consider true skin diseases, not marks that may have been left on the skin by the wrappings or losses of matter that occurred when these were removed, taking shreds of mummified epidermis. This shredding is probably what happened in the case of Ramesses IV, who seems to have an ulceration of the penis. This has given rise to a considerable amount of literature on the subject, and some observers now claim to see this as evidence that venereal disease already existed at this stage in history. Yet, syphilis in particular does not appear to have existed in ancient Egypt at that time, or at least, there is still no formal proof of its existence. Nor do the common tattoo marks present on certain female mummies indicate that during their lifetimes they were women of "easy virtue." Tattoos were worn by both prostitutes and priestesses, as cited by A. P. Leca in his book *Mummies*, but the marks seen on the faces of the pharaonic mummies Merneptah and Ramesses V date from the time of mummification and were more or less tattoos that indicated their royal status.

The skin tumors that exist on the faces of certain pharaohs, such as the reddish-brown ones on the forehead of Ramesses II (Fig. 3), were first noticed a long time ago. One possible diagnosis is the common skin disease of senile comedones of acne. I consulted with Professors Robert Degos and Jean Civatte, dermatologists at Saint Louis Hospital in Paris. They were unable to come to a definitive conclusion on this subject. They were also unable to identify the lesions present on the face of Ramesses V (Fig. 16). Around 1900 they were thought to be the result of smallpox. A microscopic study of all these lesions would yield much further information, but today one obviously cannot suggest to the Egyptian museum authorities that they take even a tiny sample from the face of the royal mummies in their care, for this would only cause further damage.

On the other hand, the skin lesions of Amenophis II, Tuthmosis II, and Tuthmosis III are of both medical and historical interest. These kings were in a direct line of descent: Amenophis II was the son of Tuthmosis III, who was the son of Tuthmosis II. From our diagnosis they all show tumors of varying sizes distributed unevenly over their bodies. In the case of Amenophis II (Fig. 17), they are clearly visible at the base of his neck, while his face itself shows the presence of whitish colonies. These colonies are a recent appearance and will be further discussed later. The skin tumors of Tuthmosis II and Tuthmosis III are easily recognizable, as seen in Figure 18. The dermatologists mentioned above were again unable to make a definite pronouncement as to the nature of these lesions, because of the changes in the original color as a result of mummification. It would be worthwhile once again to make a microscopic examination, for as we shall see, such study of mummified tissues could well provide further information for a precise diagnosis. The likelihood of a hereditary disease is quite possible, for the grandfather, father, and son were all afflicted with these same lesions.

From a historical point of view, these skin lesions affected three generations. This fact disproves the theory that only the reign of Tuthmosis II could have occurred during the time of the Exodus mentioned in the Bible. The skin lesions on Tuthmosis II have been interpreted by some to be the famous "boils" that are described in the Bible as one of the plagues of Egypt, which occurred when Tuthmosis II refused to allow the enslaved Hebrews to depart with Moses. This theory was further supported by calendar calculations made in 1960 by Jean de Miceli, who claimed to have pinpointed the exact date of the Exodus to April 9, 1495 B.C. In my book *The Bible, the Qur'an and Science* I stated my position on this theory, which I feel should be rejected on many accounts—one of those being medical. It is impossible to consider something to be specific to a single king if it is inherited by all three who are in a direct line of descent. It is simply unacceptable to present, as an argument corroborating this theory, any medical findings that are not unique to the king of Egypt in question.

Numerous traces of the various accidents and wounds that occurred during a subject's lifetime have been found on nonroyal and royal mummies. Two of the royal mummies provide examples that are extremely significant from this point of view. The first is that of Sekenenre, a king of the Seventeenth Dynasty, and the second is Merneptah, the supposed pharaoh of the Exodus, successor of Ramesses II. (I shall return to Merneptah in much greater detail later on.) Apart from the royal mummies above, there are many documents concerning physical trauma in ancient Egypt. The effects of fractures resulting from trauma are visible on many mummies; such fractures may or may not have set correctly. X rays of the mummified bodies have provided us with precise data on the lesions and their consequences. On some mummified subjects, bones still in a fractured state were even found complete with the splints. Ange P. Leca noted the large abundance of fractures of the forearm and one case where this part of the limb had actually been amputated; embalmers went so far as to compensate for this loss to the extent of making an artificial hand, very roughly fashioned in pieces of moulded cloth, in order to restore the appearance of the living person to the mummy for all eternity.

The mummy of King Sekenenre, dating from the seventeenth century B.C., is in extremely poor condition. It may well have received only a cursory mummification, performed under un-favorable conditions near the battlefield on which the king met his death. In particular, it shows signs of deep wounds about the face and skull (Fig. 19), especially to the right, below the eye socket, and the upper regions of the forehead. These wounds were most probably delivered by the weapons of the Hyksos, against whom Sekenenre was doing battle at the time of his death. From a medical point of view, these lesions exhibit features that are clearly recognizable enough to conclude that they occurred under such conditions. In particular, the lesions include the presence, in the region occupied by cranial lesions, of a bone splinter consisting of a two-by-one-half-inch fragment that re-mains attached to the neighboring bone by connective tissue. Egyptologists and doctors are indebted to Elliot Smith's book *The Royal Mummies* for this description. Concerning the type of bone lesion shown on this mummy, it occurred sometime during the subject's lifetime as opposed to during mummification or a tomb robbery. In this particular case, we can be quite sure that wounds of this kind proved to be fatal.

The mummy of the second king is that of Merneptah. It was

also an interesting example for a doctor to examine. As we shall see later on, this mummy bears multiple traumatic lesions. In all probability, some of these occurred during the subject's lifetime, but X rays are required to establish that type of diagnosis. Other data can be gleaned from different sources. Nonetheless some of these lesions leave us in doubt as to whether or not they were sustained during his lifetime or after mummification. One such lesion is, however, quite patently the result of a trauma that has occurred to the mummy, not to the pharaoh during his lifetime. It is a fracture of the middle section of the right forearm that affects not only the bones but also the muscles, tendons, and skin covering them. All of these elements are very irregularly fractured and many fragments have fallen from the place of fracture (Fig. 20). This may be explained by the fact that mummified tissues, being in a state of dehydration, are extremely fragile and will shatter into many pieces on impact (Fig. 21). When this aspect of the mummified tissues is examined, there can be no doubt whatsoever that the breakage occurred after mummification.

Although these examples give us an idea of the advantages to be gained when a medical expert examines a mummy (with regard to the diagnosis), the models selected here are by no means the most unique. It is quite possible that, in conjunction with the data observed, the use of microscopic examinations, X rays, and endoscopic exploration may additionally provide further information as to the cause of a possible lesion. The combination of these methods can help further identify features that a single method of investigation would not otherwise have accomplished with the same precision.

I shall examine in some detail, later on, the advanced data obtained through the use of radiology, in showing the existence of Ramesses II's dental lesions. I gave my X-ray documentation, collected in Cairo in 1975, to Professor Georges Rousières and Dr. François Rousières. Together we reached the conclusion that the infection of the bone marrow in the mandible of Ramesses II was osteomyelitis. We noticed on the X rays not only a defect in the bone, but a detached fragment. I had personally examined and photographed the mummy in Egypt, aided by my colleague, Michel Durigon, and although the examination was extremely thorough, neither of us had noticed the existence of a minute orifice located in the submaxillary region of the mandible. François Rousières, a specialist in dental surgery, however, was struck by this orifice from his very first visit to the Museum of Anthropology in Paris. As we all stood before the mummy, Rousières drew my attention to the indisputable existence of this opening. Through this opening an enormous abscess must have flowed, resulting from the discharge or suppuration of the bone that proceeded from the teeth. Ramesses II had certainly died with this lesion. We shall see later on what connections these findings have with the last deeds ascribed to him by certain Egyptologists. They are more in a spirit of romantic fiction than of formally established data. Ramesses II was a very old man at the time of his death, and quite incapable therefore of performing any exerting deeds, a fact substantiated by medical examination.

# 7. The Decay and Deterioration of the Royal Mummies

In Cairo in 1975, I received the necessary authorization to examine the mummy of Merneptah. I was aided by Professor Michel Durigon, whose collaboration I had requested because of his knowledge of forensic medicine. When the piece of cloth covering the body was removed (Fig. 20) so that we could proceed with our examination, my colleague and I were both dismayed.

The state of the mummy as it was found at the beginning of the twentieth century was fully known to me. Pharaoh Merneptah had been discovered in 1898. His wrappings were removed on July 8, 1907, by Elliot Smith. An account of this early examination of the mummy, illustrated with photographs, is in Smith's book *The Royal Mummies*, which was published in 1912. When I compared these photographs with the state of the mummy in 1975, it was quite clear to me that the mummy had undergone considerable deterioration. I had not expected to find such damage. When I asked the authorities at the Egyptian Museum in Cairo about it and requested information concerning the reports filed on the mummy over the last decades (taking it for granted that examinations had been carried out over the years), I was informed that there were no records whatsoever. First the Head of the Egyptian Museum, then the President of Egyptian Antiquities came to observe the tragedy we had encountered. Elliot Smith's photographs had shown the existence of a lacuna (Fig. 8), or a hole, measuring 1 ½ × 2 ½ inches in the abdominal wall of the mummy. It was situated to the left of the medial line. Two-thirds of that same wall were found to have caved in when we began our examination in 1975; a piece of bone from the right side of the thorax including the inner part of the clavicle (Fig. 22) had detached itself from the mummy's thoracic wall, and though it had been in place at the beginning of the century (Fig. 23), it was missing during our examination and has never been found again. The mummy had also disintegrated in many places, in much more depth and over a much wider area than at the beginning of the twentieth century. Colonies of fungi, in the form of whitish heaps, were to be found scattered here and there, but on the thorax in particular. A sourish smell also wafted from the mummified body. Debris from the abdominal wall that had collapsed had filled the pelvis and was mixed with small fragments of tissue.

No one at the Egyptian Museum could say exactly when this had occurred. As far as the collapse of the abdominal wall is concerned, I have often wondered whether one of the diagrams in Elliot Smith's book may have already indicated serious damage to this part of the body at that time, or whether it had something to do with the samples that were taken from the abdominal aorta, once the wrappings had been removed, as described in the famous British medical journal *The Lancet* in 1909. Was deliberate damage caused for the sake of a medical examination? Whatever the case, the mummy showed signs of both structural and biological deterioration.

Once the museum authorities were alerted, they showed me a number of other mummies in poor condition. That of Merenre I (Fig. 1), from the Sixth Dynasty, is roughly forty-three centuries old and appears to be the most complete example from the Old Kingdom in existence. In 1975, it was in an advanced state of decomposition and gave off a frightful stench. A large part of the mummy's anterior thoracic wall was missing and so were parts of the neck and mandible. (Unless something is done to rescue it now, this mummy, too, will sooner or later disappear.)

The royal mummies of Merneptah and Merenre I were probably among the worst affected by the deterioration caused by the method used to preserve them. In their cases, as well as that of Ramesses II, the findings of 1975 indicated that two kinds of deterioration were present: structural destruction and biological decay. Structural destruction requires that action be taken to strengthen the bodies of the mummies, and biological decay is stopped through a sterilization method. These mummified bodies were proved to have been invaded by various kinds of parasites and subject to damage from insects, fungi, and microbic putrefaction agents. It is quite possible today to treat the mummies with processes that will not at the same time be harmful to the mummified tissues. For many years, the only methods of preservation known were chemical. These may have been useful, but were mainly effective at surface level. Today's gamma-ray treatment (used in France to preserve works of art) acts more in depth. It was used on Ramesses II because it was shown to be of no danger to the mummified tissues, extremely adaptable, and deep reaching. I shall return to this point later.

Another royal mummy was in equally serious danger, that of Amenophis II (Fig. 17). The mummy's face had been taken over by whitish colonies, and all the evidence pointed to their being a fungal growth. This diagnosis, however, needed to be checked by microscopic examination for it to be absolutely confirmed, which I recommended to the Egyptian Museum in 1975 but without any success. When I checked on the mummy in

December of 1976, the invasion of fungi appeared to have spread.

In recording the long history of the mummies, their sepulchers, the removal of their wrappings after discovery, and their condition of preservation over the last decades, I have learned about the various factors contributing to their decay and deterioration. Apart from the damage done by tomb robbers, the mummies of the New Kingdom undoubtedly suffered far less damage in the course of the three thousand years spent in their tombs than during the few decades they have been in the open air, exposed to the ravages of their present environment. Some, such as Ramesses II, have been exposed for more than ninety years, others for slightly less, but they have all suffered as a result.

If the mummies are to be saved, we must now reproduce by artificial means the conditions that were prevalent in their tombs. Complete insulation, protection from light rays, and constant levels of temperature and humidity are the conditions I described in various works, such as the September 1976 issue of the review *Archaelogia*, under the title "The Need for Urgent Rescue," *before* Operation Ramesses and the arrival of Ramesses II in Paris. They are the very conditions, apart from the air conditioning of the display case, that were in fact created for Ramesses II (but for him alone) upon his return to Cairo in May 1977. Until then, he had been kept, like his neighbors in the Royal Mummies Room, under a protective glass that was not hermetically sealed. The individual showcase that was designed for Ramesses II in Paris should now be reproduced for the other mummies to replace their present cases, with air conditioning as well. The present display cases are not only antiquated but fail to protect the mummies from group contaminations.

When Egyptologists removed the wrappings of the mummies, it caused their several-thousand-year-old insulation to be broken. It was held at that time that mummification alone would suffice to ensure preservation. Gaston Maspero had sounded the alarm in 1916 as we have already seen, but more than sixty years passed before the problem was considered again. It is hoped that the Egyptian authorities will put the progress made to good use. If they halt their attempts to rescue the royal mummies at Ramesses II, it is unlikely that there will be any chance of saving certain others.

# Part III

---

# MODERN
# MEDICAL
# INVESTIGATIONS

# 8. Microscopic Research

## The Examination of Mummified Tissues Through the Microscope

Microscopic examination of mummified bodies casts light on illnesses suffered by ancient subjects during their lifetime. Anatomical cell formations can be identified in mummies several thousand years old that have come down to us in a satisfactory state of preservation, and these findings indicate that the process of mummification could preserve not only basic organs and tissues, both human and animal (various animals were mummified, including fish), but also their detailed structural characteristics. Mummification protected these bodies from the effects of decay and putrefaction that normally cause them to disappear after a certain time.

In 1852, J. Czermack tried, somewhat unsuccessfully, to examine mummified tissue under a microscope. For those not familiar with this procedure, there is a difficulty that lies in the fact that one cannot simply take a tiny sample from a mummy and mount it directly onto a microscope slide. The mummified tissue has to be prepared first before one can proceed to an examination. The procedure is much like the one used for a sample from a human organ taken from an operating room or from an animal in the laboratory.

To examine a freshly taken sample of tissue, the sample must first be treated with a solution called a fixative. It is then incorporated into a block of paraffin, which is readied to be cut into extremely thin sections with the aid of an instrument called a microtome. After the sections are cut, they are then bathed in various dyes. It is only then that they are ready to be viewed under the microscope.

This same process was required for mummified tissues. The dry, brittle samples first had to be transformed into tissue that was soft enough to withstand cutting, but the tissue fragment first had to be rehydrated. It was during this process that the extreme difficulty lay. The correct rehydrating solution had to be chosen, then care had to be taken not to over-rehydrate. If this occurred an unusable pulp was obtained. On the other hand, under-rehydrating had to be avoided. In the mid nineteenth century, J. Czermack tried using caustic soda (sodium hydroxide) but was unsuccessful. Many other attempts were subsequently made over the years, but seldom met with any success.

It was not until the beginning of the twentieth century that the patient work of a doctor who was also a great enthusiast of Egyptology resulted in the perfection of a technique of preparing the tissues, the basic principles of which are still valid today. Marc A. Ruffer was a Frenchman born in 1859 in Lyons. He attended medical school in England and then went on to Paris, where he studied the then recently developed science of bacteriology. After completing his studies, Ruffer went to Egypt, where he taught bacteriology and devoted his hours of research to the microscopic investigation of mummies. Ruffer was killed during a torpedo attack in World War I. Although he died before his time, he left behind a considerable number of achievements. His successors followed in his footsteps, using techniques that were little more than variations of the processes he had invented for the preparation of mummified tissues. The optical instruments used since the time of Ruffer have obviously been improved considerably.

Today, the scanning electron microscope allows us to uncover details that would have otherwise gone unnoticed. These new microscopes have considerable powers of enlargement and enable us as scientists to distinguish tiny elements inside the cell itself.

At the beginning of my research in Cairo in 1974, the knowledge of the remarkable results obtained by Ruffer led me to believe that we should be able to do as well, if not better, using our more modern equipment in Paris (I had seen the colored plates of his microscopic observations). The one difference was that Ruffer had had as much mummified tissue available for his research as he needed, sixty years ago in Egypt, whereas in France in 1974, this was no longer the case. What I was hoping for primarily was to bring back a few well-preserved fragments of mummy to France. Permission to do so is not easy to obtain, however. Museum authorities are somewhat reluctant to sacrifice a well-preserved fragment of mummy when told that it is to be used for technical tests, even if the final objective is something that will subsequently be of use when it comes to further research. In 1975, Henri Ryad, the former head of the Egyptian Museum in Cairo, and Abdel Kader Selim, the current head, were made personally responsible for the selection of samples of tissue. Two fragments were taken from the thorax of a mummy that was in excellent state of preservation. The mummy used was that of a woman (Fig. 9) who had lived during the Nineteenth Dynasty, around 1200 B.C. One of the samples taken showed a perfect preservation of the skin (Fig. 24). The pores were still visible after 3200 years. It was as if they had been those of a living person. This extremely high quality of mummification allowed us to uncover certain anatomical formations that are usually distinguished only in contemporary human tissue.

I entrusted these samples to Professor Jacques Mignot and Professor Michel Durigon. Together, they were able to quickly apply the rehydration technique and the method of fixation in the appropriate liquids that precedes embedding the specimens in paraffin. The work carried out by these two specialists is among the finest ever performed by those engaged in such delicate research. I am greatly indebted to both of them for the success I obtained in my international presentations on microscopic images of mummified tissue.

The fragment Jacques Mignot and Michel Durigon studied had various layers of thoracic covering, which were perfectly distinguished from one another. A general view of the section (Fig. 25) showed details that were extremely interesting. First, the epidermis had disappeared. This was due either to burns caused by natron salts used during mummification, which are equivalent to what we would call second-degree burns, or to the removal process of the mummy's wrappings, which may have torn the epidermis away. The underlying layers appeared to bear their natural features. The cells of the layer producing the dermis and the subdermic network of connective tissue, muscle fibers, and vessels were all able to be seen. Three elements do merit particular attention:

1. The muscular fibrillae (Fig. 26). Together, these form muscle fibers. One of their features is the transversal striation normally found only in skeletal muscles. Intestinal muscles do not have such striations. The size of the unit employed to measure these formations is $\frac{1}{1000}$mm. Mummification had kept them perfectly preserved.
2. The cells. These cells and their nuclei are visible in the dermis (Fig. 27). Usually, such cells work their way up from the depths to the surface, each layer representing its own characteristics. In the lowest layer at the base, small cells have been found with their nuclei. In the upper layers, the cells grow larger and gradually lose their nuclei.

At this point they become anuclear. These different stages of cell growth were observable with utmost clarity.

3. The blood cells. In the fragment examined, the cells were so perfectly preserved that it was possible to isolate and identify the blood cells. It is a well-known fact that these cells are extremely unstable, particularly the red blood cells (Fig. 28). Aidan Cockburn and his collaborators in the United States made the same observations. On one of our slides red blood cells could clearly be distinguished. The ability to identify blood cells after thirty-two centuries shows the extraordinary powers of preservation provided by mummification. The skill of the laboratory technicians and doctors who managed to rehydrate these cells is almost equally as significant.

I have often wondered why a mummy, such as the one that was the subject of this examination, showed differences in skin color. In this particular instance (Fig. 9), the skin color does not appear to be the result of an artificial process, as it was in the case of Ramesses V, whose face had been painted red (Fig. 16). Nor was it the use of certain resinous substances during mummification, giving the mummy a blackish appearance, as in the case of Amenophis II (Fig. 17). The mummy of Sethos I, the father of Ramesses II, was severely damaged soon after it was installed in its tomb, and it was probably repaired and strengthened in the Twenty-first Dynasty with the use of a black bituminous substance that gave the mummy its present color (Fig. 31). In the case of the mummy from the Nineteenth Dynasty (Fig. 9), there was a great contrast between the upper part of the thorax, which was grey or brownish in places, and the lower section, where the skin had retained its normal color. A sample taken from the region of the left armpit was a reddish brown. This showed that the color was due to the absence of skin in this area: the muscle was covered by only a few scattered scraps of skin tissue, and the brownish tone was thus the result of bare muscle tissue.

Less surprising, perhaps, was the fact that the bone had remained well preserved. We do possess ancient bones that are older than those of the mummies and have survived in a good state of preservation—at least as far as their external appearance is concerned. In the case of mummified bone, microscopic examinations reveal that its microscopically visible features have been absolutely perfectly preserved (Fig. 29). If one knew nothing about where it had come from one might think it a fresh bone.

As a specialist in forensic medicine, my colleague Michel Durigon was particularly interested in the mummies' hair. When we were in Cairo together in 1975, the museum gave us some hair from two mummies that were more than four thousand years old. Durigon examined them with a scanning electron microscope with under-reflected fluorescent light. This technique is among one of the most advanced forms of research into infinitely small structures, from a biological point of view. The hair structure appeared to have deteriorated only very slightly and its natural pigmentation was still visible. Aidan Cockburn's research team in the United States in 1973 also used the scanning electron microscope to explore intracellular structures on mummified tissues.

Using the fragments at our disposal, microscopic examinations were successful, above all, in showing the perfect preservation of the anatomical cell characteristics of mummified tissues. We were prepared, if need be, to carry out individual analyses using only tiny samples, because it is sometimes impossible to remove more than an infinitely small portion without damaging a mummy.

The large fragment I brought back from Egypt enabled specialists to perform technical trials: the study of this fragment provided training that was to be useful later on. Experimental studies were also carried out on the irradiation, or the X raying, of mummified tissues prior to the gamma-ray sterilization proposed for the mummy of Ramesses II. Professors Jacques Mignot and Michel Durigon collaborated on Operation Ramesses II by using their considerable technical expertise. As far as I know, this technique has never been mastered elsewhere in France to the same degree.

No research was carried out on the viscera of Ramesses II, for we did not have these at our disposal. Of all the pharaohs, I do not think that any viscera, except those of Tutankhamun, could have benefited from microscopic examination. The viscera of the other pharaohs have either disappeared or remain in certain areas of the bodies from which they cannot be removed. The heart of Ramesses II is said to have been examined at one time and appeared to be free from serious wounds, at least from a macroscopic point of view, but the proof as to the origin of the organ examined does not seem to me to have been provided. The heart of Ramesses II may have been embalmed and placed in a canopic jar and later extracted, or perhaps it was left in place in the thorax, where, until now, there has been no investigation made that confirms its presence. On the other hand, the aorta of his son, Merneptah, was indeed examined in London by S. G. Shattock, as published in the English medical review *The Lancet* in 1909. There are no illustrations, but the author claims to have found platelets, indicating the presence of lesions of arteriosclerosis. This comes as little surprise, since the X ray taken in Cairo, in 1975, also shows examples of calcification in the femoral arteries.

During the first years of the twentieth century, microscopic research helped uncover lesions in various organs. Marc A. Ruffer examined an impressive number of mummified tissues and was able to reach diagnoses *a posteriori*. Some of these discoveries were of considerable importance in the history of medicine in ancient Egypt.

It is known today that schistosomiasis, a disease where parasitic worms can invade several organs, among them the bladder, is rampant throughout the Nile Valley and especially the Nile Delta. Almost 100 percent of the country people are affected by it. Although it is possible to treat cases that are not too advanced, continued exposure to the parasite is unavoidable due to the river and canal water. It is these water areas that are responsible for the high mortality rate. This disease is well-known today, but until M. A. Ruffer's investigations in 1910, there was nothing to prove that it had existed in ancient Egypt. His microscopic examination of several mummies, dating from around 1000 B.C. revealed calcified bilharzia eggs in the kidneys. Ruffer also made several other interesting discoveries that showed the existence in the New Empire of arterial atheroma, lung infections, renal suppurations, cirrhosis of the liver, and anthracosis of the lungs. It is a shame that he did not have methods of color photography reproduction at his disposal to record the microscopic features of such lesions. He reproduced, or had reproduced, drawings of what he saw through his microscope. There is no doubt however, that his conclusions are highly relevant, and the greatest credence should be given to them. Had Ruffer possessed all the modern optical equipment including a scanning electron microscope, I am certain that he would have discovered much more. Those who benefited from his work seem, technically speaking, to have arrived at more exact diagnoses. Today, though, it is the "raw material" that is missing. There are not that many mummified tissues left to study because of plundering and the dispersion of those few specimens that were available. The rarity of mummies means that those remaining—the royal ones first and foremost—are more or less untouchable. Further research is limited because of this.

## The Discovery of Parasitical Biological Agents

Another important use of the scanning electron microscope in the study of mummies is in the discovery of parasitic biological agents. Research of this kind can be approached in two different ways, which depend on the type of mummified bodies to which it is applied.

The first type of mummies are those whose identity is often unknown and whose date and place of origin have only been approximated. These mummies exist in the reserves of many museums, where they have unfortunately been abandoned. Should one wish to acquire one of them for research purposes, however, even if this requires the taking of only the most innocuous samples, the museum curator will most likely counter this request with the fact that the mummy has been registered, catalogued, and accounted for, and that he is responsible for it. To this curator, what does it matter if the mummy decays, as long as it decays *administratively*? A curator's job is, by definition, to preserve a mummy for better or for worse, while warding off any intrusions from the outside, even by those who request to carry out scientific research for its benefit.

Things do not always happen this way. Such institutions as the Pennsylvania University Museum have had the good sense to donate, to a team of scientists headed by Aidan Cockburn of Detroit, several mummies named P.U.M. in order to determine their place of origin. Specialists from highly diversified disciplines were involved in this and a thorough exploration was made. There was obviously very little of the original mummy left at the end, but Cockburn and his team made an extremely important contribution to our medical knowledge of mummies. Such multidisciplinary research was carried out in England (The Manchester Museum Mummy Project under the direction of Dr. Rosalie David in 1975–1979). It, too, provided new and valuable information about the preservation of other mummies threatened with decay and deterioration.

These, the deteriorating mummies, form the second category of mummies, which for certain reasons we should like to rescue from danger. Authorization was given to me in Egypt to carry out certain special research studies, but I have never been able to obtain even a few cubic millimeters of sample, scraped either from the surface of Merneptah's body or from that of Amenophis II, which has been invaded by colonies of parasites. The overall diagnosis is that important mummies have not been treated properly and are slowly decomposing.

Samples taken from royal mummies are, for all intents and purposes, highly rare, even though these samples would certainly be useful in deciding which of the mummies are to be given priority treatment in the preservation process. They would reveal more than simply that such-and-such a mummy is under attack from such-and-such a biological agent. Furthermore, a sample taken from only one area that does not reveal the presence of fungi or bacteria does not mean that it is absent elsewhere. Only positive results have any value, and they must be rechecked continuously. A thorough knowledge of possible contaminants is required, particularly of contaminants that attack mummies preserved in such conditions as those prevalent at the Egyptian Museum in Cairo, and more specifically in the case of the mummy of Ramesses II.

General autopsy work has indicated that fungi, insect larvae, and bacterial agents can invade mummies. Mummies are a favorable environment for the culture of all such microorganisms. Since the essential aim is to preserve the mummies to the best degree, we cannot open or cut them. So when an extremely tiny sample is taken from one of them and one of these contaminating agents is found on the surface of the mummy, it is a signal for alarm. The reason is that we do not know what is going on underneath, inside the mummy. We are unable to reach these areas. This idea is to me as clear as daylight. But what may be clear and simple to a doctor is not always taken into consideration, as it should be, by those not of the medical profession. This became apparent to me during Operation Ramesses II at the Museum of Anthropology in Paris.

When I left Cairo in November of 1975, the mummy of

Ramesses II had been removed from the Egyptian Museum, where it had been on display, and transported to a nearby laboratory. The intention was to isolate the mummy in a separate, air-conditioned case that had been sent from Paris by the Museum of Anthropology. I must remind the reader that the initial aim of the director of the Museum of Anthropology in Paris was to transport the mummy of Ramesses II for exhibition purposes and not for medical or scientific study. The mummy was not placed at that time inside the intended case. The experts from the Museum of Anthropology, who stayed behind after my departure, sent me samples of dust and pellicles taken from various points on and near the body. These samples were examined by Dr. M. Ferly Thérizol. Those from the periphery of the abdominal orifice, used for extracting the viscera, contained spores (Fig. 30); others seemed to contain insect debris, like the legs of acarids. The spores did not grow as cultures. They looked very much like those of fungi. What further evidence was needed (in view of what we know about the research performed on other mummies) to show that the mummy of Ramesses II should have been sterilized? It was clearly being invaded by parasites, and this one fact alone indicated that treatment was needed.

This was later confirmed when several different species of fungi were found at the Museum of Anthropology in Paris. They were found existing on samples taken from other parts of the body. This confirmation was of extremely great interest. Had this discovery not been made, the problem would have remained the same. It is impossible to know *everything* about the biological contaminations. One cannot take samples from all over, and especially not from inside mummies. Therefore, a single indication of biological pollution is all that is needed. What must be avoided is the assumption that if no bacterial agents are found, then a mummy is free of them. A trained bacteriologist will easily agree with that statement.

In matters such as this, let us remember the practical conclusion to be drawn. In 1975 in Cairo, the discovery and confirmation that the mummy was contaminated by biological agents meant that it would have to be sterilized. The process was one in which, regardless of the nature of the contaminating agent and its location in the mummified body, the agent would be destroyed. These requirements called for the use of gamma rays, a satisfactory process in this particular case. Later, we shall see how this solution was arrived at and describe the precautions that had to be taken to make quite sure that it would not be harmful to the mummified tissues.

## Research in Genetics

We know that the D.N.A. carries the genes that are the support of hereditary characteristics. In every cell of a human being, the total length of the D.N.A. tape is one and a half to two meters. We are far from knowing all the genes of a human being, forming what we call the genoma. In bacteria, the genoma is considerably reduced, corresponding to its very small size: for example, in *Escherichia Coli* the length of the D.N.A. tape is about one millimeter.

Modern progress in the ultramicroscopic investigation of the cells of mummies allowed Svente Pääbo, of the University of Uppsala in Sweden to extract a short sequence of D.N.A. supporting the genes—that is, to draw out the chemical support of a minuscule part of hereditary characteristics.

Evidence of the perfect preservation of D.N.A. by mummification was shown by the possibility of including this short sequence in a bacteria, like *Escherichia Coli*, and by obtaining replicas in the descendance of the latter (cloning). We must emphasize the preservation of certain hereditary characteristics by the mummification processes. Nevertheless, we must avoid being carried away by overenthusiasm concerning the possibilities of discovering hereditary characteristics in mummified bodies.

Unfortunately French journalists and even scientists speaking on TV showed no restraint in commenting on this finding.

The only appropriate remark that I know of, from this point of view, was made by J. S. Jones, of the Department of Genetics and Biometry, University College, London: "It is important to understand *what Pääbo has not done*: we cannot of course reconstitute a functional gene (let alone a living individual) from this short repeated sequence." (*Nature*, vol. 314, no. 6012, 18–24 April 1985, pp. 644–645 and 576)

# 9. X-ray Examination

One day in 1903, a taxi driver in Cairo drove three passengers, each of whom has left his name to posterity. Two of the passengers—Elliot Smith and Wood Jones—were famous anthropologists. The third passenger, Tuthmosis III, was a former king. Smith and Jones had decided to transport Tuthmosis to a Cairo clinic where the first X-ray equipment in Egypt had been installed. Portable X-ray units did not exist at this time, so to X ray the king, there was only one possible solution: transport him to the clinic.

In 1898, an Egyptologist, Flinders Petrie, had also wanted to test the use of recently discovered X rays in his study of mummies. The feet and legs were the only parts of the body that could be X rayed however, for the unit had not yet reached a degree of perfection sufficient to provide proper images of other parts of the body.

These two "firsts," resulting from British initiative, began the X-ray study of mummies. I might add that these British applications of radiological techniques were quite extensive. Even today, modern studies are still inspired by those of P. H. K. Gray, who took many X rays of the mummies in the Leiden Museum and the British Museum in 1966. From his copious documentation, Gray gathered extremely important information, whose technical details proved very instructive for us in Cairo in 1975. In a way, it enabled us to obtain remarkably clear and precise X rays using only a portable unit.

I have taken much of the material in this chapter, from the report I submitted to the French Society of Radiology in April 1976. It was prepared in close collaboration with Dr. Clément Fauré, chief radiologist of the Paris Hospitals, and my Egyptian colleagues.

Twice I had returned from Egypt with X-ray documentation of the several pharaohs whose bodies had been completely examined. I requested Dr. Clément Fauré help me scrutinize these X rays in Paris, for I felt his comments would be extremely useful to me. Before turning to my own observations concerning the pharaonic mummies, however, I would like to review the general importance X-ray examination has in regard to mummies.

First, one has to be able to recognize a true mummy from a false one. This must be mentioned since forgery, believe it or not, did at one time exist, not for a pharaoh of course, but there were cunning forgers in Egypt who made wrappings assembled on a wooden and wire frame that gave the appearance of mummies. They managed to trick enthusiastic buyers into thinking they were taking home what they believed was a rare antiquity. X rays, to say the least, uncovered this stratagem.

Another totally unexpected result of radiological study was a case in which the virtue of a princess, Makare, who died three thousand years previously was being defended. Certain Egyptologists who were deciphering her mortuary inscription said that it suggested she was a virgin because of her status as a Divine Votaress of Amon, but others had written that she was the wife of Pharaoh Pinedjem, by whom she had had a child, who may have been the small mummy found buried next to her. Which side was right? The one supporting her virginity or those who claimed she had violated her position as a Divine Votaress? The use of radiology in 1968 brought everyone to agreement: the accompanying mummy was not of a child but that of a baboon. It was learned later that the princess had wanted her favorite animal mummified like herself and buried next to her. The image of the mummy's skeleton, as it appeared on the X ray, was sufficiently detailed for the type of ape to be identified.

Getting back to the information yielded from the X-ray studies on several royal mummies, I must stress that X rays took a very prominent position in all of the research undertaken. I later found some pertinent data in James Harris and Kent Weeks' book *X-Raying the Pharaohs*. This American team had X rayed many royal mummies, but their diagnosis did not provide enough explanation. There were too few X-ray plates in their book, and the text was open to discussion on certain points. The text actually contradicted the point made by the illustrations, one example being the results from the examination of Pharaoh Merneptah's teeth. Their investigation, due to inconclusive results, had more or less to be completely redone.

In 1975, Professor K. Kassem, Professor Ragay El Meligiy, and Dr. A. Ramsis were kind enough to honor my request and perform complete X-ray examinations of each of the following four mummies: Merneptah, Ramesses II, Tuthmosis II, and Sethos I. During this study, they also carried out a partial study of other mummies to establish certain specific points. I was given a special-grade X-ray film, by Kodak in Paris, suitable for the research we were about to undertake. The X rays my Egyptian colleagues produced are the continuing subject of praise from many specialists, particularly since they were obtained with a very simple portable unit.

The skeletal system is obviously what appears most clearly on X rays. The bones were what interested us most in the case of Pharaoh Merneptah. To start, we sought indications defining the different characteristics of the lesions that occurred during the subject's life, as opposed to those that came after mummification. It was important to distinguish the two, for our ultimate goal was to establish the exact causes leading to the death of this pharaoh, whom we thought to be the pharaoh of the Exodus.

After I had examined Merneptah, the Egyptian authorities asked me to carry out an equally exhaustive study on the mummy of Ramesses II. The examination of this skeleton was of crucial importance. The physical state of the pharaoh's bone structure had to be established so that we could decide just how solid it was. Apart from the skeleton, the pharaoh's body was, quite visibly, riddled with cracks such that we needed, in addition to a naked eye view, a very faithful radiological view of it as well. We strove to get excellent pictures of the parts of the body that were not skeletal, or in other words the soft tissues. In this manner we were able to study the full extent and seriousness of the mummy's decay.

The mummies of Sethos I and Tuthmosis II were studied because of the importance of the bone lesions that were seen on them. As a result of our first evaluation, our objective was to figure out what could be done to consolidate such badly damaged mummies. The destruction of these mummies was most likely caused when their tombs were ransacked. The mummy of Sethos I had been decapitated by tomb robbers, but had been embalmed a second time. In this second embalming process, a high collar of resin had been added to more or less hold the neck in position on the thorax (Fig. 31). The traces of decapitation at the base of the neck, however, are perfectly visible on the X rays. The X rays also show the existence of a few votive objects made of metal located in the thicker part of what is left of the materials enveloping the mummy just inside its left arm. This practice was common in many mummification processes. Various votive objects would be placed among the wrappings around the mummy. The body of Tutankhamun was surrounded by more than 100 such objects, which were found when the Egyptologists removed the wrappings from the mummy. Tutankhamun, we must remember, had not been violated. Such objects have rarely been found in other mummies, for nearly all of these others have been plundered at one time or another. Only a few other objects exist, as shown by X rays, a good example being those of Sethos I (Fig. 32).

It is interesting to make a comparison between the differences in X rays taken of the same part of the body of different mummies. With this in mind, there are two mummies that provide a fruitful comparison of the thorax, and the abdomen and pelvis. They are the mummies of Ramesses II and Merneptah.

## X Rays of the Thorax

The mummies of Ramesses II (Fig. 33) and Merneptah (Fig. 34) differ in the contents of the thorax. Very simply put, one may say that the first has a full thorax and the second an empty or almost empty one.

There is every indication that both bodies underwent similar mummification processes. The first stages of the ritual in Merneptah's case may well have been affected by his tragic death, which in all likelihood occurred while he was pursuing the Hebrews during the Exodus. This, however, is a simple hypothesis. The most likely explanation of the empty thorax is that at some time, but definitely at a time before the removal of his wrappings, Merneptah's thorax was emptied of the organs it contained. As I stated earlier, these organs were also embalmed, like the rest of the body, and then placed partly in canopic jars and partly in the thoracic and abdominal cavities. Merneptah's body underwent the same general treatment that his organs did during embalmment. When Merneptah's wrappings were removed at the beginning of the twentieth century, the abdomen (Fig. 8) was definitely closed and not wide open as was the case with Ramesses II (Fig. 2). There was an incision, though, on its lower left side, which had been made to remove the viscera.

There are practically no organs left in the thorax of Merneptah (Fig. 34). At present there is one abnormal shadow in the upper left part of the thorax that is clearly marked in the X ray by a whitish area with irregular contours. This shadow seems to indicate the presence of an organ. Apart from this, the forearms are clearly folded over the chest. Note that in the case of Merneptah, the arms are more or less symmetrically crossed.

The presence of materials filling the thorax is marked on the X ray of Ramesses II (Fig. 33), by convergent white masses. These contours are blurred and largely superimpose the image of the folded forearms. The forearms are very unevenly crossed. The right forearm is less folded back against the rest of the arm than the left and is in much more of a horizontal position than a vertical one. In contrast, the left forearm is tightly folded back and is nearer the vertical position.

What are the materials filling the thorax of Ramesses II? The only way of knowing is to compare him with what we know of other mummies and the practices of the embalmers during this time in the New Kingdom. The custom at that time was to remove all of the viscera from the thoracic and abdominal cavities, mummify them, and then to replace them. They were packed in cloth, surrounded by lichens and other various plants, sand, resinous substances, and on occasion, bags of natron salts. This was done for either all or some of the viscera without regard to anatomical considerations. The heart may just as easily have been removed as left in place. In many cases, we just do not know. What we do know about Ramesses II, however, is that it is absolutely impossible to explore the thorax through the open abdomen. We realized this from our endoscopic investigations. The reason for this is that there is no possibility of inserting an endoscope through the contents of the thorax without hitting a wall of resin that isolates the thorax from the abdomen. We had to make do with X-ray investigations in trying to ascertain the contents of the thorax.

When normal methods are employed to take an X ray of the thorax, all types of superimposed shadows appear. Their opacities vary according to their chemical characteristics. The heavier the chemical compounds, the whiter the image. The sharpness of the contours and the differences in tone of these compounds are in proportion to the sensitivity of the film. The degree to which the tones are affected by the X rays depends on the extent to which these have been arrested by the masses they cross. Whatever the case, we remain entirely dependent on *all the masses crossed from front to back* on a frontal projection. Whatever the quality of the film, the density problem remains the same.

To get the best radiographic results and thus arrive at an improved knowledge of a certain part of the body, one has to employ a process that provides plane by plane views. Everything in this process is X rayed on a predetermined plane at a certain distance from a fixed point on the body at so many centimeters or half-centimeters, for example, in relation to the shot taken from the back. In this way, it is possible to isolate each of the contents of the thorax plane by plane and to obtain, on the X ray, an exclusive view of the particular plane in question. This process, called polytomo-radiography, enables one to uncover formations that would not otherwise have been shown. I have stressed its usefulness, along with Clément Fauré, with regard to mummies, since our report of April 1976 to the French Society of Radiology. In this report we also reinforced the importance of the studies of Aidan Cockburn, an American specialist. He had used this process inside a skull to uncover extremely precise and detailed information.

It was perfectly obvious to me that the complexity of the contents of Ramesses II's thorax required this radiological process to be used. X-ray equipment capable of executing this polytomo-radiography could have been installed at the Museum of Anthropology to study the mummy. To do so, a high-tension cable would have had to be led nearly 100 yards from a power-point to supply the equipment with electricity. After all was said and done, my plan was deemed too complicated and I was unable to persuade the head of the Museum of Anthropology to perform these extremely useful investigations.

Another possibility would have been to transfer Ramesses II from the laboratory at the museum to a nearby clinic or hospital that had tomographic equipment. I must note that every Paris hospital has one of these units. Again I was met with a categorical refusal and the tomographic study was dropped. Standard X-ray studies were carried out in Paris at this time but they simply repeated those already done in Cairo in 1975.

The value of the tomographic study of mummies was plainly demonstrated at the symposium "Science in Egyptology" in June of 1979 at the University of Manchester in England. Eminent specialists from various disciplines gathered at this international meeting to present their work in this field. The radiologists of Manchester University were particularly important. I presented the results of my investigations performed on a certain number of royal mummies, among them Ramesses II. In my presentation, I did not mention tomography, although at that time it had been successfully used in centers specializing in research on mummies.

The reasons why it had not been possible to perform tomographic exploration during my investigations at the Egyptian Museum in Cairo were perfectly understood. The equipment was simply not available. The same circumstance did not apply, however, to the investigations that could have been made—but were not—when the mummy was in Paris. In fact, such investigations were deliberately ruled out for the reasons I have indicated.

The Museum of Anthropology prided themselves on having used special film in their X-ray work. The fact is that the X rays showed nothing more than X rays taken with normal film would have—at least as far as the *essentials* were concerned. Chromodensitography, like xerography, could have helped separate the masses contained in the mummy's thorax, but it did not provide any information that enabled us to establish the nature of the mummified organ. The mummified heart had been so deformed by dehydration and packing that the shape it had taken did not even indicate which organ it was. There is no definite or precise information regarding the masses filling the thorax of Ramesses II.

The frontal X ray of the mummy of Merneptah (Fig. 34) showed that the radius and the ulna of the right forearm had been fractured to the degree that multiple fragments were sited.

In my estimation the fracture was bound to have occurred after death. In this area we also see the shattered soft tissues of the mummy. On the mummy itself (Fig. 21) each extremity appears to have been torn apart. Many tiny bits of mummified tissues have detached themselves from the main cadaver.

The excellent quality of the X rays taken in Cairo in 1975 allows one to count the exact number of vertebrae. In the case of Merneptah, the vertebrae represent an anomaly, but this is without pathological significance. Instead of twelve dorsal vertebrae, Merneptah has thirteen. He also has thirteen ribs instead of twelve. The last of the dorsal vertebrae and the first of the lumbar ones are separated by intervertebral discs which are slightly pinched together but are linked by opaque bridges of paravertebral tissue resulting from mummification and not vertebral arthritis. Clément Fauré gave a clear explanation of this phenomenon in our report of April 1976 to the French Society of Radiology. The general assumption up to this time was that Merneptah suffered from vertebral rheumatism, when in fact that was not the case. Nevertheless, this does not preclude that it must have existed in ancient Egypt.

The X-ray study of the thorax of Merneptah that I conducted

showed the existence of traumatic bone lesions, which may well have occurred when the subject was still alive. Parts of the twelfth and thirteenth ribs on the right side of the body are missing. The mummy is lying on its back and so it therefore cannot be observed today, but it is known that through the work of Elliot Smith at the beginning of the twentieth century, an orifice existed in the thorax that was four inches long. A lacuna does indeed exist in the inner part of the clavicle and first rib on the right side. This orifice can be seen on the mummy (Fig. 22) at this point on the thorax. At the beginning of the century it was filled with a piece of bone. There is a photograph that was taken by Elliot Smith showing it still in place (Fig. 23). Having wondered whether or not it had fallen inside the thorax, I decided to search for it. This led me to use endoscopy as well as X rays. Let me add that the piece was never found. Although the mummy had certainly deteriorated since the beginning of the century, it is hardly likely to have disappeared on its own. The piece therefore had been removed. But by whom and why?

## X-ray Examination of the Abdomen, Lumbar Vertebrae, and Pelvis

In that the evidence of vertebral arthritis in the mummies is the subject of debate, I was not surprised to find features indicating its existence in certain very old subjects, such as Ramesses II. At over eighty-five years of age or more, it is commonplace today to have vertebral arthritis. When Clément Fauré examined the X rays of the entire skeleton of Ramesses II he seriously questioned the possibility of arthritis: "We consider that the spine of Ramesses II shows very few signs of morphological lesions. In particular, there is no serious osteoarthritis of the spine, nor any indication of 'ankylosing spondylitis.' " These are recorded from the notes in his report on the X rays taken in Cairo in 1975. The

Museum of Anthropology appears, however, to have discovered that Ramesses II did indeed suffer from vertebral arthritis. This diagnosis appeared in a medical doctoral thesis that was presented by Catherine Guillerm in 1982 at the University Pierre and Marie Curie, under the title *The pelvispondylitis of Ramesses II, a myth?* The chairman of the board of examiners was Jacques Cayla, Professor of Rheumatology. Their conclusion is indisputable. The study showed that, contrary to what might have been thought, this pharaoh was not suffering from rheumatoid pelvispondylitis.

In December of 1977, I was to give a lecture in Tunis to various members of the medical profession. The subject was to be medicine and the mummies of the pharaohs, and during the course of the lecture I planned to show various documents concerning Ramesses II and other pharaohs. Imagine my surprise when I opened a Tunisian newspaper the day before my lecture and found an article, based on data attributed to the Museum of Anthropology. The piece mentioned the "vertebral rheumatism" of Ramesses II and in particular the diagnosis given by the doctors on the nature of its development. The article pointed out that Ramesses II was known to have leaned to and favored his left side as he walked. Many experts besides myself must have smiled when they read this. During the course of my lecture the next day I exhibited documents showing that the spinal column was not damaged by such lesions. As a general rule, I went on to say, the morpholology of the spinal column may be changed during the embalmment operation and positioned by mummification in a totally artificial posture. One cannot draw any conclusions therefore as to the shape of the subject's spine during his lifetime.

An X-ray examination of Ramesses II's pelvis (Fig. 35), revealed several extremely important details.

The first noticeable thing is the incongruity between the right and left sides of the pelvis. On the left side, where the evisceration orifice is located (Fig. 2), little of the stuffing cloth was found. The X ray was rather dark in this area. On the right, however, there was a considerable amount of stuffing and hence the picture was lighter. The radiological opacity of the stuffing accounts for this difference in tone.

On the right side cracks in the pelvis are quite clearly seen. They show up as large, irregular black streaks and run horizontally or almost horizontally. They are superimposed upon one another and join together with a wide, oblique streak at the uppermost crack. These are not bone fractures—pelvic or femoral—but cracks in the tissue surrounding the bone. We can distinguish what they really are on the photograph of the mummy in Figure 2. What this frontal photograph of the abdomen does not show is the gap between the upper and lower parts of the abdomen. The upper part has sunk at least an inch and a quarter away from the lower one. I shall avoid boring you with a detailed map of the cracks and the points where pieces are missing from the mummy of Ramesses II, as seen in my X-ray examination; but I would like to simply state that valuable information was gathered for the restoration operations on the mummy itself. Certain parts of the body were strengthened with glue to prevent them from crumbling even more, for example. Such information was obtained from the X-ray examination, together with the data we observed. It was later completed by an endoscopic exploration.

On this X ray of the pelvis of Ramesses II we also find signs of the calcification of the femoral arteries on both sides. It can be very clearly seen. This is another example of the excellent quality of the X rays provided by my Egyptian colleagues in Cairo. Ramesses II died when he was over eighty years of age. It is hardly surprising, therefore, to find that he was suffering from a very large arterial atheroma. Other evidence of atherosclerosis was also observed in his carotid arteries as well. Ramesses II's successor was his thirteenth son, Merneptah. He, too, died with the same lesions. An X ray of the pelvis and upper thighs (Fig. 36) shows it present in every femoral artery and its tributaries. Clément Fauré discovered that the articulation between the pelvis and the femur is pinched bilaterally and on both the left and right sides of the body. Then came the question whether this was a sign of arthrosis of the hip or the result of mummification. Because such pinching may be caused by the mummification process it therefore may have nothing to do with any pathological causes.

## X-ray Examination of the Lower Limbs

In some cases, the results of these examinations were quite commonplace. For example, the extent of the injuries in some of the pharaohs were a result of being brutally smashed by tomb robbers. I shall leave these types of lesions aside, however, and concentrate on my further explorations of the lower limbs of Ramesses II (Fig. 37), who was not a victim of tomb robbers and therefore an excellent specimen.

My preliminary examinations of the pharaoh revealed the loss of a right toe. It was later found and reattached. This examination also revealed crevices found not only in the trunk but also in the lower limbs. Here again, these cracks affected only the soft tissues surrounding the bones, and the skeleton itself was intact, except for the missing toe.

To gain a further understanding as to the existence of these crevices let's look at the X rays of the thighs only. There are a whole series of lines mostly horizontal, affecting the soft tissues. They surround the femurs, which are themselves intact.

The X rays also provide another illustration of the lesions caused by atherosclerosis, which is found in the femoral arteries on both sides of the body. The X rays show the slightly irregular distribution of opaque accretions on each of the walls of the arteries. These are also seen on the external part of the right thigh, indicated by a black area. The absence of traces of tissue on the X ray therefore marks an important defect. A large piece of the soft tissues of the right thigh is in fact missing.

Now that we are familiar with X rays of mummified bodies, it has become quite normal to see a bone that is over 3200 years old that looks very much like a living one. Although it is possible that a bone might remain spontaneously preserved, there can be no doubt whatsoever that bones that have undergone the mummification process are in a much better state of preservation.

## X-ray Examination of the Skull and Face (Teeth Excepted)

Of all the X-ray examinations carried out, this one seems to me the most interesting, both from the point of view of forensic medicine and from a historical standpoint. The light it sheds on one of the "actors" in the drama of the Exodus, Pharaoh Merneptah, is particularly worth mentioning. This aspect of history is so subtly interwoven with medicine that the problem of situating the Exodus within the chronology of the pharaohs must be covered later in the book. But first, to understand it properly, we must proceed from the simple to the complex. We shall start by looking at general data as to what an X ray can show us of the head. First we shall describe the X ray of the head of Ramesses II.

The profile X ray (Fig. 7) is particularly instructive. The front part of the skull does not appear black or empty, in its entirety. Along the vault and in the anterior part of the skull, the white on the X ray is not due solely to the density of the bone. There seem to be traces in this area of an augmented radiological opacity. As for the rest of the cranial cavity, it would seem to be uniformly filled with a material that is impenetrable to X rays.

If the subject were lying on his back with his skull resting fairly and squarely on the back of the head (occiput), the material would in this case have a horizontal level.

Our knowledge of other mummies enables us to state the following: First, the entire brain has been removed (we mentioned this earlier and will return to it later); and second, the anterior part of the cranial cavity is three-quarters empty (corresponding to the grey, triangular-shaped area on the X rays). Here, a certain quantity of resinous substance has remained stuck to the vault. It was introduced into the skull in a liquid form by the embalmers, once the brain had been removed, through an orifice in the ceiling of the nasal cavity. The liquid substance solidified thereafter. The posterior part of the cranial cavity is totally filled with this resinous substance. As the subject was lying on the back of his head on the embalming table, the liquid ran from the point of introduction toward the back of the head where it hardened into a block.

We have explained the large areas of opacity, leading us to the following questions: by what route and how was the brain extracted? Does this show up on the X ray?

It is not difficult to answer these questions. In the case of Ramesses II, as indeed for a large number of royal mummies of the New Kingdom (and probably many others dating from this period), the putrescible organs were hastily removed, as we have seen in the section on mummification. It was explained that for the brain, access was gained through the nasal cavity. Its ceiling was perforated, and the brain removed by shredding it with sharp instruments, then flushing it out with a jet of water. Once this operation was completed, the cranial cavity was filled with resinous substances, which then solidified. Cloth was also used, which must, I suppose, have been introduced by a different route, as in the case of Ramesses V.

Other methods were also used for removal of the brain. Sometimes an incision was made in the neck to form a passage through the back of the head where the brain stem joins the brain to the spinal chord (as in the case of Pharaoh Amhosis).

Sethos I (the father of Ramesses II) and Tuthmosis II were most likely "operated on" in the same way by the embalmers. They deposited this resinous material in the cranial cavity partly to compensate for the brain that they had removed. The X rays of Sethos I (Fig. 38) are, like those for Tuthmosis II, illustrative of this point.

Comparison of the various X rays of the head of Ramesses II's mummy—frontal and other projections taken at various special angles—has enabled us to trace the passage of the instruments used by the embalmers to create an orifice that linked the nose to the forward part of the brain. We should not forget that at this point, they forced in the ethmoid bone, the precise location being the "lamina cribriformis" (perforated by very thin vessels and nerves), which was the area of least resistance. Very close examination of the X rays taken in Cairo in 1975 showed that at this point, the upper limit of the ethmoid is lost. The X ray no longer revealed traces of the lamina cribriformis or the ceiling of ethmoidal cells.

The demonstration of the fact that Ramesses II had undergone this extremely delicate "operation" performed by the embalmers 3200 years ago, would, however, have been infinitely more sensational if the Museum of Anthropology had carried out X-ray examinations using polytomo-radiography. It is a method that is very common today indeed, being used by any properly equipped X-ray clinic. Aidan Cockburn, in the United States, employed it to discover the orifice created by the embalmers to extract the brain.

When the X-ray examination was performed on the head of Ramesses II, proof was found showing an atheroma of the two inner carotid arteries carrying blood to a large part of the brain. Atheroma is a deposit of fatty lumps on the inner walls, hardening the arteries with a possibility of severe disturbances to the blood supply. On the profile X ray, they show up as small whitish formations of irregular shape, projecting themselves into the lower angle of the greyish area to be seen in the frontal X ray of the skull. The discovery of these opaque structures on a single profile X ray is not sufficient to make a diagnosis. It is the way in which they correspond to images found on X rays taken from other angles that enables us to state that they exist and put this interpretation on them. Here again, the use of tomography would most certainly have provided magnificent views of these features, which were an exceptional discovery in the research carried out on mummies.

The X-ray examination of Merneptah's skull is (apart from the question of the teeth, which we shall go into later) a topic of extreme interest, mainly because of the existence of a large cranial lacuna. As we already know, this pharaoh was the victim of a very serious trauma. One wonders whether it was just one more trauma—and if so, how violent it was—that caused the very large hole in the skull to be seen on the frontal X ray (Fig. 39).

Let us concentrate on the upper part of this X ray for a moment. On the right side, we see a lacuna projecting above the eye socket. The breach has fairly irregularly shaped contours. Near the lower edge, in the greyish surface of the breach, there is an opaque image measuring several millimeters on the X-ray reproduction, which would indeed appear to be bone. The present lacuna is not situated on the right part of the mummy's forehead, but is, in this case, the projection above the eye socket of a loss of matter located at the back of the skull in the parietal region.

The pharaoh is at present lying on this region, so the mummy cannot be moved. It is therefore impossible to reach the breach and photograph it. Luckily, however, Elliot Smith included a photograph of it (Fig. 40) in his book of 1912. Here we see it more or less surrounded by the scalp on its upper, inner, and outer edges, but not underneath, where the bone is bare. The fact that the bone is uncovered at this point is not the result of a lesion but is the work of the English anthropologist who wrote that he removed the scalp to see the state of the bone it was covering. Unfortunately, we therefore cannot draw any conclusions as to the origin of this lacuna because of the absence of scalp in this region.

It is important to stress the fact that a morsel of bone can be distinguished on the X rays, lying just above the lower edge of the hole. The bone is marked on the reproduction of the X ray by a white area and is oblong, inclined at a forty-five-degree horizontal angle. It corresponds exactly to the image shown on the photograph of the mummy's skull taken over seventy years ago, of what looks like a splinter of bone. This observation has precise significance, which we shall describe later when we come to the study of this bone lacuna.

This frontal X ray of the skull also shows other interesting lesions, whose authenticity has been verified by other X rays taken at different angles. Such lesions are the absence of a nasal septum (partition dividing the nostrils) and that of the upper and middle conchae (bony structures inside the nasal cavity) on the right side. The existence of these lesions in the nasal cavities raises the question: Were the embalmers obliged to use a wider approach route, allowing access to the interior of the skull so that they could remove the brain by the usual passage before mummification?

# 10. Dental State

In Cairo in 1975, I directed an X-ray study of several pharaonic mummies. In particular, I asked our Egyptian colleagues to provide us with X rays taken from various angles. The excellent quality of the documents I brought back with me from Egypt on my return enabled Dr. Georges Rousières and Dr. François Rousières to arrive at very precise conclusions as to the dental state of several pharaohs. The overall results were presented to the Academy of Dental Surgery (Académie de Chirurgie Dentaire) in December 1976.

These studies on the dental lesions of the pharaonic mummies, which concern Ramesses II as much as other pharaohs, were not carried out at, or by, the Museum of Anthropology during Ramesses II's stay in Paris. I point this out here because Professor Lionel Balout in his article in *Archaeologia* in February 1978 presents the studies in such a way as to make one think they were. Here, as in many other instances, he makes no reference whatsoever to the reports presented to various learned societies by the doctors and dentists who had already carried out the work beforehand. Apart from some points of detail, which I shall quote, the results of the dental studies performed on Ramesses II at the Museum of Anthropology in 1976–1977 added little to the discoveries of 1975.

Two areas were given special attention: ascertaining the subject's age and studying the dental lesions, which were of considerable importance. Of one of the pharaohs studied, we are now able to affirm that he was suffering at the end of his life from extremely serious lesions that were very painful and highly debilitating. This information allows us reject, as a result of their incompatibility with medical data, certain actions ascribed to the pharaoh in question that do not have any sound basis.

## Ascertaining the Subject's Age

This is typically a simple forensic problem, provided there exists a single tooth intact. Some forensic studies have been able to fix the age of an adult to within a few years by using a single tooth for the purposes of the study. Here, however, the problem is more complicated, because it is not generally possible to take a tooth. All one has at one's disposal is X-ray data.

The subject's approximate age is based on two observations: the thickness of the enamel and the size of the dental pulp. The enamel covering the tooth (Fig. 41) gradually becomes thinner with age. Here, however, the food eaten by certain subjects could grind the enamel down much faster than that of others, whose enamel wore much more slowly. In the subjects that concern us here, eating habits play a very important part. Examination of samples of various kinds of bread found in the tombs has shown that they were composed of flour mixed with amounts of minerals and even sand. Chewing sand must certainly have caused considerable wear on the enamel covering. Hence the extent to which the enamel is worn does not indicate much when it comes to determining the age of the tooth.

The case is different for the size of the pulp chamber and the pulp canals. The latter occupy considerable space within the young tooth, but as the subject grows older, become smaller and smaller, so that in elderly people they are minuscule. On good X rays, therefore, there is a measurable link between the dimensions of the pulp chamber, plus those of the pulp canals, and the subject's age. The X rays we brought back from Egypt in 1975 showed quite clearly the dimensions of the pulp canals of the pharaohs examined. Certain rules laid down for this kind of study by the Swedish expert, G. Gustafson, were applied by the Doctors Georges and François Rousières in their examination of the X rays taken of Tuthmosis II. They estimated the pharaohs age at death to have been thirty-five years, give or take five years.

Such measurements remain very approximate, however, for the precision of the estimate varies according to the subject's age.

It was estimated that Pharaoh Merneptah was between sixty and seventy years old when he died, and that Ramesses II's death occurred when he was somewhere between eighty-five and ninety-five years old. In this case, the dental lesions were very serious, making it much more difficult to estimate the size of the pulp chamber and pulp canals.

In fact, the figures quoted here for Ramesses II are the approximations arrived at by the Doctors G. and F. Rousières. We should not pay any heed to the information circulated at the time of Ramesses II's stay in Paris, according to which the pharaoh was exactly eighty-eight years old when he died, as established by the dental examination. In fact, investigation of the teeth can never claim to be so exact.

## Dental Lesions

Inscriptions and various documents have enabled us to obtain precise details as to the existence of "consultants" for dental troubles in ancient Egypt. I hesitate to use the term dental specialists for such consultants do not appear to have left traces of any kind of dental art. The remedies described in certain papyruses seem unlikely to have relieved the patients of much pain, either. When we find that honey was frequently used in dressings applied to dental decay, we may rightly suppose that the patients were far from having their toothaches soothed. On the contrary, their pain probably increased because of such practices. One even wonders if teeth were ever extracted. Ange Leca in his book *Egyptian Medicine at the Time of the Pharaohs* (Roger Dacosta, publ., Paris, 1971), writes: "There is nothing to prove that dental care, in the sense that we understand it today, was ever administered in ancient Egypt."

Also in his book, Leca presents an interesting point in the history of dental decay:

"Elliot Smith has found few examples of dental decay in the pre-dynastic periods, for at this time, the teeth fell out at an early age. From the Fourth Dynasty onwards, dental decay was noted in members of the aristocracy, while the common people remained unaffected by it. Gradually, however, it became more and more common, until finally, during the period of decline, every sector of the population was prey to it. This fact was linked to dietetic hygiene: food was now more rich and copious. The consumption of cooked food probably favoured dental decay in the poorer classes, who had until then been spared."

We should not be surprised therefore, to find dental lesions on the mummies of the pharaohs. Such lesions are often quite considerable, resulting from multiple points of dental decay. Ramesses II and Merneptah contain some striking examples. Destructive lesions of this kind are not present on other subjects. Tuthmosis II died between ages thirty and forty, and the dental state of Sethos I enables us to state that his death occurred at around forty years of age. Both of them were much younger than Ramesses II or Merneptah.

Merneptah was the successor of Ramesses II. He provides an

example of dental lesions of minor importance compared with his father, Ramesses II, whose lesions are quite considerable.

The general image of the teeth is not easily distinguished on the X ray of Merneptah (Fig. 39). Nevertheless, one should note the existence of a tooth lying horizontally, slightly to the left of the medial line. It is perfectly distinguishable on the profile X ray (Fig. 42), where it occupies the pharyngeal region in front of the spinal column. It is most probably a tooth that escaped from the upper jaw (left incisor) during embalmment and has remained in this abnormal position ever since. These two X rays, along with others taken at special angles, show that the pharaoh had lost many of his teeth. There appear to be only six left (the anterior ones), on the maxillary (upper jaw), and only seven premolars and molars on the mandible (lower jaw). Several of the latter show signs of dental decay. We may therefore ask ourselves the following question: Were the most seriously decayed teeth removed from Merneptah, even though the practice of extraction does not appear to have been widespread? We may definitely observe here, on the bone in which they grew, a very regularly shaped setting, strongly indicating that the bone had healed. This would imply that the missing teeth fell out (or were pulled out) much earlier—certainly before the pharaoh's death.

We may therefore affirm that Pharaoh Merneptah's dental state is characterized by the loss of numerous teeth (over half of them), some of which disappeared before his death. There is no reason to be surprised by the existence of dental decay, especially in a man who appears by the dimensions of the pulp canals, to have been in his sixties. The calcification present in certain femoral arteries, as revealed by X rays, also lends credibility to this odontological estimate.

The dental lesions of Ramesses II are by far the most sizable ones encountered. On the frontal projection (Fig. 43), the layout of the teeth looks extremely irregular on both the upper and lower jaws. The regularity of the teeth occlusion has disappeared—the teeth ride from one jaw to the other. The greyness of the upper part of this X ray is explained, as mentioned above, by the presence inside the cranial cavity of a resinous substance used to fill it.

What appears very clearly is the lack of symmetry between the two sides of the lower jaw. There is a bone lacuna in the right side of the mandible. A comparison with the left side shows us the great volume of the lacuna. We have already seen this picture on the profile X ray of the skull mentioned in the section on mummification. If we return to this (Fig. 7), we can see the extent of the irregularity found in the teeth occlusion. Many of the teeth contain dental decay and are all extremely worn down, due to considerable wear and tear on the enamel and even on the body of the tooth itself. This should not surprise us in such an aged subject.

One lesion is particularly noticeable. It is a huge hole caused by dental decay in the first lower molar (the preceding X ray showed it on the right), separating the two roots, which are easily distinguished on the X ray. Around them is an area of osteitis. Also, in the mandible there is a lacuna caused by the spread of the dental infection. One can even detect the presence of a small detached bone fragment, triangular in shape, with its apex pointing downward (Fig. 44).

Thus, 3300 years after the subject's death, a mere X-ray examination enables us to state that Ramesses II suffered, during the last years of his life, from an extremely serious dental infection, complicated by a lesion in the surrounding bone. Although the X-ray investigation tells us that he died *with* this osteitis, it does not allow us to affirm that he died *of* it. We have here, then, the case of a bone abscess, which, as frequently happens, has detached a morsel of bone and left it floating freely within the abscess. Dr. François Rousières had studied the X rays and confirmed the diagnosis we made in Cairo concerning the osseous infection of the dental area. When the mummy of Ramesses II was in Paris, Rousières noticed and showed me the traces of an unusual orifice in the region below the chin. It appeared to be the outlet through which the pus from this abscess had flowed.

Whatever the case, it is important to know that lesions such as this, when they occur in very old people, can well prove fatal—in spite of surgical and dental care, and regardless of the antibiotics that are systematically applied to such severe infections. In addition, infections of the bone and teeth on such a scale are always excruciatingly painful. There is nothing to indicate that the medicinal resources of the time were able to save the pharaoh from tremendous suffering. He must have died in terrible agony unless his age or the deterioration of his brain had made him insensitive to pain. These facts are indisputable from a medical point of view.

As far as I am aware, attention had not been drawn, in medical publications, to the state of Ramesses II at his death, until my paper was read before the French National Academy of Medicine in February 1976 (well before the X-ray study of the mummy was taken over by the Museum of Anthropology). James Harris and Kent Weeks in their book X-Raying the Pharaohs describe the considerable dental lesions they had discovered through X-ray examinations, but make no mention of the localized mandible infection, nor of the lacuna in the bone, which I was the first to make known.

## The Historical Importance of a Medical Discovery

The above discovery was of undisputed importance to the study of the famous pharaoh's last moments.

As we know, the Holy Scriptures, particularly the Book of Exodus in the Bible, tell us that during the Exodus, the pharaoh personally pursued the Hebrews at the head of his army, when, guided by Moses, they crossed the "sea of rushes" without wetting their feet. The Scriptures describe how the waters returned covering "Pharaoh and his host" so that "not so much as one of them remained." The Bible and the Qur'an are the only written sources to mention this event. There are no hieroglyphic documents on it.

Consequently, whomever we decide was the pharaoh of Egypt in the Exodus, it is clear that he must have been in good enough health to have led the pursuing army. Can we say this of Ramesses II? The medical study of the mummy does not provide the slightest grounds for us to think so. As a matter of fact, it is patently obvious that Ramesses II was totally incapable of taking such a warrior-like initiative just before his death.

# 11. Endoscopic Examination

Endoscopy is the method of exploring certain cavities of the body. It has the great advantage of enabling us to discover particular details that would otherwise have remained inaccessible. A special instrument helps us to see and photograph what is observed, but when used, the device has to penetrate through a natural or artificial orifice to reach the inside of the cavity under examination. In the first instance, for example, the endoscope may be introduced naturally through the mouth to allow for the examination of the stomach, or through the anus to investigate the rectum, or even the large intestine. In the second, an orifice has to be artificially created with a knife, so that the endoscope can be introduced through the wall of the abdomen to inspect the cavities between the organs it contains.

A mummy in a fine state of preservation has to be respected. An existing orifice therefore has to be found—an artificial one, since the natural ones are generally sealed—if one is to gain access to the interior of the mummified body. Medical endoscopy can only be extended to include the examination of a mummy when circumstances allow it. (There must already be an orifice that enables one to introduce the instrument destined to perform the investigation.)

The endoscope used is a tube inside which is an optical system that channels a luminous beam lighting the cavity to be observed. It allows the observer to receive, at the end of the tube, images of the areas thus illuminated. A camera, even a movie camera, may be attached to the endoscope. The older, rigid models have been greatly improved since the introduction of optic fiber, allowing the system to be oriented at will, hence its name: fibroscope.

To my knowledge, endoscopy had never been used to examine a mummy. I got the idea of employing it during my work at the Egyptian Museum in Cairo, since I was familiar with it from use in a hospital. While studying the mummy of Merneptah (Fig. 22) in 1975, I had noted the existence of an abnormal orifice on the right side of the thorax. At the beginning of this century, however, there had been a piece of thoracic wall at this point that was still in place (Fig. 23). Had the section quite simply fallen inside the thorax? It could not be seen with ordinary lighting, so it seemed useful to look for it with an endoscope. Once the president of Egyptian Antiquities had given me his general approval for this unprecedented exploration, I sought out a specialist in endoscopy practicing in Cairo. Thanks to the help of the head doctor at the Al Maadi Military Hospital, I found an extremely diligent collaborator, Dr. Mustapha Manialawiy. Dr. Manialawiy brought his special equipment to the museum, and the very next day we began our inspection of the thorax of the mummy, but did not find the missing piece of bone. Dr. Manialawiy took numerous photographs of the chest from inside, for we had discovered very clear anatomical formations that were mummified and in a perfect state of preservation—the ribs, the spaces between them that were filled with muscles covered by the remaining membrane of the pleura, and the clearly defined vertebrae with their rib articulations—all were carefully examined and photographed.

There was one more detail in the study of the mummy's chest that had to be focused on. It had to do with the image shown on the X ray (Fig. 34) in the upper part of what had been the left pulmonary field. The whitish shadow, indicating the presence of an abnormal formation, might be the heart, left in place and pushed upward by the embalmers. When seen through the endoscope (Fig. 45), only its whitish, irregular features could be observed. The form we had discovered did not suggest any organ in particular, and it was not possible to identify it just by looking at it. We would have had to take a sample and have it examined under the microscope. Then we might have been able to say that it was indeed the heart. As it was, the outward appearance displayed none of the heart's features. Because the terms of our study did not, at that point, include any taking of samples (on account of the extremely fragile state of Merneptah's mummy), we were unable to perform this "biopsy." Unfortunately, the nature of this mass remains a mystery. Nevertheless, endoscopy was useful in allowing us access to a region of the mummified body that would otherwise have remained beyond our reach.

At the beginning of the twentieth century, Elliot Smith had observed an abnormal orifice in the abdominal wall, in the area of the right lumbar region, at the spot where the right kidney had been (it was later removed by the embalmers). Thanks to X rays, we knew that the orifice was of sizable dimensions and affected two ribs. It had been measured by Elliot Smith; we wondered if the orifice had increased in size since then, due to the gradual decay of the mummified tissues. It was impossible to discover the answer, however, for the mummy was lying on this unusual orifice. The only way to find out was by the endoscopic examination of the interior of the body. Our inspection of these regions with the endoscope confirmed the fact that the mummified tissue had indeed deteriorated. There was nothing in our observations that allowed us to conclude that the orifice had been created by a wound received during the subject's lifetime or to state that another cause existed. We are totally ignorant, therefore, as to the origins of the orifice; although, we now know that, on this side, the mummified tissues are deteriorating.

In the Egyptian Museum in Cairo, there were other mummies containing abnormal orifices that we could study by endoscopy. I selected the mummy of Ramesses V from among many others. It seemed especially interesting since this pharaoh displayed a huge orifice in the vault of the skull (Figs. 6 and 46), and no exact hypothesis has been made yet as to its origins. Some have blamed the orifice on tomb robbers (as was the case with several other pharaohs with such cranial lacunae), since there seem to be no arguments for a different explanation. During this primary stage of our explorations, I was eager to observe the interior of the skull, since access to it was very easy. I suggested the use of endoscopy to the president of Egyptian Antiquities, who accepted, and the procedure was performed on the spot.

As I described earlier, two very important discoveries were made. It was the first time an opportunity had arisen to inspect a mummified skull and to photograph the hole through which the embalmers removed the brain.

During the early stages of our exploration, we found remains of cloth (Fig. 47) in the posterior part of the cranial cavity. They were covered in a calcareous substance and had served to fill the empty cavity. The remains probably came from the strip of material, nine meters long and three centimeters wide, that was removed, as we know, by Elliot Smith at the beginning of the century. The strip must have been inserted through the artificial orifice in the vault of the skull, bored for this purpose by the embalmers.

Next we observed and photographed the passage through the ethmoid bone (Fig. 5). This passage was used by the embalmers to remove the brain. They took this route to gain access through the nose, as I explained in the section on mummification. This orifice was used as the traditional access route for this operation for a very long time. The photographs that we now have of it have greatly added to our knowledge of the techniques employed by the embalmers of the New Kingdom. Many of their secrets have been revealed to us, as we now have precise information on many points, thanks to medical research on mummies. We cannot praise enough the skill of the embalmers for having made use of this tiny area of least resistance. It is well known to modern anatomists who call it the lamina cribriformis of the ethmoid bone. We should remember that once the brain had been removed the embalmers used this same orifice to introduce into the cranial cavity the liquid resin that subsequently solidified there.

Of this solidified resin, only a small quantity has been found: it is the blackish matter on the right edge of the hole. A fragment of this mass was removed with biopsy forceps under the light of an endoscope. Chemical analysis confirmed that it was resinous in character. We do not know what became of the rest of the resin—if there was any left after the cranial cavity had been filled with cloth. Cloth was introduced through the artificial orifice bored by the embalmers on the left side of the dome of the skull. In the case of Ramesses V, it appears to have replaced the large resinous mass found in other mummies, such as Ramesses II, Tuthmosis II, and Sethos I. These mummies do not contain any such empty spaces. Why was cloth used for Ramesses V instead of a resinous filling? There is no clue to the answer of this question.

A third mummy has benefited from the use of endoscopic examination: Ramesses II. The very first exploration of this kind occurred in 1975, also at the Egyptian Museum. Remember that this mummy's abdomen was severely damaged (Fig. 2) and contained multiple cracks that were irregular and sometimes converging. Because of the possibility of damaging the mummy, it was not possible to explore the cracks with a rigid instrument, however gingerly, to see if they affected the whole thickness of the wall.

The X rays taken at this time (Fig. 35) also provided a good topographical outline of the crevices. They did not, however, give specific information as to the depth of the crevices located on the right-side section of the mummy's abdomen, which was partly stuffed with cloth. The cloth was found at the bottom of crevices in certain places, but not everywhere. Furthermore, I suggested that I examine the crevices by transillumination (by introducing a source of light into the abdomen and looking to see whether it was visible from the outside through the cracks and crevices in the abdominal wall). The source of light was provided by the endoscope. Unfortunately, it could only be inserted to a depth of between five and six centimeters into the evisceration orifice (Fig. 48), because its progress toward the interior of the abdomen was blocked by the presence of cloth. It was nevertheless possible for us to establish that certain crevices affected the entire thickness of the abdominal wall, especially toward the right side. Thus, endoscopy was able to provide us with helpful complementary information that was useful when it came to assessing the mechanical damage suffered by the mummy.

One and a half years later, in December 1976, a second endoscopic examination was performed in Paris on the abdomen of Ramesses II. A few weeks earlier, at the Museum of Anthropology, I had seen pieces of cloth removed that had very loosely filled the abdomen. They appeared to me to be quite different from those I had observed the year before in Cairo. Evidently, the older pieces of cloth must have been changed in Egypt. Other remains of the cloth used for stuffing were present in the mummy's abdomen, in the upper part particularly, but were locked in a resinous lump, and could not be disengaged. Dr. Mustapha Manialawiy, who had come to Paris at my request to carry out the examination, used the endoscope to observe the abdomen, which had been partially disengaged by this process. As he examined it, he realized that there was an impenetrable barrier at the base of the thorax. The X rays of 1975 had shown (Fig. 33) that the thoracic cavity was stuffed with magma, clearly visible on the plates, which probably corresponded to various bundles of organs, vegetal fibers, natron, and other substances used to stuff the thorax. The only way we can form an idea of what these bundles might contain is by comparison with other mummies. All we can be certain of is that it was impossible to see through the stuffing of the thorax with an endoscope and, therefore, to identify its contents. I was not present at the endoscopic examination performed on Ramesses II in Paris, but my Egyptian colleague showed me the photographs he had taken. It was quite clear from them that the thorax could not be explored.

Furthermore, the Museum of Anthropology later declared that the heart of Ramesses II was indeed in place inside the thorax. We may be sure, however, that endoscopy did not make it possible to identify this organ. We have already seen why the radiological techniques used in Paris could not provide a valid argument in favor of this assertion, so we must conclude that the heart of Ramesses II could not have been identified by any reliable means.

However, it was interesting to take microsamples with the use of endoscopy. Pieces were taken of various substances that had been used to fill the cavities left after the removal of the organs (especially the thoracic cavity of Ramesses II)—samples of cloth, for example, which must have been very old, not only on account of their appearance, but also because they were very deeply buried. Dr. Mustapha Manialawiy again used biopsy forceps, as we had in Cairo, to take samples. Here we have another example illustrating the usefulness of endoscopy: the ability to direct the taking of tiny quantities of various substances.

Thus, endoscopy was shown to be doubly helpful. It provided us with not only images of otherwise inaccessible regions, but also the opportunity to take minuscule samples.

# 12. The Royal Mummies and the Problem of Their Cranial Lacunae

Egyptologists have always been intrigued by the lacunae found in the skulls of several pharaonic mummies. Modern medical knowledge should, in some cases, be able to shed light on this problem. For this to be possible, it was necessary to examine the lacunae of each of the mummies concerned, so that comparisons could be made. We gave a detailed account of our observations and the hypotheses that might be formed from them in a report read before the French Society of Forensic Medicine on April 12, 1976. The scope of the work went beyond the strict framework of the cranial lacunae to include more general considerations, and, in addition to those participants cited earlier, we were joined by Professor Pierre F. Ceccaldi, head of the Police Forensic Laboratory in Paris.

Cranial lacunae can be seen on six of the mummies preserved at the Egyptian Museum in Cairo. They date from dynasties that existed between the seventeenth and eleventh centuries B.C. (Seventeenth to Twentieth Dynasties). Obviously, problems similar to those described here may apply to mummies dating from other periods, but the only ones in a sufficiently decent state of preservation to permit such study are those of the following six kings:

| | |
|---|---|
| Seventeenth Dynasty | Sekenenre |
| Nineteenth Dynasty | Merneptah |
| Twentieth Dynasty | Sethos II, Ramesses IV, Ramesses V, Ramesses VI. |

The first mummy, Sekenenre, was discovered in 1881 at the hiding place of Deir El Bahari, where Ramesses II and his father, Sethos I, were also discovered.

The other five were found in 1898 in the Tomb of Amenophis II in the Valley of the Kings. Once the second discovery was made, conclusions were quickly drawn by comparison as to the origins of the cranial lacunae. There could be no doubt that two of the mummies in this group had been disembowelled by tomb robbers, those of Sethos I and Ramesses VI, and that they displayed severe cranial lesions. It was then deduced, very summarily, that the same must be true of the other three. At the beginning of the nineteenth century A.D., Merneptah, Ramesses IV, and Ramesses V were thought to have been subjected to the same pillagings. The abnormal cranial orifices must therefore have been cut by tomb robbers in the course of their visits to the tombs in search of precious objects that might have been left inside the skull. There were exceptions, however, and some Egyptologists were unwilling to make definite pronouncements concerning Ramesses V. In fact, it would require much greater circumspection than this to come to a decision.

A. Leca, in *Egyptian Medicine at the Time of the Pharaohs*, states that it is impossible for us to credit the ancient Egyptians with having bored trepan holes for magical or therapeutic reasons. He examines ten cases from this point of view, but regards only one as possible: that of a Twenty-fifth Dynasty princess (seventh century B.C.) who is said to have undergone an operation of this kind, but perhaps not in Egypt. In more recent times, however, after the birth of Christianity and under the influence of the Romans, there seem to have been cases of voluntary trepanation.

The subjects may even have escaped premature death; signs have been discovered that possibly indicate the regeneration of the bone on the circumference of the orifice. As far as accidental lesions are concerned, several pieces of evidence have been found, such as the skull of a child, cited by Ange Leca (Egyptian Museum, No. 61051), which presents a large lacuna with bone splinters. Elliot Smith also cites such a case.

Studies on mummies other than those of the pharaohs therefore lead us to eliminate, for all practical purposes, trepanation performed for ritualistic or magical reasons. The only cases we shall deal with are those where the lesions are the result of an accident. There is good reason to believe that this last category may apply to the pharaohs, for there is no indication here that trepanation was performed while the subject was alive. Nevertheless, we shall have to bear in mind at this point the possibility of voluntary trepanations. These may have been carried out not during the subject's lifetime but at the time of embalmment. We shall also deal with another very special category of lesions: those due to tomb robbers. These last represent the main cause of the damage likely to have occurred in the tombs themselves. Nor should we rule out, at least from a theoretical point of view, the possibility of damage caused by animals, although proof of this has yet to be produced.

## Lesions Caused by Tomb Robbers

Two of the six mummies examined appeared to have skulls that had been broken into, and in one case both the skull and face were damaged by tomb robbers.

The cranial lesions of Ramesses VI (Fig. 49) are extremely typical, not only because of their appearance but also their context. This mummy, which dates from the Twentieth Dynasty, was discovered in the Tomb of Amenophis II. With it, there was formal, unambiguous proof that pillagers had visited the tomb.

The state of the wrappings surrounding the mummy in its coffin, bear their signature: the tomb robbers brutally smashed the skull and face using tools such as axes and knives. Mummified tissues, dehydrated soft tissues, and even bone itself are all extremely brittle. Violent blows make them literally shatter into pieces and can cause far-reaching damage. We only have to look at the mummy to see the extent and depth of the damage. An X-ray examination was not carried out on this mummy because it would not have provided any useful information—one look at the mummy and the origin of the damage was totally obvious.

An irregular hole, five centimeters in length at its widest point, is visible on the mummy of Sethos II. It appears in the left parietal bone near the medial line of the skull, and is the result of blows inflicted on the mummy's skull and other parts of the body.

Thus, two out of the six cases in question may be labeled as victims of tomb robbers' blows: Ramesses VI and Sethos II. The remaining four (Ramesses IV, Ramesses V, Sekenenre, and Merneptah) do not, in spite of what has been said, particularly of Merneptah, appear to have been violated by tomb robbers. I believe I have found arguments that permit us to suggest alternative explanations of their lesions: trepanations performed at the time of embalmment, in the case of two mummies; and for the other two, accidental injuries sustained by them during their lifetimes.

## Embalmment Trepanations

There is evidence to suggest that in some cases embalmers bored trepan holes in the vault of the skull to accomplish certain operations. It was with this in mind that we compared the cranial lesions of Ramesses IV and Ramesses V, and presented the two cases to the French Society of Forensic Medicine.

The mummies both date from the Twentieth Dynasty, roughly 1160 B.C. The cranial lacunae are on the left side in both cases and on the same bone, the parietal bone. In Ramesses IV, the hole is located on the posterior part of this bone. It is very regular in shape and has a diameter of five centimeters. In Ramesses V (Fig. 6) the orifice has been bored much further forward, near the medial line. It extends sideways and measures 3.5 centimeters at its widest point. A most important observation is that these two orifices have very regular edges, free of any detached fragments of bone clinging to their circumference. The absence of such splinters (which are found in the case of accidental lesions that occurred during the subject's lifetime) should be kept in mind. From this point of view, the radiological appearance of the orifice in Ramesses V shows it to be a particularly clean cut.

Unfortunately, Ramesses IV's cranial lacuna is known only from the descriptive documents and photographs left by Elliot Smith, for the pharaoh has been lying on the cranial hole since the beginning of the century. Elliot Smith has not provided a description of the scalp surrounding the circumference of the hole. We have attached great importance, however, to the state of Ramesses V's scalp on the periphery of the cranial lacuna, as shall be seen.

The fact that Ramesses V's lacuna is situated in the anterior part of the left parietal bone has made it easy for us to observe all the features of the lacuna, especially the state of the scalp surrounding it. All or most of what is now bare bone, including the surface of the unusual bone orifice, was once covered with scalp. The scalp has been folded back and appears in a normal mummified state. This allows us to reject the hypothesis that a hole was made in the bone after mummification, while making extremely plausible the hypothesis that the orifice is the work of the embalmers, who would have drawn back the scalp and mummified it in this position.

The above leads us to believe that the hole was bored by the embalmers and used, so it appears, for embalming operations. The particular practice in question, although not very common, was definitely performed; it consisted of inserting the cloth destined to stuff the inside of the cranial cavity through the orifice. Elliot Smith used the same hole to extract the cloth when he removed the mummy's wrappings. The strip of material was nine meters long and three centimeters wide. The embalmers would not have been able to insert a mass such as this through any other orifice linking the cranial cavity to the outside.

Furthermore, in spite of the existence of the hole in the dome of the skull, the embalmers proceeded to remove Ramesses V's brain by the same route—the usual one for this period—through the nose and the ethmoid bone. When the mummy's cranial cavity was examined with the endoscope, as described in the preceding chapter, we found and photographed the orifice of the ethmoidal lamina cribriformis, through which the brain had been extracted, passing through the nasal cavity. The embalmers would not have been able to insert the long strip of cloth through this route. Elliot Smith extracted it through the orifice in the vault of the skull. The function of the cloth therefore becomes perfectly clear; although, we do not know why the embalmers in this case chose to fill the cranial cavity with cloth rather than a mass of resin.

There is another feature that may be accounted for by the present hypothesis (that in the case of Ramesses IV and Ramesses V, the holes were bored by the embalmers): the location of the hole. From Ahmosis and the kings called Tuthmosis down to the mummy of Ramesses V, it has been observed that the embalmment operations of the New Kingdom were all carried out on the left side of the body. As we have seen, evisceration was always practiced from this side.

The hypothesis that the embalmers created an orifice to help them in their surgical operations is the most logical explanation of the presence of the cranial lacunae found on Ramesses IV and Ramesses V.

# The Lacunae of Traumatic Origin

In the case of the two remaining mummies, Sekenenre and Merneptah, it seems that the lacunae are of traumatic origin. We know this for certain in Sekenenre's case, because we are aware of the circumstances of his death. The trauma is less certain, but still highly plausible, in Merneptah's case. The circumstances surrounding his death are the focus of a later chapter.

The mummy of Sekenenre, a king of the Seventeenth Dynasty (seventeenth century B.C.), is quite unique: it has traumatic lesions that are known to have occurred during the subject's lifetime. In the course of a battle, the young king fell victim to several blows, either from a lance or an axe, which damaged the skull and face (Fig. 19). The blows were responsible for the lacunae in the bones of the right frontal region and various other places in the face. The mummy of Sekenenre was not X rayed in Cairo in 1975, but the description of it given by Elliot Smith in his book *The Royal Mummies* (1912), provides us with extremely important details concerning the features of the lesions. The English anthropologist had in fact examined the mummy at the beginning of the century and discovered the existence of a bone splinter. It was a large fragment, measuring fifty by eighty millimeters, that had remained joined to an edge of the upper frontal orifice on the right, held in place by a fibrous shred of the dura mater (the outermost fibrous membrane covering the brain). The presence of this bone fragment, still in contact with the periphery of the orifice, indicated an accidental lesion. It was known that Sekenenre had died in the course of a battle against the Hyksos—weapons belonging to them had even been matched with the cranial and facial lesion and shown by this comparative study to fit perfectly. So in this case, historical and forensic data matched perfectly, confirming that the cranial lacunae were indeed of traumatic origin.

As far as Pharaoh Merneptah is concerned, certain data must be explained before we can arrive at a definitive description of the circumstances surrounding his death, so we shall leave them to another chapter.

Merneptah's cranial lacuna (Fig. 40), already described, has the appearance of a loss of matter in the right parietal bone. The location alone is enough to make us rule out the idea that it is the work of the embalmers, since we know for a fact that those of that period carried out their operations from the left side, as in the cases of Ramesses IV and Ramesses V. Although Merneptah and Ramesses V were separated by a period of some sixty to seventy years, there is nothing to suggest that the customs and practices of the embalmers changed during this interval. Operations were also performed from the left side before Merneptah, as in the case of Ramesses II, for example. Therefore there can be no question here of an orifice created for embalmment.

Observation of Merneptah's cranial lacuna is, unfortunately, not possible today. The pharaoh is lying with his head resting on this abnormal orifice. The mummy had been seriously affected by gradual deterioration from the beginning of the century, so it was impossible to move the mummy, given the conditions of preservation in 1975, to perform an endoscopic examination. Our only sources of information were the descriptions and photographs from the beginning of the century. These two sources of information, although limited, nevertheless seemed sufficient to give us an idea as to the origin of the lacuna.

Elliot Smith had put forward a hypothesis suggesting that tomb robbers were responsible for the cranial orifice, based on comparison with other mummies. Merneptah's mummy had been found in the same place as certain others, among them those of Sethos II and Ramesses VI, which had undoubtedly been damaged by pillagers. Smith also wondered whether the lacuna visible on Merneptah might not have been deliberately created for some occult reason. Possibly the simplest way of imagining what actually happened is to carefully examine the photograph taken by Elliot Smith at the beginning of this century.

Looking at this photograph (Fig. 40), we must remind ourselves, once again, that it is necessary to discount the fact that the scalp, both underneath and inside the lacuna, is missing, for it was Elliot Smith himself who removed it to observe the state of the underlying bone. In so doing, he uncovered the meeting point of the two parietal bones with the occipital, known as the lambdoid suture. In view of the above, two observations can be made. First, the hole in the bone is not prolonged near the periphery. There is no apparent destruction of the scalp around the edges. The skull has not been smashed at the periphery, nor has the covering skin been torn. This does not coincide with the theory that a violent blow was struck by tomb plunderers. Moreover, the X ray of the skull shows that the neighboring bone is intact. Second, what appears to be a splinter of bone may be seen on the photograph taken by Elliot Smith. It shows up as an irregularly shaped image in white against the black of the hole and is situated on its lower edge. Was this really a bone splinter?

This question was answered in 1975 by the use of radiology, for by that time it was no longer possible to move the mummy to observe the orifice itself.

The shading of the X-ray image (Fig. 39) clearly indicated that there was indeed a morsel of bone still present in exactly the same place as over sixty years ago, when photographed by Elliot Smith. It was therefore possible to state that the parietal lacuna in the skull of Merneptah was bordered by a bone splinter, which remained clinging to the edge of the hole, in spite of the various moves the mummy had been subjected to since the beginning of the century.

Therefore, there was every reason to compare the case of Merneptah and his lacuna to the traumatic lacuna of Sekenenre. Hence the most plausible diagnosis for Merneptah was a skull fracture forcing the skull inward and damaging the brain. The large piece of bone and sizable fragments that shattered under the effect of the trauma are lost today. With the exception of the tiny splinter mentioned, they were not to be found inside the skull of the mummy when X rayed.

It is likely that a craniocerebral wound of this size alone would have been sufficient to bring about the death of the subject very rapidly, if not instantaneously. We therefore have reason to believe that Pharaoh Merneptah came to a tragic end. We shall return later to the other traumatic lesions that medical study of the mummy has enabled us to uncover. For the moment however, we may state that the craniocerebral injury alone was capable of causing sudden death.

The importance of this medical observation lies in the fact that this pharaoh, the son and successor to Ramesses II, must, in my opinion, be the one who pursued the Hebrews as they fled from Egypt under the guidance of Moses. As the Holy Scriptures tell us, the pharaoh lost his life in the process. In the following chapter I will explain the reasons that lead us to believe that Merneptah was the pharaoh of the Exodus.

*Part IV*

—

# THE PHARAOH
# AND MOSES

# 13. The Problem as It Stands: Existing Documents

The issue raised at the beginning of this study was the attempt to situate the Exodus within the chronology of the pharaohs. It led to medical research into the pharaonic mummies and caused us to compare various data gleaned from three different sources: the texts of the Holy Scriptures (Bible and Qur'an); documents of Egyptian archeology; and medical findings concerning the mummies of pharaohs who may, according to diverse hypotheses upheld until now, have been affected by the events surrounding the flight from Egypt.

I began by giving a detailed account of the main research carried out on various mummies, and I showed that some of the data acquired have led us to an exact pronouncement concerning the principal cause, if not *the* cause, of Pharaoh Merneptah's death. We shall now return to the evidence that has led me to believe that he is, in all likelihood, the pharaoh of the Exodus. Some of my reasoning is based on history and archeology, coupled with the events related in the Holy Scriptures. The rest is of a medical order, for I would not have dared to maintain a particular theory, if the arguments arising from the examination of the mummy had conflicted with nonmedical data.

This study is the first of its kind because it assembles and compares data from several extremely diverse disciplines. If information from one discipline contradicts observations from another, it implies that the theory that at first seemed plausible can no longer be held to be so, and must therefore be rejected.

The complex questions dealt with here are approached in a very different spirit from those of Egyptologists and experts in Biblical exegesis—their field of inquiry being limited to knowledge of their own particular subjects. Of course, I am well aware that there are some in both groups who are willing to examine, without prejudice, data that lie outside their own familiar territory. It must be stated, however, that genuine multidisciplinary studies are almost totally lacking in this field.

What is especially lacking is the method of reasoning particularly cherished by doctors. When faced with a difficult case, the doctor will not be satisfied with simply establishing a diagnosis based on relevant arguments, but will subject the proposed diagnosis to critical tests. This consists of trying to refute, as it were, the diagnosis, using counterarguments, the validity of which may be gauged when they conflict with what is supposed to have been proved. If the diagnosis withstands this challenge, it must be the correct one.

What theories are offered as far as Moses is concerned? The answer is sometimes hypotheses of a purely philosophical kind, containing only one small aspect of the data, and sometimes hypotheses that one would like to see supported by more or less similar points of view that arose at a specific time in history. Thus we soon find ourselves on a speculative path, taking no account whatsoever of hard facts that rule out the product of purely abstract considerations. In particular, I am thinking of those who claim, without a shred of material evidence, that Pharaoh Akhenaten, who was responsible for encouraging monotheism, must have inspired Moses.

Alas, such methods of reasoning are very common today, for

visionaries have overtaken objective thinkers. It is no surprise, therefore, to find grave shortcomings in methods of approaching such problems. The flair with which an argument is expressed camouflages its inherent mediocrity. It is a fact that a large number of theories concerning Moses are based on extremely weak data. Comparisons and challenges have not been carried out on them, even though these are absolutely indispensable. In my study of these works which focus on situating the Exodus in the history of the pharaohs, I was staggered to find theories sometimes based on a single fact. Their authors were not the slightest bit interested in knowing whether other observations existed that formally disproved their theory. Take, for example, the commentator who used the calendar to calculate the position of the Exodus to within one day. He placed it under the reign of Tuthmosis II, but could not have realized in so doing, that he had situated the entry of Joseph and the sons of Jacob into Egypt at a time when Abraham was still alive. We might also mention those who have been swept along by "Ramesside Romanticism," ascribing to Ramesses II initiatives and abilities that occurred at the end of his life, no matter how incompatible they are with formally established medical data. One has to know how to keep to a moderate line of thought in a field where this kind of overenthusiasm can lead one's reasoning astray.

When dealing with the issue of Moses and the Exodus, it would seem of prime importance to refresh our memories as to the documents in our possession. It is also indispensable to recognize the true value of the imaginative theories of many commentators whose main objective is to present history in the light of their own personal point of view, whether religious or metaphysical, while paying scant attention to questions of objectivity. It is for this reason that an examination of certain theories on the subject leaves us astonished by the fact that there is no concrete evidence to uphold them.

We should first know what documents we possess on the story

of Moses. Essentially, they consist of the Holy Scriptures—the Bible and the Qur'an. Unfortunately, however, there is nothing in them to indicate the exact identity of the kings of Egypt reigning at the time the events took place. The Old Testament version of the story of Moses is described in the Book of Exodus, the second part of the Pentateuch. It constitutes the main source for the Judeo-Christian doctrines on this subject. The Qur'an often mentions the story of Moses. Out of the 114 suras the Qur'an contains, the story is spoken of in more than ten of them. The name Pharaoh, the main character on the Egyptian side, is repeated seventy-four times, occurring in twenty-seven suras. The Biblical and Qur'anic narrations coincide as far as the essentials are concerned. The Qur'an provides additional information on certain points, but it is the Biblical narration that gives us the most detailed data, putting us on the track of the identities of the two pharaohs concerned. For as we shall see later on, the Bible tells us that at least two pharaohs reigned during Moses' life.

Egyptology can offer us no data whatsoever either on Moses himself or on the Exodus. There are, however, several hieroglyphic documents alluding to forced laborers who may well have been the enslaved Hebrews, since the hieroglyphic name sounds very similar to that of Jacob's descendants. Furthermore, the famous Stele of Merneptah provides the only hieroglyphic transcription known of the word *Israel*. We shall see the meaning it has in this inscription.

Apart from these two sources, one religious, the other secular, there are no further documents known that might enlighten us.

My initial research was twofold, including both the historical and the medical points of view. The historical aspect was concerned with the following questions: Bearing in mind the written documentation in existence, at what period was Moses in Egypt? Under which pharaoh was he born? Under which pharaoh did the Exodus take place?

Only when satisfactory answers had been found to the above

questions, and it seemed possible to construct a hypothesis based on solid arguments, could comparison be made with the medical aspects. The description given in the Holy Scriptures was compared with the data obtained from the various medical examinations performed on the mummified body of the pharaoh who seems most likely to have been the pharaoh involved in the Exodus. Later on, we shall see that, in the case of Merneptah, the narrations contained in the Scriptures and the findings of medicine are perfectly compatible. We shall also realize that this is by no means the case for other pharaohs, Ramesses II in particular.

# Data Contained in the Holy Scriptures

## The Biblical Passages

(The following quotations are taken from the Revised Standard Version.)

The Book of Exodus begins by recounting how Jacob and his son entered Egypt to rejoin Joseph. The Bible does not tell us how many kings of Egypt Joseph had known, but the story begins with a new King "who did not know Joseph" (Exodus I: 8). This was the period of the oppression. Since Jacob's time, the Hebrews had become a large group, or community, so the pharaoh imposed on them the construction of the cities named in the Bible as "Pithom" and "Ramesses." This detail is of crucial importance. Because the Hebrews had become "too numerous" in the country, the pharaoh decided that each newborn son would be cast into the river. Moses was born into this generation. At the age of three months, he too was sent up to the river, but his mother placed him in a rush basket on the river's edge. It was here that the pharaoh's daughter discovered Moses and took him home. One of Moses' sisters had watched to see what became of the abandoned infant. She then intervened with the pharaoh's daughter, pretending not to recognize Moses, arranging things in such a way that his mother was chosen to be his nurse. Thus, miraculously saved, the child was later treated at the king's court as if he were one of the pharaoh's own sons, and he was given the Egyptian name of Moses.

As a young man, Moses went to live in a country called Midian. There he married and lived for many years. The Bible relates a second detail of great importance: "In the course of those many days the king of Egypt died." (Exodus 2: 23).

According to the Scriptures, God then ordered Moses, in the episode of the Burning Bush, to go and find the pharaoh and lead his brothers out of Egypt. He was accompanied on this mission by his brother Aaron. The pharaoh who received him was the successor to the one under whose reign Moses had long ago been born.

The new king of Egypt refused to allow the Hebrews to leave. Once again God revealed Himself and ordered Moses to repeat the request. The Bible tells us that Moses was eighty years old at this time, another detail that will help us situate him in the chronology of the pharaohs. The request was rejected again by the pharaoh, even though Moses had demonstrated that he possessed supernatural powers, and in spite of the trials God later sent down upon Egypt, such as the famous plagues that afflicted the entire country.

In the face of the pharaoh's intransigence, the Hebrews escaped, led by Moses. The number to have supposedly left the City of Ramesses was six hundred thousand, "besides women and children" (Exodus 12: 37). This figure has surely been grossly exaggerated.

The Exodus is described in the following terms: "Pharaoh made ready his chariot and took his army with him, and took six hundred picked chariot. . . the king of Egypt pursued the people of Israel as they went forth defiantly." (Exodus 14: 6 and 8). At the edge of the sea, Moses raised his staff and caused the waters to part. Thereupon, his people crossed without wetting their feet, followed closely by the Egyptians, who had caught up with them. "The Egyptians pursued and went in after them into the midst of the sea, all the Pharaoh's horses, his chariots and his horsemen." (Exodus 14: 23). "The waters returned and covered the chariots and the horsemen and all the host of Pharaoh that had followed them into the sea; not so much as one of them remained." (Exodus 14: 28–29).

The Book of Exodus is quite clear. The pharaoh had perished because "not so much as one of them remained." Furthermore, we again find this detail of the Bible repeated in the Psalms. Psalm 106, verse 11, and Psalm 136, verses 13 to 15, are an act of thanks to God "Who divided the Red Sea in sunder, and made Israel pass through the midst of it. . . but overthrew Pharaoh and his host in the Red Sea." The French Ecumenical translation of the Bible (Paris, 1975) talks of "the Sea of Rushes." Once one has read this, how can one doubt the fact that the king of Egypt lost his life in the course of the pursuit? Those faithful to Judaism are certain that the pharaoh lost his life during the Exodus. For them, the texts speak for themselves. Strange as it may seem, however, there are Christian commentators who disagree, as we shall see in a moment. The Bible does not, however, give any indication as to what became of the body. It is the Qur'an that provides information on this point.

## The Qur'anic Passages

In their broad outlines, the Biblical and Qur'anic descriptions are similar. The Qur'an does not, however, provide a continuous narration, so it must be reconstituted from the disparate elements scattered throughout numerous passages. Nor is the pharaoh mentioned by name, any more than he is in the Bible. The only additional information on this point is that one of the pharaoh's counselors was named Haman. However, this detail still does not enable us to establish which royal council he belonged to.

In the Qur'an, the pharaoh is described as the Jews' oppressor, but the Qur'an does not give the name of the cities constructed by the Hebrews as forced laborers. There are a few variations concerning details of the Biblical and Qur'anic narrations, but they are of no practical consequence for our specific purposes. It should be pointed out, however, that the indications in the Bible as to the number of people who took flight—the Bible tells us that six hundred thousand men, plus women and children, spent a long time in the wilderness—are not found in the Qur'an, nor is the description of the route taken by the Exodus in the Bible.

The pharaoh's death during the Exodus is described in great detail by the Qur'an. Furthermore, the description differs from the Biblical narration in that indications are given as to what became of the body once it had been covered by the returning waters. Sura 10, verses 90 to 92, tells us that the body was found on the very same day—an important detail to remember.

## Data Taken from Hieroglyphic Texts

### The Habiru

From the Bible, we know that the Hebrews spent a long time in Egypt. The total length of their stay in this country was 430 years (Exodus 12: 40).

From Pierre Montet to Daniel Rops, it is thought today that the first Hebrews—Jacob and his sons, including Joseph—arrived in Egypt at the same time as the Hyksos did in the seventeeth century B.C. The four-century stay of a rapidly proliferating population must have left traces in the literature of the times. This is a legitimate question to ask when faced with allusions in hieroglyphic documents to certain categories of workers called Apiru, Hapiru, or Habiru, or "forced laborers," as the Hebrews were to become. The sound of the word is curiously close to that of *Hebrews*, so it was not long before commentators associated the two. In fact, it is very difficult to discern what the word really means.

The name Habiru includes harvesters, agricultural laborers, and construction workers. In the *Ancient History of Israel*, Father R. de Vaux notes, "they are not members of the local population, they do not identify themselves with a class in society, they do not all share the same occupation or status."

By the fifteenth century B.C., under Tuthmosis III, the Habiru were employed as "workers in the stables." During the reign of Amenophis II, 3,600 of them were brought back from Canaan as prisoners. Father R. de Vaux tells us that they had constituted a considerable portion of the Syrio-Palestinian population living there. Nearer the period with which we are most concerned, around 1300 B.C., under Sethos I, these people are again mentioned because of the disturbances they caused in the Beth-Shean region. Under Ramesses II, they are alluded to in hieroglyphic texts as laborers or workers engaged in transporting piles for building the Great Pylon of Ramesses Miamon. It was at about this time that the Bible mentions the fact that the Hebrews had built the Northern capital, the city of Ramesses. The last reference to them comes in an Egyptian text of the twelfth century B.C., roughly one century after the period in which Moses and his followers took part in the Exodus to the Promised Land.

We may therefore state that the word *Habiru*, or its equivalents, appeared in hieroglyphic writings at roughly the same time as the Hebrews were living in Egypt. The word may also be applied, however, to other groups or communities living outside Egypt and not just those Habiru inside the country. As I have written in *The Bible, the Qur'an and Science,* "we might perhaps draw an analogy with the word *suisse* (Swiss), which has several different meanings in French. It can mean an inhabitant of Switzerland, a mercenary soldier of the old French monarchy who was of Swiss extraction, a Vatican guard, or an employee of a Christian Church." When seen in this light, the word *Habiru* might just as easily refer to the origin of these people as to their activities and functions; it may have been current both during the Hebrews' stay in Egypt and at a period that was very distant in time from the Exodus.

## The Inscription of the Word Israel on the Stele of Merneptah

When the stele relating the triumphs in battle of Ramesses II's successor, Merneptah, was found in his funeral temple in the necropolis in Thebes in 1895, Egyptologists were amazed to find the word *Israel* written in syllabic hieroglyphic characters. So far, this is the only mention of the word expressed in hieroglyphics. The inscription dates from the fifth year of Merneptah's reign and is most certainly from the very last decades of the thirteenth century B.C., although commentators have not yet pinpointed the exact date at which Merneptah ascended to the throne. The stele records a "devastated Israel which has no more seed."

As a result, people immediately jumped to the conclusion that this was proof of the fact that the Jews must have settled in Canaan by the fifth year of Merneptah's reign, hence the Hebrews' Exodus from Egypt had already taken place. Even today, I have heard the so-called argument put forward that the Exodus took place under Ramesses II, whose reign preceded Merneptah's.

In fact, we should take a closer look at the meaning of the word *Israel* on this stele written in hieroglyphics. We should inquire into its precise origin to help us understand the exact meaning of the inscription. The stele was produced to glorify the pharaoh's exploits in battle. It is known that on his father Ramesses II's death, Merneptah had to reestablish order along the borders of this country. The stele records his victories and the names of foreign places and lands. In the inscription, names are followed by what is known as a generic determinative, designed to avoid any misinterpretation of the hieroglyphic characters. All the names mentioned in the list of Merneptah's victories are accompanied by a generic determinative indicating "foreign country." There is only one exception, the word *Israel*. The generic determinative qualifying *Israel* has nothing to do with a "foreign country" it signifies a "human community or group," meaning a collection of men and women. The hieroglyphic inscription shows this beyond any shadow of a doubt. We may state, therefore, that on the stele of Merneptah the word *Israel* designates a human foreign community or group, not a country. This makes it hard to believe the interpretation placed on the word by those who think it means the already occupied Promised Land.

We should note, furthermore, that the stele dates from the end of the thirteenth century B.C., and it was only much later, around 931–930 B.C., that the Kingdom of Israel was formed, lasting until 721 B.C., when it collapsed. It is difficult, therefore, for the word *Israel* on the stele to take on the sense of a "political entity." It quite obviously refers to a more modest human group, and there is nothing to stop us from thinking that this group or community was living in Egypt at the time.

Once one knows the origin of the word *Israel*, everything becomes clear—it was the nickname given to Jacob, Abraham's grandson, after Jacob had wrestled with the Angel (Genesis 32: 29). The great ancestor in Egypt of the Hebrews was Jacob. Why should we be surprised, therefore, to find that the group descended from him had adopted their great ancestor's name as the title of their community? In all probability, the *Israel* on the stele of the fifth year of Merneptah's reign designates the Hebrews in Egypt, a foreign group or community still present in the country when Merneptah came to the throne. The Egyptologist Pierre Montet in his book *Egypt and the Bible* (Delachaux et Niestlé, publ. Neufchatel, 1959) offers this very explanation.

# 14. The Exodus and Its Place in the Chronology of the Pharaohs

## Previous Hypotheses as to the Position Occupied by Moses in the History of the Pharaohs

Those who have tried to find the period occupied by Moses in history have placed it at various points ranging from Tuthmosis II to Merneptah, from the middle of the fifteenth to the end of the thirteenth centuries B.C. Most attempts have tried to locate Moses in time according to whichever king of Egypt may have played a part in the Exodus. We do indeed need the help of data provided by Egyptology, for what the Bible tells us is not sufficient on its own. It is only after we have compared Biblical with Egyptological data that we can locate the era of Moses and the date of the Exodus.

There is one book of the Bible that does in fact seem to enlighten us on this point. Unfortunately, however, it contains one item of information that quickly appears untenable. The book in question is Kings I (6, 1). It places the time Moses left Egypt at 480 years before the construction of the Temple of Solomon, around 968 B.C. According to this estimate, the Exodus would therefore have taken place around 1450 B.C. and the entry into Egypt in roughly 1850 B.C. Now, this period more or less co-

139

incides with Abraham, for, still according to the Bible, approximately 250 years separated him from Joseph's date of entry into Egypt. The inaccuracy of the chronological date contained in Kings I is quite obvious, hence we cannot base our answer on the Holy Scriptures alone.

The Exodus was an extremely important event, marking the flight from Egypt of the Hebrews, who had been resident in the country for over four centuries. It was of great consequence in the story of Moses, and also in the history of Egypt. It cannot be emphasized enough that, according to what the Holy Scriptures tell us of pharaonic history, the Exodus, following on the terrible plagues sent down on Egypt, marked a tragedy for its sovereign—the god-pharaoh was defeated and lost his life in the process. Painful events such as these should normally have left traces in historical documents, stelae, and various inscriptions. But in fact we find nothing of the sort, because it was unthinkable that the sovereign, who was also god, could have been defeated and killed during a warlike event. What pieces of evidence can today's investigator turn to in this case? There is one thing that has come down to us—the mummified body of the pharaoh himself. In the twentieth century, we have methods at our disposal that can help us carry out investigations to determine the causes of a subject's death. Hence any evidence uncovered that points toward a tragic death immediately assumes considerable historical value. This has been the subject of my research linking Scriptural data to medical observation.

To situate Moses in time, reference is mainly made to the Exodus. If we are looking for a hypothesis as to the identity of the pharaoh who took part in the Exodus, we have to go back a long way in time. Since the Bible says nothing on the subject, it is in extra-Biblical sources that we may perhaps find a clue to his identity. The oldest information on this point has mainly been handed down by tradition. As Gaston Maspero, the famous Egyptologist of the beginning of the century, wrote in 1900 in

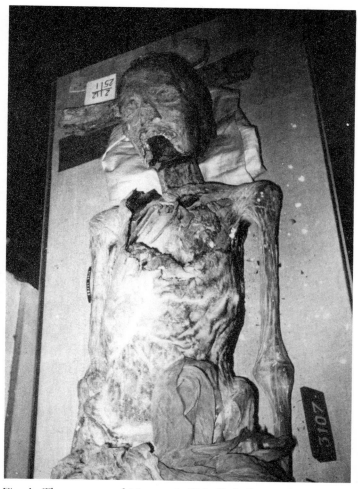

Fig. 1. The mummy of Mernere I. This Sixth Dynasty king reigned roughly forty-three centuries ago and was buried in the area of the Sakkara pyramids. The mummy has lost the upper part of the thorax (a part of the neck and mandible) and is in a state of decomposition. This is probably the oldest and most complete mummy we possess at present.

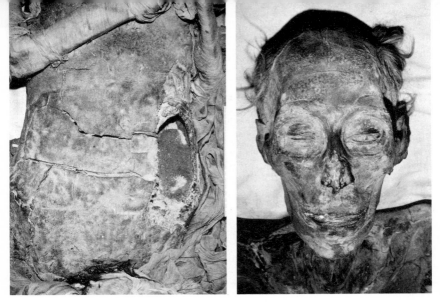

Fig. 2. *(above left)* Ramesses II—view of the abdomen. The mummy is 3200 years old. On its left side, there is an enormous evisceration orifice. The embalmers subsequently sealed it with a plaque, which is now missing. Many crevices may be seen in the abdominal wall, indicating the deterioration of the mummy.

Fig. 3. *(above right)* The mummy of Ramesses II. Apart from the remaining hair, which was dyed yellow by the embalmers, there are small, brownish skin tumors on the forehead (senile comedones of acne).

Fig. 4. Embalmment instruments. View of a display case at the Egyptian Museum, Cairo, containing scalpels, forceps, needles, and other instruments.

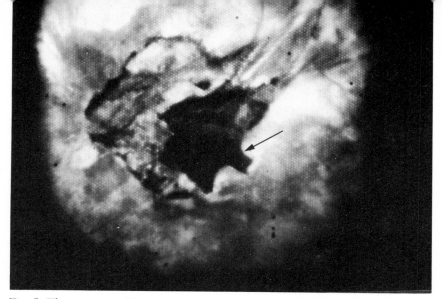

Fig. 5. The mummy of Ramesses V. The ethmoidal orifice bored by the embalmers between the upper part of the nasal cavities and the base of the cranium, allowing the brain to be removed via the nose. The arrow indicates the edge of the hole. This photograph was taken during an endoscopic examination.

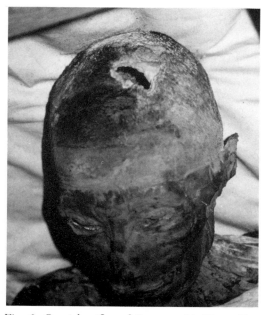

Fig. 6. Cranial orifice of Ramesses V. The orifice was probably bored by the embalmers to perfect mummification, not to extract the brain.

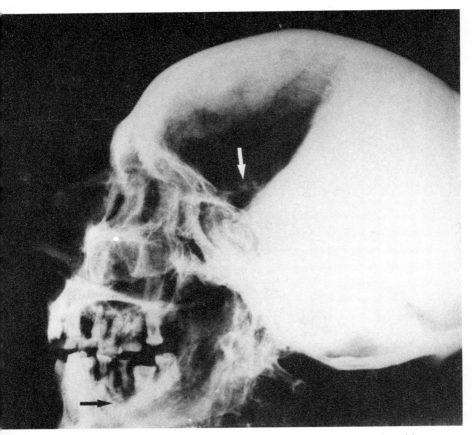

Fig. 7. Ramesses II—profile X ray of the head. The view shows the dental lesions; an infection inside the lower jaw (mandible), indicated by the black arrow; the partial filling of the cranial cavity with a resinous material; and plaques of arteriosclerosis inside the skull, indicated by the white arrow.

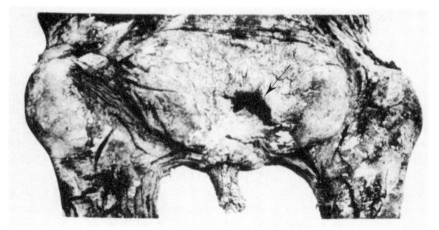

Fig. 8. The mummy of Merneptah—lower abdomen. The photograph was taken after the removal of the wrappings by Elliot Smith in the early twentieth century. It shows a slight deterioration of the abdomen in the form of a cavity, measuring roughly 4 × 6 cm, on the left of the medial line, indicated by the arrow. The left evisceration orifice was resealed by the embalmers. Part of the genitals are missing.

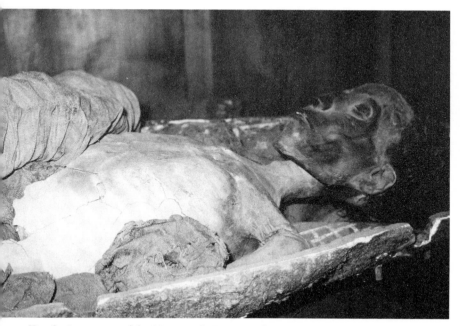

Fig. 9. A mummy of the Nineteenth Dynasty (about 3200 years old). The subject may well be Queen Twosret. The surface coloring of the mummy is not uniform, probably from the disappearance of skin in certain places. It is also possible that the face was painted on the left cheek.

Fig. 10. View of the Giza plateau and Pyramids. Cephren's pyramid can be seen behind the Sphinx. This necropolis dates from the Old Kingdom (around 2600 B.C.), i.e., the Fourth Dynasty.

Fig. 11. Tutankhamun in his tomb in the Valley of the Kings. The sepulcher was discovered almost intact in 1922. Nearly all of its contents were removed except the stone sarcophagus containing the coffin in which the remains of the mummy now lay.

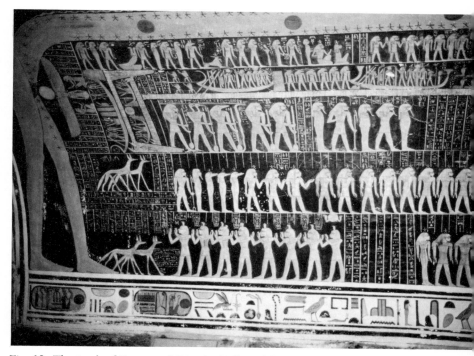

Fig. 12. The tomb of Ramesses VI in the Valley of the Kings. The fact that the wall paintings on the vault have been perfectly preserved after three thousand years indicates the excellent climatic conditions prevalent in the tombs. These conditions have also helped to keep the mummified bodies in a good state of preservation.

Fig. 13. View of Zoser's Pyramid (Sakkara). This pyramid was constructed around 2700 B.C. by the famous architect, Imhotep. It predates the regularly shaped pyramids on the Giza plateau and belongs to the oldest group known.

Fig. 14. Entrance to the tomb of Ramesses VI in the Valley of the Kings. During the New Kingdom, protection from robbers was sought by digging deep tombs at the foot of the rocky cliffs of the Theban necropolis. Originally, the entrance was unobtrusive and sealed. In modern times, it has been enlarged and modified to allow visits by tourists.

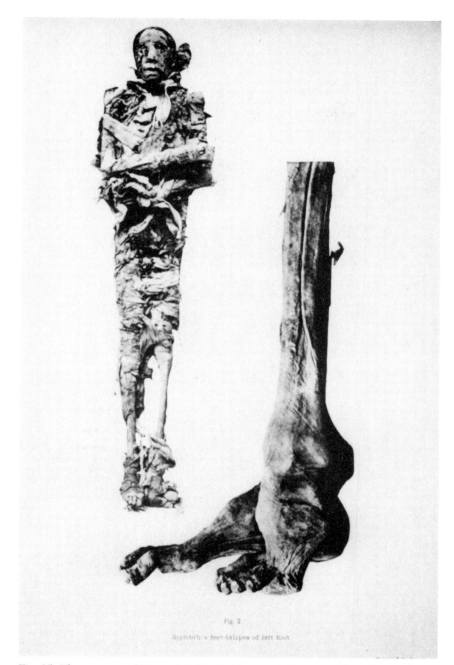

Fig. 15. The mummy of Merneptah-Siptah (Nineteenth Dynasty). Three thousand years ago, the pharaoh was afflicted with poliomyelitis. Its effect on the bones can be seen on the left lower limb (shortening, atrophy, and club foot). Photograph by Elliot Smith.

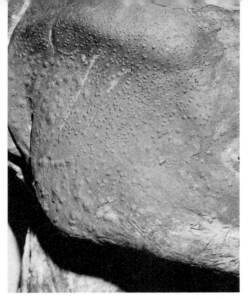

Fig. 16. Ramesses V—lesions of the face. The face has been painted red by the embalmers. It is also the site of small tumors that were long thought to be smallpox but whose nature is not definitely known.

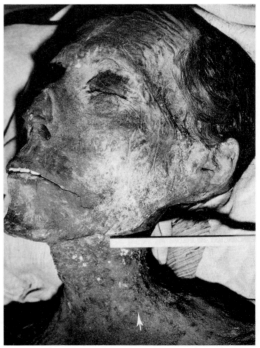

Fig. 17. Amenophis II. The embalmment resins have given the mummy an artificial color and highlight the whitish colonies that have invaded the face (probably fungi). Arrow: skin tumors on the mummy's neck, especially around the lower part. They are also present elsewhere on the body.

Fig. 18. Tutmosis II, Tutmosis III, and Amenophis II. These three pharaohs are directly descended from one another. They all show signs of multiple skin tumors, all of the same kind, suggesting a hereditary illness. This photograph shows the skin lesions of Tutmosis II.

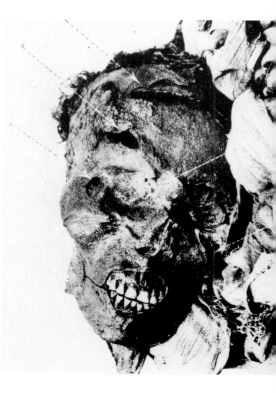

Fig. 19. Penetrating wounds in Sekenenre's face and skull. This Seventeenth Dynasty king (seventeenth century B.C.) died in battle from blows delivered by the weapons of the Hyksos. Medical study of the lesions has corroborated historical information by showing that they were traumatic in origin. Photograph by Elliot Smith.

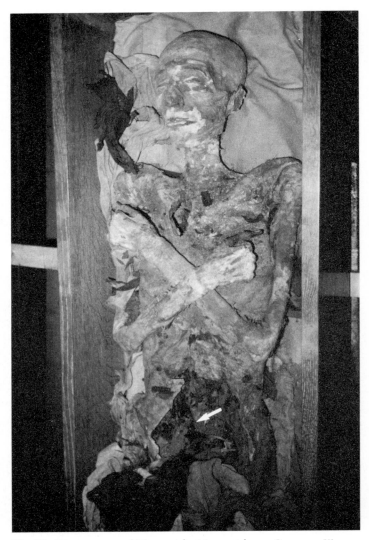

Fig. 20. The mummy of Merneptah. Merneptah was Ramesses II's successor. The mummy appeared to have been greatly damaged by 1975, when compared with its state at the turn of the century (see Fig. 23). The anterior abdominal wall has been two-thirds destroyed, as indicated by the white arrow. A small section of the thoracic wall on the right has vanished. The fracture of the right forearm is a lesion that occurred after mummification.

Fig. 21. Merneptah—fracture of the mummy's right forearm. There are many broken fragments around the fracture, which follows a jagged line.

Fig. 22. Merneptah—view of the thorax. Abnormal thoracic orifice created by the disappearance of a section of the thoracic wall. The small white spots around the medial line of the thorax and at the lower part of the neck resemble colonies of fungi.

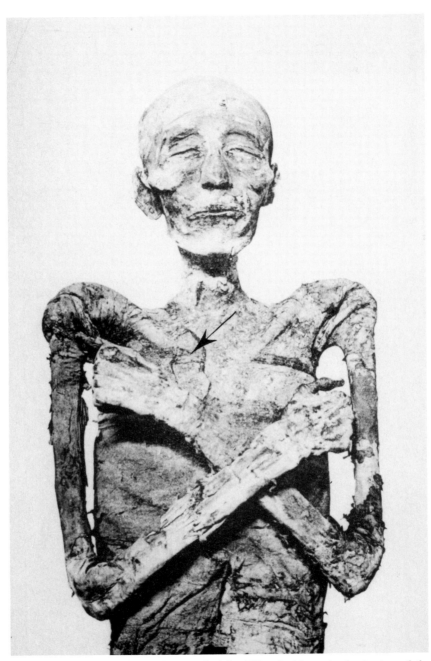

Fig. 23. Merneptah. When photographed by Elliot Smith at the beginning of the century, the mummy appeared to be less damaged than it is today. At that time, the piece of the thorax now missing was still in place in the area of the right clavicle.

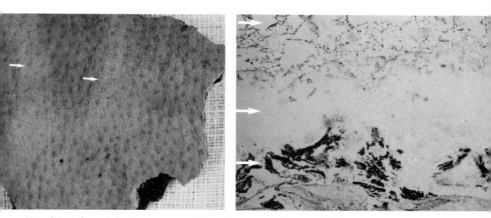

Fig. 24. *(above left)* A mummy of the Nineteenth Dynasty (thirteenth century B.C.). An example of the perfect preservation of the thoracic covering, from which the ribs are seen to protrude *(arrows)*. Mummification has preserved the pore orifices, which are clearly visible. The underlying muscle appears as an indentation: it is red in color.

Fig. 25. *(above right)* A mummy of the Nineteenth Dynasty. General view of the section of the skin covering part of the thoracic wall, as seen under a microscope. On the top is the dermic layer *(arrow)* and identifiable structures of the skin; in the middle is the subcutaneous tissue *(arrow)*; and below are the layers of muscle *(arrow)*. At every layer, anatomical structures can be recognized through the microscope.

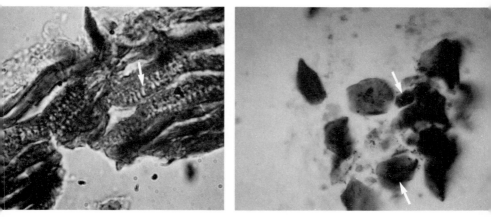

Fig. 26. *(above left)* A mummy of the Nineteenth Dynasty. When united, the muscular fibrillae form the muscular fibers, but here mummification has separated them. They are marked by transversal striations, a feature of the skeletal muscles, and may be measured in units of 1/1000 mm.

Fig. 27. *(above right)* A mummy of the Nineteenth Dynasty. Malpighi's cells of the skin: small cells with nuclei *(upper arrow)*, and larger cells with nuclei that are gradually disappearing due to the normal evolution of the dermis *(lower arrow)*. These features have been perfectly preserved.

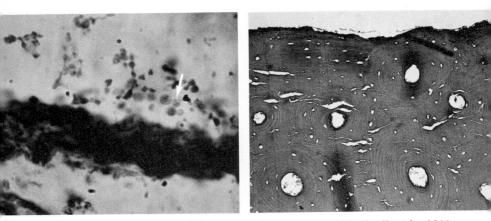

Fig. 28. *(above left)* A mummy of the Nineteenth Dynasty—red blood cells. After 3200 years, red blood cells can still be identified. This finding is very rare in view of the extreme fragility of blood cells.

Fig. 29. *(above right)* Merneptah—tiny fragment of bone fallen from the fracture of the forearm. Mummification has preserved all the details of the microscopic structures of the bone—just as if it were a freshly taken surgical sample.

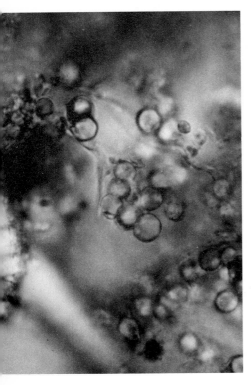

Fig. 30. Ramesses II—spores of fungi. The discovery of these spores, in the form of rounded bodies, which surround the abdominal evisceration orifice (see Fig. 2) provides conclusive evidence of the biological contamination of the mummy and the need to sterilize it.

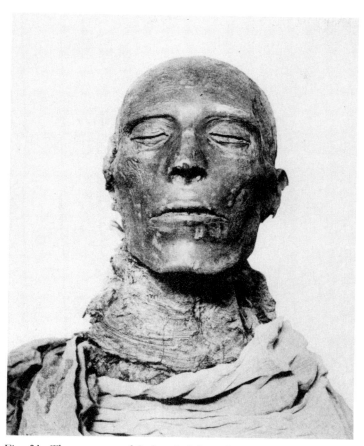

Fig. 31. The mummy of Sethos I, father of Ramesses II. The crude collar was added to the mummy after it had been decapitated by tomb robbers and reembalmed. The face is blackened by mummification resin. Photograph by Elliot Smith.

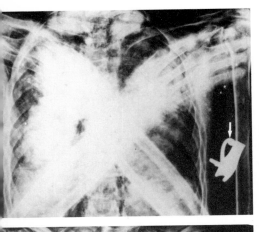

Fig. 32. Sethos I—frontal X ray of the thorax. The X ray shows the unhomogeneous contents of the thorax; the forearms folded over the chest; and on the left, an amulet representing the "Eye of Horus" (*arrow*), which was incorporated into the resins enveloping the mummy.

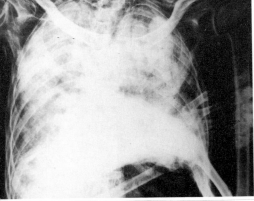

Fig. 33. Ramesses II—frontal X ray of the thorax. As in the case of other mummies, the thorax is thought to be partly filled with the organs. These would have been removed by the embalmers, then treated and wrapped. No attention was paid, however, to replacing them in their correct anatomical position. They were accompanied by various materials used in mummification, and it has been absolutely impossible to identify the contents of the thorax, in spite of what some have said to the contrary.

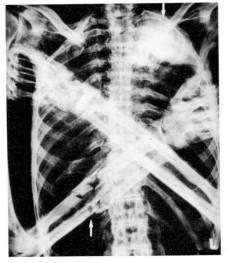

Fig. 34. Merneptah—frontal X ray of the thorax. An example of an almost empty thorax, which nevertheless provides numerous radiological details. Of note is the opaque mass in the upper part of the left side of the thorax (*arrow*) and the fracture of the right forearm (*arrrow*). (The other lesions and anomalies that this X ray reveals are discussed in the text.)

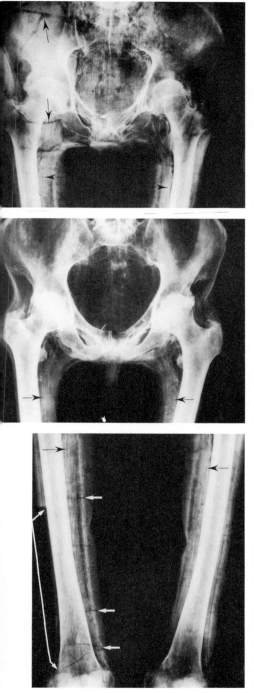

Fig. 35. Ramesses II—frontal X ray of the pelvis. The evisceration orifice, which has been left gaping open, is marked by a black area on the left side. On the right, the multiple crevices of the soft tissues (*arrows*) can be seen clearly; also visible is the cloth filling the abdomen, which was later removed. Note also the calcifications in the two femoral arteries (*arrows*).

Fig. 36. Merneptah—frontal X ray of the pelvis. The pelvis is empty and the skeleton is perfectly outlined and totally normal. Calcifications may be seen in the femoral arteries (*arrows*).

Fig. 37. Ramesses II—frontal X ray of the femurs. The two bones are unfractured. The two femoral arteries contain calcifications (*black arrows*). The multiple cracks in the soft tissues show up as black and are marked by horizontal lines (*white arrows*). On the outer side of the right femur, the soft tissues do not show up as a whitish shadow because the bone is bare at this point on the mummy (*two white arrows*).

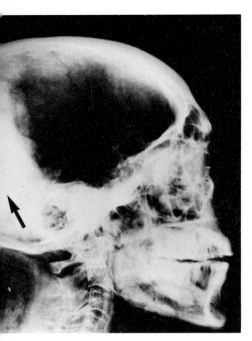

Fig. 38. Sethos I—profile X ray of the head. The teeth are in fairly good condition—in contrast to those of Ramesses II and Merneptah. The cranial cavity has been filled in its posterior part by a resinous material, introduced through the nose after the brain was removed.

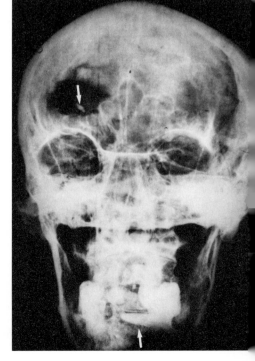

Fig. 39. Merneptah—frontal X ray of the head. The X ray shows the clearly defined lacuna on the right side (see Fig. 40), its position, and also a bone splinter. The latter shows up as a tiny patch of white near the lower edge of the hole. It corresponds to a detail in the photograph (Fig. 40) and is marked here by a white arrow. *Lower arrow*: a tooth lying horizontally (see Fig. 42).

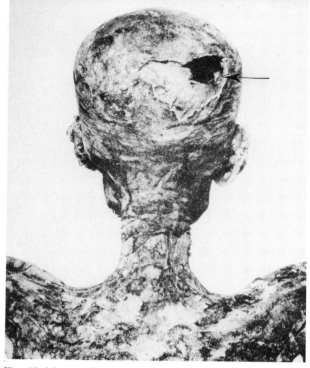

Fig. 40. Merneptah—posterior view of the head. On the right, the bone lacuna can be seen with its tiny splinter (in white) on the lower edge in the extension of the arrow. The scalp, missing beneath this edge of the lacuna, was deliberately removed by Elliot Smith to allow for observation of the underlying bone. Photograph by Elliot Smith.

*Young Tooth*                    *Aged Tooth*

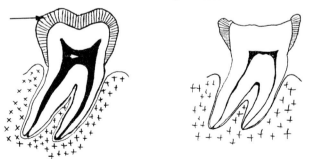

Fig. 41. Diagram of dental evolution as related to age. The young tooth is shown with its thick layer of enamel (*black arrow*) and broad pulp chamber (*white arrow*). The pulp chamber reaches down to the roots and the pulp canals are wide. (The aged tooth is characterized by worn enamel and a pulp chamber and pulp canals of reduced volume.) Illustration by F. Rousières.

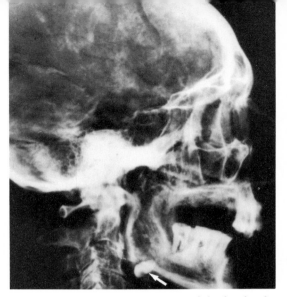

Fig. 42. Merneptah—profile X ray of the head. The foremost teeth of the maxillary (upper jaw) are still present. The teeth of the mandible (lower jaw) are better preserved. Some posterior teeth are still in place but there are several cases of decay, especially in the molars. A tooth has been detached by embalmment and has lodged in the pharnyx, where it is superimposed on the angle of the lower jaw (*white arrow*).

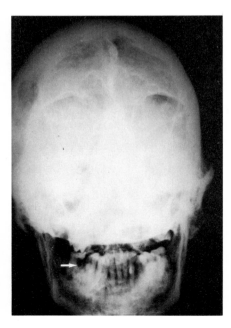

Fig. 43. Ramesses II—frontal X ray of the head. The greyish area in the upper part of the X ray is explained by the presence in the cranial cavity of a resinous material introduced after the brain was removed (see Fig. 7). Severe dental lesions may be seen, with a lacuna in the right part of the lower jaw (*white arrow*). See also the profile X ray (Fig. 7).

Fig. 44. Ramesses II—diagram showing the dental lesion of a molar (*Drawn by F. Rousières*). Dental decay has caused the separation of the roots, an osseous abcess and lacuna in the mandible, and a bone splinter in a zone of osteomyelitis (*arrow*).

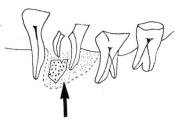

Fig. 45. Merneptah—endoscopic view of the thorax. The abnormal mass revealed by the X ray (see Fig. 34) in the left part of the thorax is again shown in this view. Nevertheless, it does not allow us to confirm whether the mass constitutes the heart, which might have been left in place and covered with calcareous salts, another anatomical formation, or even a foreign body in the mummy.

Fig. 46. Ramesses V—close-up of the cranial orifice. The scalp, which had covered the area of the orifice, has been folded back and mummified (*arrow*). This hole was probably bored by the embalmers.

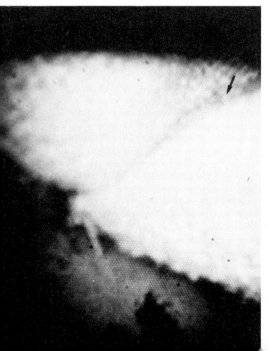

Fig. 47. Ramesses V—endoscopic view of the cranial cavity. In the posterior part of the cranial cavity, the presence of a fragment of cloth has been observed. The interweaving of the fibers may clearly be distinguished. A material that seems to be calcareous has been deposited on the cloth.

Fig. 48. Ramesses II—attempt at endoscopic examination. An attempt was made to insert the endoscope into the abdomen through the abdominal evisceration orifice. However, it was only possible to penetrate to a depth of a few centimeters. The light at the end of the endoscope was used for examination by transillumination. It was discovered that the crevices on the right passed through the entire thickness of the abdominal wall.

Fig. 49. Ramesses VI—cranio-facial lesions. This photograph was taken by Elliot Smith shortly after the mummy was discovered at the turn of the century. It shows the extent of the lesions caused by tomb robbers. The mummified tissues around the skull and face have been shattered.

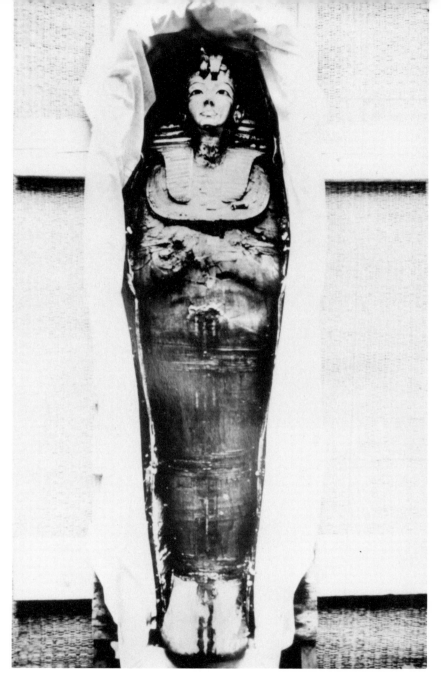

Fig. 50. The mummy of Tutankhamun after the opening of the innermost gold coffin. The outermost wrappings appear to be in perfect order. Deterioration is superficial. The upper part of the mummy is covered by the mask. Photograph from the Griffith Institute–Ashmolean Museum.

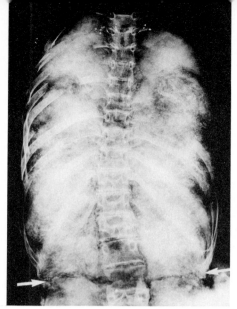

Fig. 51. Tutankhamun—X ray of the trunk. A large number of bones (ribs) are missing. Between the arrows, the section of the trunk deliberately cut by Derry is perfectly visible and passes through the third lumbar vertebra. Photograph courtesy of Professor R. G. Harrison.

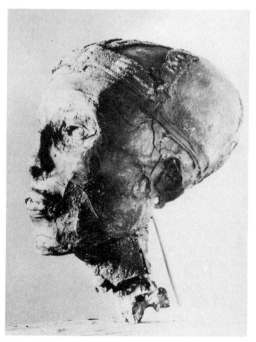

Fig. 52. The head of the mummy of Tutankhamun detached from the body. The photograph shows the damage done to the lower part of the neck. The head is maintained in an upright position by a support strut. Photograph from the Griffith Institute–Ashmolean Museum.

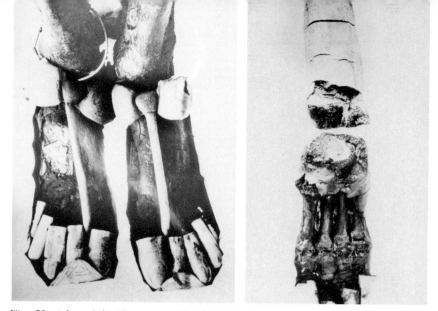

Fig. 53. *(above left)* The mummified feet of Tutankhamun almost intact. The gold sandals and toe stalls are in position. The feet and ankles have only suffered superficial damage. Photograph from the Griffith Institute–Ashmolean Museum.

Fig. 54. *(above right)* The left foot of Tutankhamun after removal of the sandals. The ankle has been disarticulated and the soft tissues of the foot have disintegrated. The metatarsal bones are bare. Photograph from the Griffith Institute–Ashmolean Museum.

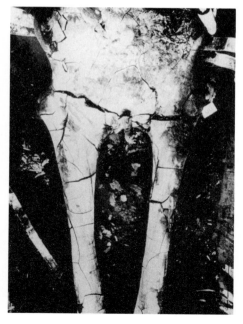

Fig. 55. Tutankhamun—lower abdomen and upper part of the legs. The multitude of deep cracks shows the degree of deterioration of the mummy. Photograph from the Griffith Institute–Ashmolean Museum.

Fig. 56. *(left)* The body of Tutankhamun reassembled in 1925. The multiple remains of the mummy after the dismemberment were reassembled, like pieces of a jigsaw puzzle, and laid down on a bed of sand. The empty spaces left by the missing parts were filled with resin and glue, giving a rough semblance of a human body, which did not look as if it had been damaged very much. Photograph from the Griffith Institute–Ashmolean Museum.

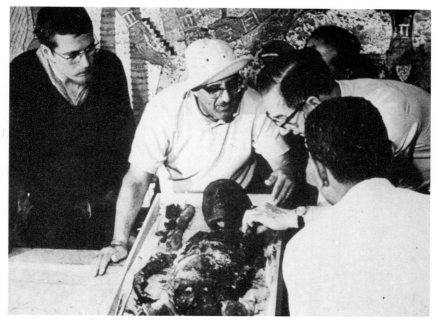

Fig. 57. The British expedition inside the tomb of Tutankhamun in 1968. The artificial reconstitution of the body is unmasked. Henceforth the body is seen to be made of dislocated remains with numerous pieces missing (see X ray of the thorax, Fig. 51). On the right side of the body, segments of the upper limbs are separated from one another and the trunk. Photograph courtesy of F. Filce Leek.

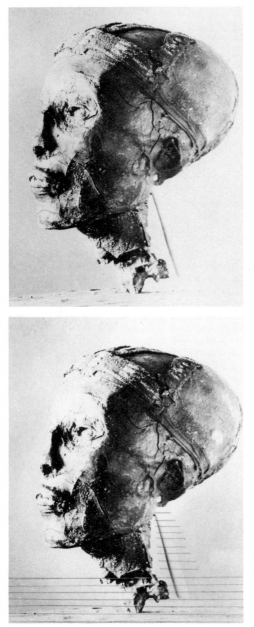

Fig. 58. A subtle procedure. *(above)* The detached head of Tutankhamun. Photograph from the Griffith Institute–Ashmolean Museum. *(below)* Figure 134 of "Tutankhamen" by Christiane Desroches-Noblecourt, who presents this document with the plinth of the head invisible, thus camouflaging the decapitation.

his *Visitor's Guide to the Cairo Museum,* Merneptah "was probably, according to the Alexandrian tradition, the Pharaoh of the Exodus who is said to have perished in the Red Sea." I was unable to find in Egypt the documents from which Maspero drew his conclusions, but we may attach great weight to them, because he was a very eminent Egyptologist. There can be no doubt that before Alexandria was destroyed by the Roman conquest, documents were kept on the history of antiquity, which would make very interesting reading today.

Apart from Pierre Montet, there are very few Egyptologists or specialists in modern Biblical exegesis who have studied arguments either for or against the above hypothesis. In fact, in the last few decades, we have witnessed a profusion of different hypotheses that have been produced with the sole intention of satisfying a single concordance with one precise point in the Holy Scriptures. Their authors have had no regard for other aspects of the same texts, which flatly contradict the hypothesis they are upholding. It is not enough in this instance merely to compare history and archeology; one has to go much further.

Since we had in our possession the mortal remains of one of the participants in the drama, and an examination of them might have provided information, we decided to make use of that fact. Those who usually specialized in such questions could not undertake the research since experts with literary backgrounds could not have personally performed medical investigations. The only people able to do so were doctors.

Before going into the elements supporting my theory, it is essential to describe other, previously formulated, hypotheses while mentioning the arguments that render them either unacceptable or unlikely.

One of the strangest appears to me to be Jean de Miceli's theory (1960), which claims to be extraordinarily accurate. It places the Exodus to within one day, April 9, 1495 B.C., relying entirely on calendar calculations. Because Tuthmosis II was king of Egypt at that time, he must have been the pharaoh of the Exodus. J. de Miceli thinks he has found another argument supporting his theory in the fact that skin lesions have been found on the mummy of Tuthmosis II. He describes them as leprosy (I never discovered why) and claims that Tuthmosis II's leprosy corresponds to one of the plagues of Egypt described in the Bible as skin boils.

This remarkable construction does not, however, take into account another piece of Biblical evidence of prime importance. The Bible tells us that the enslaved Hebrews built the cities of Ramesses and Pithom, today known to be situated in the eastern part of the Nile Delta. The modern Qantir and Tell Retabeh correspond to these ancient cities. This was where Ramesses II established his Northern capital, another reason why we cannot conceive of the Exodus before his reign.

As for the skin lesions of Tuthmosis II, it should be remembered that Tuthmosis III, his son, and Amenophis II, his grandson, also show signs of similar lesions, suggesting nothing more than a disease that ran in the family. It does not therefore seem feasible to connect them with one of the plagues of Egypt at the time of the pharaoh of the Exodus.

In his book *The People of the Bible (Le Peuple de la Bible)*, Daniel Rops names Amenophis II the pharaoh of the Exodus. This theory does not seem to be any better founded than the previous one, for the author of the above work does not cite a single factual argument to support it.

In contrast to this, the hypothesis advanced by Father de Vaux, in his work *The Ancient History of Israel*, at least has the advantage of putting forward a significant element of hypothesis found in the biblical narration: the construction of the cities of Ramesses and Pithom under Ramesses II by the Hebrews into whose group Moses was to be born. This information from the Bible implies that the Exodus could not have taken place before Ramesses II came to the throne, either in 1301 B.C, according to suggested chronologies. Nevertheless, it seems to me very difficult for us to follow the theory that Father R. de Vaux subsequently advances. He places the Exodus in the first half or toward the middle of Ramesses II's reign. There are two arguments against this theory. The first is that if we are to believe what the Bible and the Qur'an—the only sources of information on the subject—tell us, then the Exodus was accompanied by the death of the pharaoh pursuing the Hebrews. The Books of Exodus and Psalms are quite clear on the subject: Pharaoh "made ready his chariot and took his army with him" (Exodus 14: 6); "the king of Egypt pursued the people of Israel" (Ibid. 14: 8); and "the waters returned and covered the chariots and the horsemen and all the host of Pharaoh. . . not so much as one of them remained" (Ibid: 14: 28–29). They talk of Yahweh "Who overthrew Pharaoh and his host in the Red Sea" (Psalms 136: 15).

Either we attach no importance whatsoever to the Biblical and Qur'anic texts, in which case there is no point in talking about Moses, or we take them into account and must therefore consider the Exodus to come at the end of a reign. It would indeed be the last act of the reign, for the king who was at the head of his army pursuing the fleeing Hebrews died as a result of it.

The impartial observer who examines all the hypotheses advanced on this subject is indeed surprised to find that a clergyman of no mean ability in this field—Father R. de Vaux, the former head of the Biblical School of Jerusalem—should have constructed a theory of the Exodus that does not take into account certain explicit passages of the Biblical text concerning the pharaoh's death during the Exodus. There is something disconcerting in this, which I am well aware is not just a tendency of Father R. de Vaux and others in ecclesiastic circles, and among Biblical commentators. There are many Jewish exegetes who have read the Bible and given the words their meaning as it stands, unhesitatingly believing that the pharaoh of the Exodus really did die during the pursuit.

The second point that has puzzled me when examining Father R. de Vaux's theory, which places the Exodus in the first part or the middle of Ramesses II's reign, is that the Bible states quite clearly that the king of Egypt died during Moses' stay in the land of Midian, before the Exodus. How can one maintain that Moses was born when the enslaved Hebrews were building Ramesses II's capital, and that the Exodus took place under this same Ramesses II, if the king of Egypt is supposed to have died, according to the Bible (Exod. 2: 23) during Moses' lifetime? At this point, Father R. de Vaux thinks he is waiving the objection by telling us that he doubts the Biblical source for this verse in the Book of Exodus. Why should he rule out this piece of Biblical evidence, having refused to take account of another part of the text that is perfectly accepted by others?

While on the subject of Ramesses II and his connection with the Exodus, we might also mention the theory held by those who claim that this extremely old man, suffering as he was from the disease described earlier, was still able to take part in battle expeditions. We should know by now that to think of this romantic hypothesis is a product of wishful thinking. It is formally contradicted by the medical data resulting from the examination of the mummy.

There is one last hypothesis that tends to arouse great interest. It claims that Merneptah was the pharaoh of the Exodus *in the course of his reign*. It is put forward by Pierre Montet in his book *Egypt and the Bible*. He admits that Moses may have been born under Ramesses II, and that it was under the reign of his successor, Merneptah, that Moses returned from the land of Midian to request the freeing of his brethren. Montet considers that in the fifth year of Merneptah's reign the enslaved Hebrews were still in Egypt, as indicated to him by the famous "Israel" stele mentioned earlier. This Egyptologist therefore situates the Exodus after the fifth year of the reign, but does not give any precise date.

Montet has carefully examined the Biblical text. What appears

144

to disturb him is that the Bible states that Moses was eighty years old when he returned to speak to the pharaoh of what was to become of his brethren, although Montet only ascribes a reign of ten years. This, added to the sixty-seven-year reign of Ramesses II, only makes a total of seventy-seven years, which is not enough to tally with his Merneptah theory. In fact, Merneptah's reign was longer than this. Manethon says it was twenty years; Rowton mentions the same figure for the reign in his chronology (1224–1204 B.C.). All we can really be sure of is that Merneptah reigned for at least ten years—Father de Vaux reminds us that the tenth year of the reign is mentioned in documents. Beyond the ten years, there is not the slightest piece of supporting Egyptological data. What we do know for certain is that after Merneptah's reign, Egypt went through a very serious period of internal strife lasting more than a quarter of a century.

In spite of its inaccuracies, Montet's Merneptah hypothesis seems to be the most credible. In it, he resumed the original Alexandrian tradition, mentioned earlier and recalled by Maspero at the beginning of the century. Montet also adopted the standard Christian tradition, as expressed at the turn of the century in religious history books, such as Abbé H. Lesètre's work, written for religious instruction. In them, it was intimated that Merneptah was the pharaoh at the time of the Exodus, but no details were given. In most cases, Moses was linked with a single pharaoh. It would seem to me, however, to be much more in keeping with the combined religious and Egyptological data to link Moses with *two* pharaohs. A more precise appraisal will follow.

## Thirteenth Century B.C. Historical Data

One may link Moses to the history of the kings of Egypt who reigned during most of the thirteenth century B.C.

The pharaoh who ruled Egypt for more than two thirds of that

145

century was Ramesses II. In fact, at the beginning of the 13th century, during the rule of his father Sethos I, the young prince Ramesses actively participated in the government of the country, sharing power with the titular pharaoh. Thus, the construction of the Northern capital, which was to become the "City of Ramesses" (Piramesses of the Bible), was begun during the reign of Sethos I, and, since the Bible tells us that Moses was born when the enslaved Hebrews helped build the city, one might just as easily suggest that Moses was born during the reign of Sethos I.

Ramesses II is renowned for the extraordinary number of temples, palaces, statues, and inscriptions that remain as witnesses to his reign. The temples of Abu Simbel in Nubia, the Ramesseum in Thebes, and important parts of the temples of Karnak and Abydos are well-known places of interest for tourists in Egypt. There are also the vestiges of Memphis and Ramesses' Northern capital, recently excavated by the Egyptologists of the Pelizaeus Museum of Hildesheim in West Germany or discovered earlier in the site of Tanis. These vestiges had been transported from the old capital to the most recent one in the Nile Delta.

His sixty-seven-year reign was accompanied by remarkable political stability—there were no internal crises, and the period saw an influx of riches of many kinds, which flooded in from foreign countries subjected to the power of the pharaoh. Prosperity characterized these sixty-seven years. The rule of the sovereign was absolute—was he not a "son of god Amon?" Was he not represented in statues and bas-reliefs as equal to the gods? However, the last years of Ramesses II's reign were not so prosperous.

The continuation of such a long period of supremacy was inconceivable without a certain amount of military activity beyond the borders of the country—in other words, a supremacy achieved without embarking on campaigns, at least during the period of time necessary to establish authority in surrounding countries, and particularly in order to thwart the attempted hegemony of the powerful Hittite Empire.

The main enemies of Sethos I had been the Hittites, who ruled vast territories in Asia as far as the Northern part of modern Syria, the nearest territories to Egypt. When Sethos I died, peace was made with the Hittites and their sovereign Muwatallis. In spite of this, though, historical data indicate that between the fourth and the twenty-first year of his reign, Ramesses II headed many campaigns in Asia against the Hittites and their allies.

In their book *Egypt*, Etienne Drioton and Jacques Vandier describe the motives for this renewed hostility as follows: "Ramesses II was a young man, full of energy and ambition. Since Muwatallis was not without ambition as well, he naturally tried to take advantage of the accession to the throne of Egypt of a young man—supposed to be short of experience—in order to extend his territories in Asia. New fights became unavoidable, but the clash between them did not occur immediately."

The first campaigns of Ramesses II led the pharaoh and his armies to Palestine and the territory of modern Lebanon. Then Muwatallis formed a coalition grouping many peoples in Syria and Asia Minor against the pharaoh. During the fifth year of the pharaoh's reign, the Egyptian armies and the Hittite forces fought fiercely along the Orontes River, at Kadesh, most likely without a decisive result. The bravery of Ramesses II was glorified everywhere, but particularly in the famous Pentaour Poem engraved on a broad bas-relief in the temple of Abu Simbel in Nubia. A new series of campaigns in Asia began in the seventh year of his reign, with other battles against the Hittites. It is likely that the pharaoh had to fight the Libyans as well.

In the end, during the twenty-first year of his reign, Ramesses II signed a treaty of mutual defense with the Hittites, which is said to have remained a model for the future and guaranteed forty-six years of peace between the two sides, as testified by Hittite and Egyptian texts that survive today (in hieroglyphs on walls at Karnak and the Ramesseum in Thebes). Each sovereign made considerable efforts to respect the treaty. Unfortunately for Ramesses II, the decline of the Hittite Empire seems to have favored threats of invasion from the Asian borders of Egypt, and Merneptah, successor of Ramesses II, had to face many dangers from foreign countries.

Except during his youth, Moses could not have experienced the period of Egypt's supremacy while living in the country. He had left his native land early, while his brothers, the Hebrews, remained enslaved in Lower Egypt, where he joined them again after the death of Ramesses II, under the rule of Merneptah.

## The Ramesses II–Merneptah Theory

In *The Bible, the Qur'an and Science,* I expanded on the Ramesses II–Merneptah theory by representing Ramesses II as Pharaoh of the Oppression and Merneptah as Pharaoh of the Exodus.

I stressed the fact that Ramesses II was the king who seems to have pushed the forced labor of the Hebrews to its utmost in the construction of great edifices. What most characterized Merneptah was that he had the misfortune of being the sovereign of the Exodus, having had to endure unpleasant preliminaries, such as the plagues of Egypt mentioned in the Scriptures.

The Bible may not have given us the pharaoh's name, but it has mentioned the names of the two cities constructed under his reign, one of which was Ramesses. Thus, along with the lists of Manethon and the *Annals* of Tacitus, the Bible is the only ancient work to hand down to us the word *Ramesses*. In the text of the Bible, it designates a town built by the slave labor of the Hebrews. Now we know that it was under the reign of Ramesses II that the famous city became the Northern capital of Egypt. The Bible tells us that Moses was born during its construction.

There is a second important piece of information contained in the Bible. It is the fact that Moses is described as being eighty years old when he petitioned the pharaoh to free his brethren (Exodus 7,7). A third item of fundamental importance provided by the Bible is the fact that the king of Egypt died during Moses' lifetime when the latter was living in the land of Midian (Ibid. 2, 23). This implies that Moses must have lived under these two pharaohs. If he were eighty years old when, on God's order, he addressed his request for the release of the Hebrews to the second pharaoh, it follows that Moses must have lived during a period in Egyptian history when the total length of two successive pharaohs' reigns was greater than eighty years.

We know for certain that Moses could only have lived during the New Kingdom, and there is no one who claims to place him in another period. But to which of the two successive reigns included in the New Kingdom does the above piece of information refer? From a *mathematical* point of view, all we can derive from the chronological data is the addition of the duration of Ramesses II's reign and that of either his predecessor or his successor.

It is generally agreed that Ramesses II's reign lasted sixty-seven years and several months. The reign of Sethos I, Ramesses II's predecessor, could not have lasted long enough to be concordant with the events that occurred during the stay of Moses in the land of Midian. Furthermore, this hypothesis would clash with what we know about the construction of the city of Ramesses, in the course of which Moses was born, and with the fact that it was impossible for Ramesses II to have been the pharaoh of the Exodus. Hence the Sethos I–Ramesses II succession cannot be upheld. The only one possible is Ramesses II–Merneptah.

We said that although we do not know exactly how long Merneptah's reign lasted, it was at least ten years and could perfectly well have been twenty. Etienne Drioton, and Jacques Vandier admit both hypotheses in their famous book *L'Egypte* (*Egypt*) in the collection *Les peuples de l'Orient Méditerranéen* (*The Peoples of the Near Eastern Countries Bordering the Mediterranean Sea*), published by Presses Universitaires de France, Paris, 1962. This book remains the "bible" of modern Egyptology.

This therefore leads us to a total of eighty-seven years for the duration of the two reigns combined. Hence there is no disagreement between the theory advanced here, which is based on the Bible, and the data provided by Egyptology. We have to admit that the most plausible hypothesis is one claiming that Moses was born during the period of the oppression of the enslaved Hebrews and that the Exodus, led by Moses, was the last act of Merneptah's reign.

## An Apparent but Untenable Objection, Based on the Bible

In order to fully present the issue, I would like to raise an apparent objection to my thesis, suggested by the First Book of Kings (6, I). It places the Exodus from Egypt 480 years before the building of the Temple of Solomon (around 968 B.C.), i.e. around 1450 B.C. Such a statement contradicts other Scriptural data, but it is well known that the historical and chronological data of the Books of Kings are open to discussion (cf. The Book of Judges, II,26).

In the Ecumenical Translation of the Bible, the Old Testament, p. 634, emphasizes that this evaluation of the First Book of Kings is debatable, because "It is the result of a clever and late calculation based on the number of priests in office from Aaron to Sadoq multiplied by 40 (this being the traditional duration of one generation)." If we suppose that the average duration of the office of these priests was 20 years, the method of calculation would reduce their total duration of office to 240 years. We know that the Temple of Solomon was built during the fourth year of Solomon's reign, around 968 B.C. Consequently the corrected calculation would lead us to believe that the Exodus took place in 968 B.C. plus 240 years, or 1208 B.C. This calculation would be in accordance with what I have suggested, thus the results of our confrontation between the Bible and archeological and historical data would be satisfactory.


## The Hebrews in Egypt

Three hypotheses (A, B, C) have been suggested by commentators:

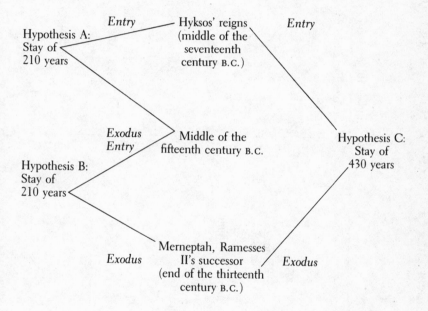

*Entry* — Hyksos' reigns (middle of the seventeenth century B.C.) *Entry*

Hypothesis A: Stay of 210 years

*Exodus* *Entry* — Middle of the fifteenth century B.C.

Hypothesis B: Stay of 210 years

Hypothesis C: Stay of 430 years

*Exodus* — Merneptah, Ramesses II's successor (end of the thirteenth century B.C.) *Exodus*

Only hypothesis C seems to the author to be tenable.

# The Most Probable Concordances Between the Bible and Egyptian History*

around 1750  The Hyksos in Egypt

around 1640  Jacob and Joseph in Egypt

between these two dates, Hebrews in Egypt for 430 years

around 1550  The Hyksos leave Egypt

around 1314  Nineteenth Dynasty: Ramesses I

around 1300  Beginning of Ramesses II's reign

Sixty-seventh year of Ramesses II's reign

Building of Pi-Ramesses    Birth of Moses

1235–1224   Ramesses II's death

Beginning of Merneptah's reign

Fifth year of Merneptah's reign, Israel Stele

Moses still in the land of Midian

Unique hieroglyphic mention of the word ISRAIL

Moses speaks to Pharaoh at age eighty

around 1204  Merneptah's death

around 1204  The Exodus

*All these dates (B.C.) are approximate, only the duration of Ramesses II's reign seems to be definitely established.

## Recent Discoveries Strengthening My Thesis

In the Holy Scriptures, there is no other Hebrew named Jacob with the exception of the eponymous ancestor of "Israel." The semitic name Yakub (Jacob) is mentioned—as far as we know written for the first time in hieroglyphic characters—in the list of the last Hyksos kings. In other words the family name Yakub was introduced at that time among the patronymics of the Hyksos aristocracy, and consequently implies that the entry into Egypt of Jacob and his first descendants took place during the period of the Hyksos kings; the Hyksos king concerned here was [MER.USER.RE–YAKUB–HER], whose hieroglyphic name means: "The one who loves the power of Ra. Jacob is happy." (Ra is the sun god of ancient Egypt.)

The most recent data about the construction of the city of Ramesses mentioned in the Bible appear to be decisive. The archeological findings at the site of Qantir, in the eastern part of the Nile Delta, are extremely important when one considers the Biblical text of the Book of the Exodus. In 1974, long before the recent excavations at this site begun, I visited fields planted with crops in this area. Suddenly my eye was caught by several whitish blocks of masonry on the edge of a field, which looked as if they had been transported here by a villager bothered by their presence while plowing. I discovered a cartouche (an oval figure containing the name of Ramesses II) on one of the blocks. I took photographs of the image and the field, and kept them in a safe place, since they seemed to be arousing curiosity—eminent Egyptologists from Cairo had told me that it was probable that the old city of Ramesses had been located there. At the time I did not pursue the matter any further.

My interest was revived by data found in the review *Orientalia* (edited by the Pontifical Biblical Institute in Rome), which reported the results of the excavations in that area carried out by

Arne Eggebrecht, Edgar B. Pusch, and their collaborators from 1980 to 1986. These Egyptologists were able to provide evidence of the beginning of the building of the city during the reign of Sethos I.

This finding gives further support to my thesis concerning the concordance of Biblical teachings—the eighty years that elapsed between the participation of the enslaved Hebrews in the construction of the city and the action of Moses facing Pharaoh—and the Egyptological data concerning the accumulated durations of the reigns of Sethos I, Ramesses II, and Merneptah.

In addition, in 1988, I found photographic documents in the catalogue of the "Ramesses The Great Exhibition" (edited by Rita E. Freed and J. P. Barger, Chairman of the Board, Boston Museum of Science) of the foundations of a part of the buildings under excavation by the above-mentioned Egyptologists of the Pelizaeus Museum in Hildesheim, West Germany, and several illustrations of the remains of the city of Pi-Ramesses, the Northern capital of Ramesses II. Among the photos are those of the ceramic faience tile decorations on the walls of the palace, representing aquatic life, a woman crowned with a lotus flower, and the gigantic toes that remain from a colossus of the king. Moreover, the catalogue included interesting articles concerning life at Pi-Ramesses.

All of these documents provide evidence of the existence of a flourishing city in the area near the Pelusiac branch of the Nile. Today we know that approximately two centuries later, during the Twenty-first Dynasty, a number of obelisks, statues, and various parts of buildings of the city were moved to the new capital at Tanis, not far from Qantir. Despite this partial relocation, the findings quoted here still authenticate the Biblical narratives concerning the city of Ramesses, in the building of which the enslaved Hebrews took a painful part. The easiness of dating the city, thanks to Egyptological knowledge, gives us an accurate dating of this Biblical event, which preceded the Hebrews' Exodus guided by Moses.

# 15. The Body of Merneptah, Pharaoh of the Exodus, and What Became of It

The Bible contains no information as to what became of the pharaoh's body once he and his army had been covered by the waters of the sea. As stated earlier, it is the Qur'an that tells us how, the very same day, the body would be saved to become a sign for those who came after.

It is interesting to note that this very precise piece of data in the Scriptures has hardly been given any importance by those who have studied the question. In fact, I have found a very strange assertion on the death of the pharaoh of the Exodus made by Father B. Couroyer, a professor at the Biblical School of Jerusalem. He writes the following in his commentary on the Book of Exodus in the Bible: "The Qur'an refers to this (sura 10, verses 90–92), and popular tradition has it that the Pharaoh who was drowned with his army (an event which is not mentioned in the Holy Text) lives beneath the ocean where he rules over the men of the sea, i.e. the seals."

In fact, the Qur'an alludes more than once to the pharaoh's death, and the Bible—I have good reason to believe that it is indeed the Bible that Father B. Couroyer is referring to when he uses the phrase "Holy Text"—quite indisputably describes the death of the pharaoh. The so-called legend suggested by the Biblical exegete in question, contrary to what he would have us believe, has absolutely nothing to do with the Qur'an.

In sura 10, verses 90–92, the Qur'an tells us that the pharaoh, as he is about to be drowned, begs God's pardon for his faults. God refuses to grant it, and warns the pharaoh that he will become a sign to future generations.

It was at the end of the nineteenth century that the bodies of all the pharaohs mentioned earlier in this book as "candidates" in the search for the pharaoh of the Exodus were found in the necropolis in Thebes on the other side of the Nile from Luxor. Whichever of the pharaohs was the pharaoh of the Exodus, his body is now lying in the Egyptian Museum in Cairo. The truth, therefore, is a far cry from the ludicrous legend wrongly attributed to the Qur'an by Father B. Couroyer.

We now possess all of the evidence linking the Biblical event to Merneptah. To make the proposed study complete, we have to compare the data gleaned from the examination of the body with what we had learned from Scriptural documents.

The body of Merneptah, discovered by Victor Loret in 1898 in Thebes in the Valley of the Kings, had been transferred to a tomb not Merneptah's own, but that of Amenophis II. Merneptah was then transported to Cairo. Elliot Smith removed the wrappings on July 8, 1907. In his book published in 1912, *The Royal Mummies*, he gives a report of the proceedings and precise details as to what the mummy looked like. At that time, the mummy of Merneptah showed signs of deterioration in several places, but, as I mentioned earlier, the passage of time had done little to damage it. Today, the mummy is severely damaged. As I indicated, two-thirds of the abdominal wall have subsided, and the body, especially the thorax, has been invaded by fungi. None of this appeared to be known at the time I began my study of the mummy in Cairo in 1975. At that time, visitors saw only the head and neck, for the rest of the body was hidden under a piece of cloth. It was so well hidden in fact, that the museum did not possess any photographs of the mummy subsequent to those taken by Elliot Smith at the turn of the century.

When the parts of the pharaoh's body that had remained covered were compared with the first photographs by Elliot Smith, it became clear that there had been deterioration, and that several pieces of the body had vanished. It was also apparent to my colleague Michel Durigon and me that mummification had been carried out with perfect success on the body, although all those around us said that the pharaoh had drowned. On a subject that had died by drowning, and had subsequently spent a long time in the water, mummification would not have been so effective. It is known that mummification does not work on tissues that are already in a state of putrefaction. Whether Merneptah died by drowning and remained in the water for a brief moment or met with some other brutal end, the body had been well preserved by mummification. Visual examination of it was not enough, however what we needed was material proof. This we obtained by microscopic analysis of a tiny fragment of the mummy. Permission to take the sample was given as a very special privilege.

The sample was a tiny morsel of the left psoas, a pelvic muscle that extends from the lateral parts of the lumbar vertebrae to the upper extremity of the femur. It was examined under the microscope by Professors Jacques Mignot and Michel Durigon. They were thus able to show the perfect preservation of the smallest anatomical details visible—the transversal striations of the fibrillae, as we have already seen on other mummies (Fig. 26). For it to have retained these microscopic features to this day, the body must have been embalmed while in good condition, otherwise decay and putrefaction would have set in.

Apart from the microscopic study of a sample taken from the mummy of Merneptah, we also employed the X-ray and endoscopic investigations described earlier. I must add, however, that of all the mummies studied, it was Merneptah's that invited the most research.

There are mummies that show a large number of fractures or losses of matter, but whose tissues are in fairly good condition. It soon becomes clear that the instances of dilapidation are the result of various injuries suffered after mummification, which are either the work of tomb robbers or more commonplace accidents that may have caused damage to the mummy as it was transferred from one sepulcher to another or, more recently, during various transportations.

For Merneptah, we have mentioned many hypotheses dealing with each of his lesions. They are summarized again as follows:

—The fracture in the upper extremity of the right humerus could just as easily be due to an accident during the subject's lifetime as a break in the mummified bone.

—The lacuna in the right part of the thorax (Fig. 22) may well be the result of an injury sustained during the subject's lifetime. There is less likelihood that tomb robbers smashed the body in this place in the thorax because there is no "breakage" of mummified tissues—bones or soft tissues— around the abnormal orifices.

—The fracture of the right forearm bones is quite obviously a fracture of the mummy.

—There is little to say about the lacuna in the right lumbar region on which the mummy is lying. All we possess is a view of the orifice seen from the inside by endoscopy. The lesion is not visible from the outside, however, and we do not possess a photograph of it taken by Elliot Smith, who gave the account of the examination of the mummified body after he had removed the wrappings.

—The cranial lacuna (Fig. 40) is of great forensic importance. As I stated in the preceding chapter, its presence may suggest a craniocerebral lesion received during the subject's lifetime—a fracture with a penetrating wound seriously injuring the brain. In all likelihood, this lesion caused a very rapid death.

The Holy Scriptures simply state that the pharaoh was drowned. It would therefore be totally in keeping with the Scriptural narration for him to have fallen victim, on the return of the water, to a trauma causing wounds to various parts of the body. These were described earlier and among them we find the penetrating craniocerebral injury. This would have brought on death very quickly, the body having been submerged either before or after the pharaoh was killed. Whatever the case, he does not appear to have stayed in the water very long. This has been formally proved by medical examination and fits perfectly with the passage in the Qur'an on the rapid retrieval of the body.

I have searched for a contradiction of any kind between our medical observations and the narrations of the Exodus contained in the Book of Exodus in the Bible and in the Qur'an, but I can find no argument to oppose the theory I hereby maintain. Given the present state of our knowledge, the only valid hypothesis that can be advanced is that Merneptah, Ramesses II's successor, met a tragic end during the Exodus.

# Part V

# THE MUMMY
# OF
# RAMESSES II
# IN PARIS

# 16. Difficult Preliminaries

The results of the studies presented so far are part of an enterprise whose initial aim was scientific. Practical implications have been derived from the observations made. The fact that modern methods helped reveal the danger threatening the pharaonic mummies led to the secondary project of saving the mummy of Ramesses II in France. Before it arrived, reports on the scientific studies carried out were either read before various learned societies, notably the National Academy of Medicine, or included in articles containing medical information. All those who knew about these scientific studies were well aware that there was an obvious link of cause and effect between the publication of the studies and the sensational arrival of the mummy in Paris several months later.

While the scientific studies were in progress, the mummy of Ramesses II was also the subject of discussion about a possible exhibition. Initially the reasons for this had nothing to do with medical research on mummies. At that time, preparations were being made between France and Egypt, on the initiative of Christiane Desroches-Noblecourt, for an exhibition on the period of

Ramesses II. Since she was the organizer of the exhibition, she hoped that its high point would be the mummy of the pharaoh. As often happens in such cases, the fact that museum pieces are to go on display abroad provides an opportunity for various kinds of restoration. Hence there was talk of restoring the mummy of Ramesses II, in the same way people spoke of restoring a particular sarcophagus or Tutankhamun's bed. There are, however, differences between the two types of rescue operation. It is obvious that for mummies, certain specific biological problems arise. Similarly, the various medical explorations of the mummy require the mummy to be seen from a point of view that is very different from the approach required for objects in stone or wood or paintings. Furthermore, Desroches-Noblecourt did not order a medical examination of the mummy before May 1975, the point at which the President of Egyptian Antiquities asked me to undertake the study with my colleagues. Doctors were obviously the only experts competent in this field, and it was equally clear that if treatment of the mummy was necessary, their advice would once again be required. Close collaboration between doctors and museum curators was absolutely indispensable.

The medical specialists required to help with the project came from many different disciplines, as we saw in part II of this book, "The Medical Examination of Mummies." In addition, my own personal experience made me realize that even a specialist, when isolated and engaged in a precise aspect of exploration, *was capable of committing very serious errors of interpretation if he knew nothing about the problems as a whole.* Thus the collection of numerous half results might impress those ignorant of these problems simply by the impressive quantity of details collected. The interpretation of such results can be inaccurate if the interpreter is unable to synthesize them. It is as if, in medicine, only the multiplicity of the examinations were relied upon, while there was no doctor capable of treating the patient by assembling the data and drawing relevant or useful conclusions from them.

When I was asked to give an opinion concerning the state of Ramesses II's mummy, I immediately saw that the problem France had raised for the Egyptian authorities required answers to be given from a medical point of view and could carry important consequences. A preliminary assessment was rapidly made, thanks to the speed with which my Egyptian colleagues—radiologists and one endoscopist—set about the required investigations. Furthermore, I had come to Cairo to carry out studies into the causes of Pharaoh Merneptah's death and was accompanied by my colleague Michel Durigon, a specialist in forensic medicine who also helped me greatly in the study of Ramesses II's mummy. I communicated to the Egyptian authorities my opinions as to the state of the mummy: the prognosis for the skeleton was good, for it was solid; there was a danger of deterioration in the soft tissues, the site of multiple cracks—and it would be possible for even more fragments to detach themselves from the mummy; judgment was withheld regarding biological decay, for samples had not yet been taken for examination. I informed Christiane Desroches-Noblecourt of these results and stressed the fact that any "restoration" of the mummy would have to take into account the medical findings, especially the possibility of biological deterioration, which I knew was already to be found on other mummies.

Furthermore, I urged the Egyptian high authorities to take steps to prevent the decay of the mummy of Merneptah, for it was much more severely affected than that of Ramesses II, and I had reason to believe that Merneptah had played a historic part in the story of Moses.

I asked myself which French specialists would be best suited to this seemingly double task. First, each mummy had to be given individual protection by insulation in an artificial environment where both temperature and humidity were constant. This seemed to be the task of conservation specialists in museums, for their job is to place each object in conditions most favorable to

165

its preservation—away from light, if possible, and from variations in the ambient atmosphere. There was, therefore, an absolutely basic problem to be solved concerning museum conservation. There was also the problem of "disinfection," as it were, for while we did not yet know anything, in the summer of 1975, concerning the biological decay of Ramesses II's mummy, we were aware, however, of an article produced by Aidan Cockburn's eminent group of researchers in the March 28, 1975, issue of the periodical *Science* under the title "Autopsy of an Egyptian Mummy," which dealt with the various biological agents that can attack mummies. I intended to contact certain qualified specialists at the laboratories of the Museum of Anthropology in Paris about a means of protecting the mummies.

I later learned that the head of the Museum of Anthropology, Professor Lionel Balout, had journeyed to Cairo, at the request of Desroches-Noblecourt, in July 1975 to investigate the possibility of transporting the mummy of Ramesses II to Paris and putting it on display there. As Professor Balout wrote in an article released to the press in January 1977 under the title "The Stage Reached in the Treatment of Ramesses II at the Museum of Anthropology," the project was for an exhibition of the mummy in Paris and *not for treatment of it*.

In the fall of 1975, Dr. Gamal Mokhtar, President of Egyptian Antiquities, came to Paris. He met with Desroches-Noblecourt and Professor Balout. In the course of the meeting, I once again stressed the medical problems concerning the mummy of Ramesses II and other royal mummies, pointing out that urgent treatment of them was required. I learned that, thanks to the benevolence of Elf Erap (a petroleum company), experts at the Egyptian Museum and the Museum of Anthropology had equipment and material at their disposal to ensure that the objects exhibited would receive proper insulation and protection from light. The material these experts used could also serve for the possible transport of the mummy to Paris. I journeyed to Cairo in November 1975, at the invitation of the Egyptian Government, where I joined Desroches-Noblecourt and Balout.

The visit gave me an opportunity to exchange points of view with Professor Balout on the mummies' medical problems. As we stood before the mummies, I was able to explain to the Egyptian specialists in antiquities the data already collected, while at the same time recapping the new information that had been provided by the investigations carried out on the mummies of Tuthmosis II and Sethos I with the help of our colleagues, the Egyptian radiologists. During my stay, several meetings were arranged with the President of Egyptian Antiquities, the Head of the Egyptian Museum and the museum board. It was quickly decided that the first rescue measures would be taken on the mummy of Ramesses II, not that of Merneptah, which seemed to be of lesser interest to those taking part in the discussion, perhaps because it already appeared to be too damaged. We reviewed the various plans of action. Professor Balout suggested placing each mummy in a sealed display case, constructed of a plastic (altuglass), which would filter out ultraviolet rays while allowing the visitor to see the mummy. His suggestion was approved by all present. Moreover, material was expected to arrive from France that would insulate the mummy.

Our sole objective was to preserve and insulate the mummy. I was also concerned with the treatment of it. Examinations had to be carried out, by sending samples to biologists, in an attempt to prove that the mummy was under attack from biological agents. The difficulty of planning a biological study to complement the other investigations already carried out was soon evident. This was especially true since we were faced with a commission composed of people whose views differed considerably from ours. I realized how hard, if not impossible, it would be to carry out in Egypt the work that appeared to be most important. It had already been difficult enough to reach an agreement as to the investigations to be made, so there was good reason to think that tackling the problem of treatment would be quite futile.

In my conversations with the authorities of the Egyptian Museum, there was never any question of transporting the mummy of Ramesses II to Paris to include it in an exhibition. This was a project that had absolutely nothing to do with me. The Egyptian authorities had invited me to take part in the discussions in Cairo entirely on account of the studies made on the mummy. Nevertheless, I did learn some of the Egyptians' reactions to the question of exhibiting the mummy abroad. The great majority of them were very reluctant to see Ramesses II transported to France for such a purpose. Those Egyptians who joined Professor Balout and myself in examining the measures to be taken for the rescue of the endangered mummy were probably also thinking about the planned exhibition, to which I imagined they were not at all kindly disposed.

Throughout the discussions that took place in November 1975 in Cairo, Professor Balout and I were concerned solely with the problem of preserving the mummies. In a report dated November 20, 1975, for President Sadat, which I presented during a visit to Mrs. Sadat, the only points raised were the technical problems of conservation and preservation of the royal mummies. In particular, the report dealt with the mummies of Ramesses II and Merneptah, since we hoped that these would receive treatment first. I had already had the honor of being received twice by President Sadat himself and of describing to him the serious risk involved in keeping the royal mummies in the unfavorable conditions at the Egyptian Museum in Cairo. I also explained my research to him. At the time I submitted the report, bearing Professor Balout's signature and my own, I took the opportunity of reminding Mrs. Sadat of earlier recommendations I had made while taking into account the discussion that had just taken place at the Egyptian Museum with members of the museum commission.

Before leaving Cairo, I decided to request an audience with His Excellency Bruno de Leusse, at that time the French Ambassador to Egypt. I wanted to inform him of the main results of the medical research performed, and indicate my own feelings as to the reactions caused by the projects then being examined, especially since the President of France was due to arrive in Cairo on an official visit in ten days' time.

The French President's visit was marked by a discussion between the two Presidents on various questions concerning the mummy of Ramesses II. I shall describe the discussion by quoting the account of it given in the Egyptian press. The following is a translation of the article which appeared in the largest Cairo newspaper, *Al Ahram*, on January 23, 1976:

### THE FULL STORY OF RAMESSES II'S MUMMY AND ITS JOURNEY TO PARIS

What is the story behind the fact that the mummy of Ramesses II is to be sent to Paris along with the antiquities that are to go on display there?

Several months ago, Dr. Maurice Bucaille, a French scientist, requested an audience with President Sadat on an important and pressing matter. During this meeting, Dr. Bucaille informed President Sadat that, while visiting the museum, he had noticed that a certain number of pharaonic mummies were exposed to gradual destruction and that their embalmment was no longer able to ward off the effects of time. "What is to be done about it?" the President asked. Dr. Bucaille replied, "The only solution is to carry out experiments and analyze samples taken from the mummies, so that the cause can be established and treated." The French scientist added, "There is only one answer: to transport the mummy to Paris for examination and perform analysis of it in French laboratories." The President assured Dr. Bucaille that he would study the question.

While President Valéry Giscard d'Estaing was visiting Egypt in December, he asked President Sadat whether the antiquities that were to be exhibited in the French capital might also include the mummy of Ramesses II.

Thereupon, President Sadat related to President d'Estaing what he had heard from the French scientist Dr. Bucaille, and added, "We shall kill two birds with one stone. First, we shall comply with the request of Egypt's dear friend, President d'Estaing, by sending the mummy of Ramesses II to Paris as an expression of our deep gratitude for the service he has rendered to Egypt; second, we shall take advantage of the opportunity by enabling Dr. Bucaille to study the cause of the gradual destruction of the pharaonic mummies."

President Sadat resolved that once the cause of this gradual destruction was known, a new method of protecting the mummies would be adopted, to be employed in the new museum that has recently been prepared.

It seemed as if, in principle, everything had been decided. But the mummy of Ramesses II was not to arrive in Paris for another eight months.

# 17. A Useful Decision

Not long before President Giscard d'Estaing's visit to Cairo, which was to be so crucially important to the future of Ramesses II's mummy, the famous remains had been transferred at the end of November 1975 from the Egyptian Museum to a former laboratory nearby. The transfer took place in my presence. The mummy was to be relieved of the dusty, decaying tissues surrounding it, leaving nothing but a few remaining wrappings. In early December 1975, during one of these dusting operations, minuscule samples were taken by the Egyptians. These samples were sent to me very obligingly by experts at the Museum of Anthropology; the experts in question soon returned to Paris without—so they tell me—doing more than watch the dusting operations performed on the mummy. As I mentioned earlier, spores of fungi were found in the samples. Until September 1976, the mummy remained the exclusive responsibility of the specialists at the Egyptian Museum in Cairo.

President Sadat's decision to send the mummy to France for treatment was the only aspect of the statement made in *Al Ahram* that concerned me. Once I had received confirmation of his decision from Egypt, preparations had to be made for the "hospitalization" of the mummy. The collaboration of those who had carried out the preliminary work was secured, and other specialists were to be called to join them if necessary. I felt the Museum of Anthropology had the laboratories and conditions that were best suited to the hospitalization and preservation of the mummy. The Museum afforded optimum insulation, which would be necessary while we proceeded to the examinations that would help decide on treatment. I felt the collaboration of doctors and museum experts could be set up under the aegis of Professor Balout, the head of the Museum of Anthropology. Therefore I asked him if he would agree to receive the mummy in his museum. His reply was affirmative, and he invited me to visit the anthropology laboratory of the museum. While in the presence of Professor Robert Gessain, he asked me what I thought of the arrangements planned for the reception of Ramesses II. It was suggested that the mummy be placed in a small room, away from ultraviolet rays and where air conditioning would ensure strict regulation of the thermal and hygrometric levels. The mummy was to be removed from the air-conditioned room to a neighboring one, where specialists would be able to spend several hours a day working on it. It was not necessary to put Ramesses in a strictly sterilized atmosphere.

A few months later, in the French and American press, articles appeared that mentioned a "sterile chamber" that had been specially installed at the Museum of Anthropology to receive Ramesses II. In fact, there was never any question of installing a "sterile chamber"—the most favorable conditions for keeping the mummy being those initially chosen.

Once the plans for the hospitalization of the mummy had been decided upon and the assistance of the collaborators secured, Professor Balout and I sent a letter, dated March 15, 1976, to both the Egyptian and French Presidents to inform them of the arrangements made. We assured the Presidents that everything would be ready at the Museum of Anthropology once they made the decision to transport it to France for treatment. There it would be made as "healthy" as possible, so that when the mummy returned to Egypt, it would no longer be contaminated or subject to either the physical or biological damage that could cause its inevitable destruction. All the arrangements made were in accordance with the joint report submitted to President Sadat on November 20, 1975. The letter included a list of the principal collaborators who were to carry out research in Paris, resuming the work that had been carried out in Cairo a year earlier. I was to head the medical team.

During this period of waiting, my collaborators and I submitted several studies to various learned societies (on February 17, 1976, to the Academy of Medicine; on April 12, 1976, to the French Society of Forensic Medicine; and on April 26, 1976, to the French Society of Radiology), which were preceded by the presentation of the first microscopic examinations of mummified tissues to the Society of Anatomy on May 15, 1975. The studies were followed by a paper read by Doctors Georges and François Rousières before the Academy of Dental Surgery on December 3, 1976, which dealt with the dental aspects of the investigations. Professor Balout invited me to give two lectures on *The Medical Aspects of the Study of Pharaonic Mummies* in May 1976 at the Institute of Anthropology, of which he was head. I also prepared a long article for the review *Archaelogia* in which I gave an account of all the work carried out so far. It appeared in the September 1976 issue, a few weeks before the mummy of Ramesses II arrived in Paris.

At this point a new factor emerged: spores had been discovered on the mummy itself. (I had entrusted this aspect of the examination to Dr. Madeleine Ferly-Thérizol). We therefore had proof, before any other research was carried out, that the mummy had been attacked by biological agents.

The results of the above work were brought to the attention of the Egyptian high authorities even before they were published in detail in France. Just as I completed the first studies, assisted by my Cairo colleagues, the Egyptian press announced the results of the first investigations. On June 9, 1975, the newspaper *Al Ahram* devoted a complete page to them. In particular, it described the endoscopic research that had been performed on mummies for the first time ever. The text was illustrated with several photographs taken in the Royal Mummies Room of the museum. One of them—the uncovered body of Pharaoh Merneptah—showed the moment when the endoscope was being inserted through the thoracic orifice.

The following year, while Ramesses II was away in France, the Egyptian illustrated review *Broadcasting and Television,* on October 23, 1976, published an excellent account, with photographs, of the studies performed on the mummy of Ramesses II in 1975. It showed a picture of the damage done to the abdomen; the view was similar to the photograph of Merneptah just mentioned. Throughout the course of 1976, there were many other articles in the Egyptian press concerning the research carried out by doctors on the decay and deterioration of the pharaonic mummies. They all expressed the hope that a means to rescue the mummies would be found.

I have mentioned the above facts because I want to highlight the great interest in these questions shown by the Egyptian high authorities—especially the two successive Egyptian ministers of Information at the time. In Egypt the decision announced by President Sadat to have the mummy treated was favorably viewed, and the people were extremely grateful to the French doctors who had first suggested this project. The public was pleased to hear of the scientific studies performed by the French, for they showed that President Sadat's decision was well-founded. The Egyptian President had reached his decision as a result of the conclusions drawn from this research.

We should also bear in mind, however, that the Egyptians

have a sentimental attachment to their pharaohs that the French can scarcely claim to have for Vercingetorix or Charlemagne.

How many people know, for example, that when the mummified remains of the greatest pharaohs of Egypt were discovered at the end of the nineteenth century in the necropolis at Thebes and the authorities decided to transfer them to Cairo in Lower Egypt, the simple countryfolk turned out in masses on the banks of the Nile? The people wished to pay their respects to the pharaohs as they passed by on the boat carrying them to Lower Egypt, and did so in the manner traditional for the passing away of a dearly beloved person.

Never before had a pharaoh left Egyptian soil after his death, although it was indeed acceptable for them all to leave the country if their remains were to be preserved, since they had wanted their bodies to exist for all eternity, which is why they had been embalmed and mummified. This was exactly what was being suggested—to preserve the body with the aid of the most modern methods. But to accept the idea that the pharaoh would leave Egypt to go on show in a foreign country was a thought that troubled the Egyptians' deeper feelings.

According to the French press, this "Egyptian sensitivity" was perfectly understood by President Giscard d'Estaing. In fact, a few days before the Paris exhibition of *Ramesses II* opened at the Grand Palais, the newspaper *Le Monde* published extracts from a letter that the French President had sent to the President of Egypt. In it President Giscard d'Estaing asked him not to send the mummy of Ramesses II to Paris: "In consideration of Egyptian sensitivity, we would prefer to drop the project," reported *Le Monde*. The French President added, however, that the laboratories of the Museum of Anthropology were ready to receive the mummy and he offered to send a military airplane to Cairo to ensure the best possible conditions for the mummy's transfer to Paris and subsequent return to Cairo.

In this and the preceding chapter, an account has been given of the occurrences pertaining to the research, discoveries, discussions, and diverse contacts in which I played a part. At first my role was unsolicited, but later proved decisive for the project of transporting Ramesses II to Paris.

I now invite the reader to compare my own account with others allegedly describing the motives that are said to have led the Egyptian Government to entrust the mummy to France. One of these accounts appeared in the official organ of the French National Centre for Scientific Research, the *Courrier du C.N.R.S.*, April 1978, under the title *The Odyssey of the Pharaoh* (L'Odyssée du Pharaon). It forms the introduction to an article by Professor Lionel Balout entitled *The Mummy of Ramesses II at the Museum of Anthropology* (La Momie de Ramsès II au Musée de l'Homme).

After the anonymous author of this introduction reminds the reader of the ancient history of the mummy, he goes on to praise Christiane Desroches-Noblecourt, the organizer of the Ramesses II exhibition at the Grand Palais in 1976, describing how, on this occasion, her intentions were to "render the best service to the king's remains." The writer continues as follows:

> these remains, which had deliberately been prepared to last for centuries and remain the witness to an instant of human life, showed all the symptoms of incipient disintegration. This opinion was, of course, shared by many informed visitors to the Museum and applied to all the royal mummies. It was necessary, therefore, if the mummy of Ramesses was to be returned to its proper state, to grapple with two essential points:
> —the findings of specialists, and
> —the finding of financial resources.
> Once the agreement of the Egyptian authorities concerned had been obtained, Christiane Desroches-Noblecourt was able to acquire the necessary funds thanks to a donation from the Elf-Erap Company. At her instigation, close collaboration was arranged between the Museum of Anthropology, the Natural History Museum and the Egyptian Museum in Cairo. It quickly became clear that more detailed work was needed in a perfectly

176

sterile atmosphere. The difficulty of obtaining such conditions on the spot obliged the museums to follow our Egyptian colleagues' advice and have the mummy analyzed and treated completely in France, then later provide a protective covering that would allow it to be exhibited thereafter in Cairo. The journey has remained unique until now and can only be described as a "new Ramesses Miracle." To attain this end, Christiane Desroches-Noblecourt appealed to the support and understanding of the President of the Arab Republic of Egypt and the French President. In Paris, Professor Balout arranged the "state apartments" of Ramesses at the Museum of Anthropology, preparing them scientifically to receive him.

The closing lines of the article sum up very briefly the mummy's arrival in France and its stay in Paris.

I shall return later to the erroneous nature of the motive given in the account—the so-called necessity of treating the mummy "in a perfectly sterile atmosphere" as a means of justifying the mummy's transfer to Paris. As for the original reasons, the basic facts described in this book have been silently ignored in the *Courrier du C.N.R.S.*, which, by its omissions, offers its readers a version that does not correspond to reality.

# 18. The Mummy at the Museum of Anthropology

Museum specialists are well educated in the art of transporting extremely fragile objects over long distances. The skeleton of Ramesses II was intact—apart from a lesion on one toe—and the sturdiness of the bone structure augured well for avoiding such risks. Nevertheless, simple observation of the mummy, and of radiological data, had revealed cracks and crevices in many areas of the soft tissues, abdomen, and lower limbs in particular (Figs. 2, 35, and 37). In the Egyptian Museum, the mummy had lain on a mattress of thin cloth inside its wooden half coffin—an oak coffin without a lid—and there was no way to remove the mummy from it. The open oak coffin was similar to the one in which Merneptah lies (Fig. 20). Likewise, Ramesses II's arms were crossed over the front of his thorax. It was important in transportation to avoid jarring or even exerting the slightest pressure on the mummy, for this might have caused a fracture in the mummified tissue of one of the upper limbs, as had been the case for Merneptah.

Such considerations highlight the importance of wedging and packing the various parts of the mummy for its voyage. The

Museum of Anthropology sent special materials for this purpose to Cairo, along with outer casings for the half coffin, so the mummy could travel in safety. A huge packing case had also been prepared for it.

The French and Egyptian authorities agreed upon transportation dates. Miss B. Coursier and Mr. J. Richir, both specialists at the Museum of Anthropology, brought to Cairo all the equipment prepared for transportation of the mummy. Christiane Desroches-Noblecourt was appointed to oversee the mummy's trip from Cairo to Paris in a Transall airplane provided by the French air force. One stopover was made in Italy, and another at Istres, France.

The pharaoh arrived at Le Bourget Airport on September 26, 1976, where he was received with full military honors. The case containing the mortal remains of the king was removed from the plane. Readers may remember the photographs that appeared in the press at the time, showing the representative of the Egyptian Ambassador standing in front of the precious cargo. Next to him we see Alice Saunier-Saïté, then Secretary of Higher Education, Christiane Desroches-Noblecourt, and Professor Balout. Not a single doctor was present at Le Bourget for the ceremony, since none of those who had originally engineered this prestigious event had been invited.

From the airport, the mummy was transferred to the Museum of Anthropology for "hospitalization" in one of the specially prepared rooms. From the moment the great king arrived in Paris, those in charge of Operation Ramesses II paid full attention to him. One of the two obelisks of Luxor, transported to France in 1831 and erected on the Place de la Concorde in 1836, bears an inscription testifying to the pharaoh's glory. On July 29, 1977, *Paris Match* reported that the truck containing the packing case and its occupant was ordered to pass by the obelisk "so that the ancient monarch's soul could contemplate his glory inscribed on stone in dithyrambic terms."

A few days after his arrival, specialists at the Museum of Anthropology proceeded to the delicate task of unpacking the pharaoh and removing the mummy from its wooden half coffin. The operation was very tricky. It would have been most imprudent to lift the body out, even if belts had been passed underneath it at several points, allowing it to be raised, or even if the mummy had been uniformly hauled up. Professor Balout described the method he used in *Archaeologia*, February 1978. The modern oak coffin was sawed open at the mummy's feet and the body slipped out. As stated, the pharaoh was lying on a thin cloth mattress. Between the mattress and the bottom of the coffin, a sheet of transparent plastic altuglass was inserted, sufficiently thick to allow for maneuvering and for the support of the mummy, while adapting itself perfectly to the bottom of the coffin. The altuglass sheet made it easy to pull the body out of the coffin, giving the technicians access to all sides.

In order to observe and take minuscule samples from the surface of the posterior part of the mummy, it was also necessary to remove the cloth mattress on which the body was still lying. The mattress was cut into sections and extracted piece by piece. Over several decades, small morsels of the mummy had fallen onto it. Once their position in relation to the body had been plotted, the pieces of cloth and debris were sent to the laboratories for analysis. Indications as to the nature of the fallen fragments were quickly obtained, which confirmed the biological attack discovered by Dr. Thérizol and described in part II.

Now that the mummy was on the plastic sheet, it was possible to view the posterior part of the body, hidden until this point. For the purposes of the work carried out at the Museum of Anthropology, it was very easy to slip the mummy from its case by this method, and, at the end of each session, to slip it back again on the altuglass sheet into the open end of the half coffin, which lay on a hospital stretcher on wheels. By aligning the level of the altuglass sheet with that of the working table, it was possible to safely remove the mummy from its case and place it in the required spot.

Between each session, lasting a few hours at the most, the mummy was confined to its air-conditioned room. Here it was sheltered from ultraviolet rays, by a filter in place of the original windowpanes. The temperature of the room was gradually lowered to 19° centigrade and the humidity to fifty-five percent, these two readings being regarded as the optimum conditions for the mummy.

We should note that the descriptions given in the French and American press at that time, claiming that the mummy was installed in a "sterile surgical theater" at the Museum of Anthropology, were totally inaccurate, as was that in the *Courrier du C.N.R.S.*—in April 1978: "It quickly became clear that more detailed work was needed in a perfectly sterile atmosphere. The difficulty of obtaining such conditions on the spot. . . obliged the museums. . . to have the mummy analyzed and treated completely in France."

The above led the uninformed reader to think that the program, alleged to have been the reason for the mummy's transportation outside Egypt, had already been carried out and that the body had been placed in a "perfectly sterile" atmosphere at the Museum of Anthropology. This was never planned nor carried out by either Professor Balout or myself, for it would have been totally unnecessary.

The author of the assertions on the imaginary sterile surgical theater for Ramesses II in Paris, published in *France-Soir* and the *International Herald Tribune*, as quoted above, was Christiane Desroches-Noblecourt. When the *Courrier du C.N.R.S.* referred to a perfectly sterile atmosphere, it used different words to express the same idea.

It is highly regrettable that President Giscard d'Estaing was led to take personal responsibility for this idea. The newspaper *Le Monde*, in a May 1976 report, which was not subsequently denied, states that in a letter of April 30, 1976, the text of which has been published, the President of the French Republic wrote to President Sadat to let him know that he was abandoning the project of exhibiting the mummy. The letter confirms the proposed treatment of the "royal corpse" at the Paris Museum of Anthropology as follows: "It seems very useful that the latter now be treated in an aseptic atmosphere. . ."

One may suppose that this detail was in fact a suggestion made to President Giscard d'Estaing: subsequently, he officially promised to place the mummy in a special environment. . . of which there had never been any question, except in the fertile imagination of his advisor.

A sterile surgical theater is a very elaborate installation. There are several of them in Paris, used for organ transplants and a certain form of chemotherapy that breaks down the body's defenses, both instances in which the patient must be protected from outside infection. Only those who are perfectly familiar with sterilization procedures are allowed inside the theater. They enter through a series of air-locked chambers where surgical clothes must be worn and various apparatuses make those present "aseptic" from head to foot. Similarly, only objects that have been thoroughly sterilized beforehand may be brought into the theater. All doctors are aware of the constraints put upon them when treating a patient under such conditions. This type of installation, however, has nothing whatsoever in common with the arrangements made for Ramesses II's "hospitalization."

On November 11, 1976, the mummy was shown on French television in its room surrounded by numerous figures in white wearing face masks. (Neither I nor any of the doctors who had collaborated with me were present.) The television shots could well have misled the viewers into thinking that the kind of rigorously sterile atmosphere that prevails in an operating room had been required for Ramesses II. In this particular case, it was not true at all. Obviously, when visiting a patient in hospital it is advisable to wear a surgical gown and face mask for one's own, as well as the patient's, safety. This may explain why the precaution was taken for Ramesses II, but one should not imagine that the mummy was ever, at any time, in a sterile atmosphere.

It was Professor Balout, aided by his assistants at the Museum of Anthropology, who devised the very practical installations used for the operation. Over the course of several sessions of work on the mummy, I had the opportunity to discover the ease and safety with which the installations could be maneuvered. It was requested that I attend several sessions during the first weeks of Ramesses II's stay in Paris and from then on become a consultant doctor in rare instances, with regard to points of detail.

Hardly a month had passed since the mummy's arrival in Paris when I read an article in *The Times* of London on October 22, 1977, accusing Professor Balout and myself of, among other things, refusing to sign a document in Cairo stating that the mummy of Ramesses II was in good condition and had not suffered any deterioration since the turn of the century, followed by a fictional report of declarations that Professor Balout and I were alleged to have made with regard to a nonexistent fracture in the mummy's leg.

To recognize the true value of such blatant untruths, the reader has only to turn to Figures 2, 35, 37, and 48, where he will find illustrations proving once and for all the spuriousness of such attacks. No document of any repute could seriously prove that the mummy was in good condition. Who could blame us for not signing a declaration that contradicted a truth that was patently obvious?

Ramesses II's journey to Paris was described as a subterfuge aimed at gaining prestige, while the "illness" of the pharaoh was labeled a diplomatic one. The *New York Times* on November 8, 1976, took up the attack by reporting declarations allegedly made by an American dentist that it was impossible for a mummy to be infected because it was very well wrapped. The newspaper also mentioned other statements, attributed this time to an Egyptian

Egyptologist on a visit to the United States, claiming that the mummy of Ramesses II was "in good condition." A few days later, the same information was to be read in the *International Herald Tribune* as well as the French and Egyptian press.

Reports such as these were reflective of a certain bitterness that surrounded the operation. This is only human. To accuse us of scientific dishonesty as some did in the *New York Times* on November 8, 1976, or the *International Herald Tribune* on November 10, 1976, is downright slanderous.

It goes without saying that the reason Egypt sent the mummy to France for treatment was because the Egyptian authorities knew that it really had deteriorated. They had been alerted to this fact by work that we had already done on the mummy in Egypt. I am most grateful to Dr. Gamal Mokhtar, the President of Egyptian Antiquities, who had asked me in June 1975 to study the mummy of Ramesses II, for intervening in this debate. Having described the alleged political motives reported by certain English and American newspapers as "absurd," he declared, "The reason Ramesses II is in Paris, and not in London or the United States, is because the French were the first to discover the damage and offer their help" (*L'Aurore*, November 15, 1976).

In France, the work carried out by the doctors was never mentioned in the replies made to these accusations by those in charge of Operation Ramesses II. Their work, or most of it at least, had already been published by that time. When under attack of this kind, it is not expressions of righteous indignation that convince people, but documentary evidence. It became my responsibility to provide the press with concrete proof that the mummy was most definitely damaged. I gave them a highly revealing photograph taken in Cairo in 1975.

By fortunate coincidence, the day after the accusing article had appeared in *The Times*, the Egyptian review *Broadcasting and Television* published the article quoted in the preceding chapter. Among the illustrations accompanying the article was the photo just mentioned (Fig. 48), which showed the deterioration of the abdomen.

Many investigations and examinations were carried out on the mummy in Paris. Those performed by the group of doctors I had assembled in 1975 were made again, a year and a half later in France. Two of the Egyptian colleagues who had been with me in Cairo came to see their famous "patient." First, there was Dr. El Meligiy who had taken the first X rays, at my request in 1975. He was passing through Paris at the beginning of November 1976 and had a productive meeting with his French counterpart, Dr. Clément Fauré, who at the time was planning the radiological investigations to be undertaken. Then later in December 1976, Dr. Mustapha Manialawiy arrived in Paris. He and I had been the first to perform an endoscopic examination of a mummy in 1975. He now came forward to complete this investigation of Ramesses II, as described earlier.

Many of the examinations performed in Paris were repetitions of the work already done in Cairo in 1975, adding nothing new to what had already been published. As often happens, certain points were clearly ascertained and the new data thus provided a better knowledge of the mummy. Progress may have been made in one direction, but it was still very annoying to find that, in another, no investigations were carried out at all. It was also a pity that certain conclusions were reached without the reservation that should normally be applied.

For example, the radiological studies performed included the use of xerography and chromodensitography. The aim was to obtain a more sharply defined picture of the soft tissues of the mummy. The above techniques did indeed provide more precise details, such as the localization of tiny foreign bodies that were apparent on the standard X rays of 1975. I must remind the reader of the diagnosis made on the presence of the "heart" contained in Ramesses II's thorax, which was arrived at by the use of chromodensitography. In Figure 33 one can see the frontal projection of the thorax, can notice that, as the standard X rays clearly show, under the left clavicle and across it, what may well be the organ. Generally speaking, its contours are well defined. The embalmers usually replaced the viscera in cavities of the body from which organs had been removed, but without reconstructing the anatomy. In view of this, we should be very wary of making statements as to the nature of the images shown on the X rays. An intestinal loop placed in the thorax can very easily look exactly like the arch of the aorta. When one knows accurate and precise data on the mummification process, one is less likely to jump to hasty conclusions. I shall not try to justify my considerable skepticism as to the so-called discovery made in Paris of Ramesses II's heart in the thorax by stating that it had been examined in Lyons long before. In view of the present state of the thorax, sealed as it is on all sides, the heart could most definitely not have been removed in modern times. It is highly likely, however, that the heart was preserved in a canopic jar, from which a doctor could have removed it for examination. There remains considerable uncertainty, therefore, as to what became of Ramesses II's heart.

As far as the dental studies are concerned, I shall limit myself to repeating what Dr. François Rousières has said. He examined the dental X rays with me and informed me that the new views taken in Paris did not reveal anything of importance compared with the discoveries already made in this area in Cairo in 1975.

When it comes to interpreting the various samples taken from the mummy, we should bear in mind the mummified body's history. The following is a brief summary:

The body was buried over 3200 years ago in the Valley of the Kings at Thebes. In spite of the precautions taken, it was the prey of tomb robbers. In all likelihood, the precious objects and items of jewelry that were placed in contact with the body have disappeared. Violations such as these led the priests of the Twenty-first Dynasty, roughly two hundred years later, to remove the royal mummies to a safer place, thus repeating what they had done for Pharaoh Pinedjem. The priests of Amon did the best they could to repair the damage, and they once again swathed the mummified bodies in wrappings. The mummy of Ramesses II was treated in the same way and finally removed to the hiding place at Deir El Bahari near the Valley of the Kings. It was here that it was discovered in 1881. Even here, however, the royal mummies were yet again subjected to the violations of modern thieves. The mummy was transferred to Lower Egypt, where most of its wrappings were removed in 1886. Unfortunately, its misfortunes were not yet over. The mummy was mishandled, stored in various places, and even exhibited in a standing position. Finally, it was removed to the Egyptian Museum in Cairo, where it remained until coming to Paris.

It is clear that whenever anything is found that is foreign to the actual body itself, either on the surface or inside the mummy, one cannot always attribute it to either the first embalmment or the second treatment carried out when the priests of Amon restored the body. The moment we know that tomb robbers or pollutants may have introduced foreign bodies into the mummy, we can no longer affirm that such bodies date back to ancient times.

After the wrappings were removed 100 years ago, the abdomen was left gaping open at the evisceration orifice. Therefore it was no longer possible to attach any importance to the presence inside the abdominal cavity of whatever material was to be found there, since the material could have come from the surrounding environment. This accounts for my surprise upon hearing the Museum of Anthropology declare that the discovery of morsels of tobacco in the mummy's abdomen was proof that the ancient Egyptians were familiar with the plant long before it was introduced in the West. I am not disputing the fact that a fragment of vegetation was identified, but it seems impossible to me, even if the fragment was found adhering to the resins on the body, to state that it was introduced in ancient times.

There are two reasons why it was easier to take samples at the

Museum of Anthropology than it had been in Cairo. First, we had access to the posterior side of the body, except the points on which it rested, which were quite small because of the pronounced curve of the spinal column. Second, the materials used to stuff the abdominal cavity through the evisceration orifice on the left had been removed so that a degree of access was made possible to the area of the abdomen located near this orifice.

The samples taken provided absolute confirmation of the results I had already published before the mummy arrived in Paris, thanks to the work of Dr. Thérizol. Obviously, the samples from the actual mummy itself were of more interest, for those tiny fragments and debris that had already fallen from the body were less likely to offer the chance of new discoveries. In both the first and second instances, however, proof of biological contamination was established as a result of the work done by J. Mouchacca and J. R. Steffan at the Cryptogamy and Entomology Laboratories of the National History Museum in Paris. With regard to insects, J. R. Steffan showed that traces of dermestids indeed existed, and that there was even a coleopterous parasite of tobacco (*Nicotiana*) present. The latter seemed to have nothing whatsoever to do with the biological damage suffered by the mummy, however. The fungi were mainly held responsible, but a distinction must be made between those fungi that may have launched a parasitic attack on the materials placed in and around the mummy, and those that had affected the mummy itself.

In his article published in *Archaeologia* in February 1978, Professor Balout included excellent photographs of the spores of a basidiomycete that is highly active on cellulose, and therefore likely to have attacked the linen cloth incorporated into what remains of the resinous shield covering the body of the mummy. In the abdominal cavity, another species of fungi was found and identified.

Figures were given listing sixty, then later almost ninety different species identified. These included various types of fungi found on the body, or from the materials surrounding it. Some even derived from inside the wooden case in which the body had lain for several decades.

It has been claimed that eighty-nine species of fungi attacked the mummy of Ramesses II. The differences of opinion between Professor Balout and myself on the significance of this supposed discovery were quite considerable. The disparity of our views became quite apparent at a meeting of the French Egyptological Society (Société Française d'Egyptologie) on September 19, 1978. Professor Balout showed photographs of the fungi and stated that the cultures taken of Ramesses' fungi at the Anthropology Museum had even been put on display.

I mentioned that an article by Professor Balout in *Archaeologia* in February 1978 stated that this impressive collection of fungi in fact originated from four different sources:

—debris from the case containing the mummy
—growths on the cloth swathed around the mummy
—growths on the vegetable matter placed inside the cavities of the mummified body
—the body of the mummy itself

Only the last kind, the fungi from the mummy itself, had any obvious importance. Their full significance was revealed when they came from decaying areas of the mummified body, as was the case with a fungus isolated in Paris. It was located on a deteriorating segment of the posterior side of the mummy's trunk, inaccessible in Egypt. This was also the case with spores identified on samples taken in Cairo before the mummy's arrival in Paris. These were taken from the evisceration orifice of the front side of the abdomen. The discovery of them showed, for the first time, the biological contamination I had pointed out when the body of Ramesses II was still in Egypt.

I draw an analogy between the results presented by Professor

Balout and the following example: Imagine that we have a patient suffering from a sore throat. Not only have we taken a culture from the throat, following classic medical practice, but in addition we have sent the handkerchief into which the patient has expectorated to the laboratory so that the same bacteriological research can be performed on it. Obviously, the laboratory finds numerous microbes on all the cultures, especially in the case of the handkerchief.

Now my question is: How readily would we have believed the results of laboratory tests if the large number of microbes discovered in the laboratory had been put forward as characteristic of the gravity of the infection? Doctors know perfectly well that only those microbes present in the affected areas are to be taken into consideration. That is why I concluded my remarks by saying: "Eighty-nine species are just too many!"

The presence of biological contamination was more than abundantly proven, but we should remember that not all parts of the body had been explored; therefore, the list of biological pollutants is far from complete. Furthermore, samples were taken only from the areas accessible on the surface, so it is quite possible that other species may have existed in places where they have yet to be discovered. We just do not know. Nor shall we ever be able to ascertain all the varieties of living organisms that may have attacked the mummy. This means that the treatment of the biological contamination had to include a method with a large range of effect, operating not only at surface level but also in depth.

The choice of treatment therefore ruled out any method that affected the surface only. In his article in *Archaeologia* in February 1978, Professor Balout states that he rejected gas disinfection, even though the Museum of Anthropology is well equipped for this method. He explains his reasons in the following terms: "We were unable to predict how the mummy would react to a chemical substance. Moreover, the Egyptian authorities, represented at the Museum of Anthropology by Dr. Nakhla, would not consent to its use."

Heat treatment was also unfavorable because there was a risk of severely damaging the mummified tissues, especially the resins. Similarly, treatment at low temperatures was discarded, so Professor Balout tells us, even though it was offered by an American laboratory. Only one solution remained: gamma-ray irradiation.

Before going into the practicalities of this technique, it is worth saying a word about the samples that may be taken aided by endoscopes, from otherwise inaccessible cavities. In this case, Dr. Mustapha Manialawiy took advantage of the endoscopy carried out in December 1976 for medical exploration purposes, to obtain samples of tiny pieces of cloth located on the borders of the abdomen and thorax. The fibers were of different hues, probably dating from the time of embalmment. There can be no doubt that Egyptologists will benefit from the information to be gleaned from the various examinations that may be performed on such samples.

# 19. Irradiation and Conservation

## Gamma-Ray Irradiation

Gamma-ray irradiation was the only sterilization method that could be seriously considered for the mummy of Ramesses II. The specialists at the Nucléart section of the French Atomic Energy Commission had used this method to treat numerous works of art threatened by deterioration from various biological agents. It was they who suggested to the Museum of Anthropology that, with the help of gamma rays, the mummy could be rescued from the living organisms attacking it. I was not surprised to hear this suggestion: not a day passes without a surgeon or doctor using instruments that have been sterilized by gamma rays. Plastic syringes, needles, compresses wrapped in paper, various kinds of probes—all these items are sterilized exclusively by this now common method.

To return to the radiosterilization of the mummy, we should note that eminent specialists had already used the technique with extremely fragile objects: not only Nucléart, but also the Research Center for the Conservation of Graphic Documents at the Natural History Museum. The two institutions were able to provide precious information that was of great help for the mummy.

The project was of great interest to me, so I accepted Professor Balout's invitation requesting my presence at the discussions set to take place at the Museum of Anthropology on November 3, 1976. The representatives of Nucléart in Grenoble, Robert Cornuet and Christian de Tassigny, would also be there. On this occasion the principle of gamma-ray irradiation for the mummy was carefully studied. The following day Christian de Tassigny, Professor Jacques Mignot, Professor Michel Durigon, Dr. Alain Haertig, Professor Jacques Heim, and I met at the Museum of Anthropology.

Research was planned in Professor Heim's laboratory, including taking samples of mummified tissue for the gamma-ray irradiation experiments. Professor Mignot and Doctors Durigon and Haertig were to monitor the histological aspect of the proceedings. A program was drawn up of the experiments to be performed.

There remained, however, one difficult but vital point still to be decided. We had good reason to believe that a sufficient dose of gamma-ray irradiation would destroy all life in the tissue, and hence any contaminating agent active within the mummy. Similarly, we were certain that the structure of the mummified tissues would not be adversely affected—not that this prevented us from planning microscopic checking experiments. However, we still had to decide how irradiation would affect the materials forming amalgams with the mummified tissues, the materials being generally termed "resins." We knew well that, under the effect of gamma-ray irradiation, polymerization phenomena occur, which, although they do not change the chemical nature of certain compounds, can modify their physical characteristics, by inducing a change of color, for example. Clearly it was impossible to risk altering Ramesses II's appearance by employing a gamma-ray irradiation treatment that entailed such consequences. We therefore had to establish beforehand the effect gamma-ray irradiation would have on what are commonly called embalmment resins. It goes without saying that there was no possibility of experimenting on a sample fragment taken from the mummy of Ramesses II. The only viable solution was to perform a trial irradiation of embalmment resins dating from the same period. I was aware that such samples existed in Cairo. They had been taken from remains found in the tombs and probably from the canopic jars in which mummified organs were preserved. I suggested asking the Egyptian Government to donate a small quantity of the resins so that they could be subjected to physical and chemical experiments both before and after irradiation. A month later, I had the pleasure of bringing back the requested samples from Cairo, thanks to the collaboration of the Egyptian Government. They were then transferred to the experimental laboratories at the Grenoble Nuclear Center.

A further problem remained: irradiation might cause damage to the pharaoh's hair, which had been well preserved by mummification and artificially dyed yellow by the embalmers. Professor Balout ordered copious experiments to be performed on the possible effects of irradiation, following which the treatment could then be carried out without fear of the hair falling out. The mummy was subsequently returned to Cairo with the hair intact. Professor Balout gave an intriguing account of the precautions taken prior to the actual irradiation treatment in his article published in *Archaeologia* in February 1978.

Experiments were made on the material sent to the Nuclear Center at Grenoble and to the Nuclear Power Plant at Saclay, on the embalmment resins, and on mummies or fragments of mummies other than Ramesses II. Once these had been performed, it was decided that the mummy could withstand twelve hours and forty minutes of irradiation at 1.8 megarads (i.e., 1.8 million units of absorbed ionizing irradiation). The radiation dose was calculated according to the desired aim: the destruction of the main contaminating agent—fungi. The dose was also sufficient, however, to eliminate the other possible biological agents that might have invaded the mummy, as shown in examples studied by Aidan Cockburn and his team.

The above are the main data on gamma-ray irradiation. There are many theoretical considerations worthy of detailed discussion regarding this method of sterilization. Their importance became evident to me once Operation Ramesses II had been completed and the mummy returned to Egypt. Due to the publicity inevitably given to this unprecedented venture, it was not long before critical remarks were voiced. It seemed, however, that much of the criticism was prompted more by prejudice than by objective reasoning.

Although I had absolutely no contact with Professor Balout regarding Ramesses II from mid-December 1976 onward, I did not lose interest in the mummy. I tried to establish just how well-founded some of the criticism was, while at the same time attempting to interpret the replies to it that appeared in the press, and in a very small number of scientific publications.

Unfortunately, the replies were more often than not couched in terms that suggested triumphant pronouncements rather than cogent arguments. I remained neutral throughout the debate, for having once helped "set the train in motion" as it were, I had no say in determining the route it was to follow. I might add, however, that the details provided by the members of the Atomic Energy Commission convinced me of the excellence of their work. In particular, the information contributed by Robert Cornuet and J. Laizier showed me the care, prudence, and skill they had used when carrying out the procedures.

What convinced me that the mummy of Ramesses II had not been exposed to any risk were the facts I learned about the safeguards taken with the gamma-ray doses applied to it. This was based on the prior experience in the irradiation of works of art, and on data pertaining to the sterilization of meat. Also taken into account were the detailed calculations described by experts concerning the distribution of gamma-ray doses to avoid overheating the mummy. Later on, I shall examine the theoretical observations made in some quarters on this point and the replies they call forth.

## Conservation

The conservation measures mainly concerned the following aspects of museum preservation:

—Closing crevices in the soft tissues. (It was not possible, however, to close the largest cracks such as the one in the abdomen that was over thirty millimeters wide.)

—Rearrangement of the remaining wrappings on the feet, hands, and upper limbs.

—Draping Ramesses II in a linen cloth, leaving the head, neck, arms, and feet bare.

—Placing the mummy in its original coffin brought from Egypt and sterilized at the museum by heat treatment. Professor Balout described the damage to the coffin, which led to its restoration. The mummy can more easily be removed today, since it is now lying on the floor of the coffin, which has handles allowing it to be grasped.

—Installation of the coffin and mummy inside a sealed display case containing an electric sterile-air ventilation system and protection against ultraviolet rays.

Everything, however, had to be sterilized by gamma rays in Paris, then transported to the Egyptian Museum in Cairo and installed there *while remaining sterile*. This was done by use of a well-known system involving an inflatable sterile tent that allows one to manipulate objects inside it with the aid of sleeved gloves. The system requires the instruments and materials needed for the operation to be placed inside beforehand. Thus all the equipment, plus Ramesses II in the case wedged inside the coffin, entered the gamma-ray irradiation chamber at the Saclay Nuclear plant and was then flown intact to Cairo on May 10, 1977.

On arrival, the tent was reinflated, the display case opened, and the mummy's protective packing and wedges removed through the tent. The airtight display case was then closed and the ventilation system set in motion.

The ventilation system was designed to permanently inject air through antibacterial filters and at the same time keep the pressure level inside the case slightly higher than that of the atmospheric pressure outside. It was intended to foil the harmful effects that would ensue if, at some future point, the outside air were to penetrate the case, which might result from a defect in the airtight sealing of the case at the points where it had been joined together. The number of joints was kept to a minimum by the use of two altuglass shells, the upper one forming the ceiling and side walls of the case. The sterilized-air injection system was electrically powered, and a bank of accumulators stood ready for use as a back-up power source in the event of a blackout. A special system of airlocks was devised to ensure that when the antibacterial filters were changed, the interior of the case would remain uncontaminated. It should be noted, however, that this arrangement did not include any form of air conditioning. Neither the temperature nor the humidity level of the air injected into the case was regulated.

Since its return to Cairo, the mummy of Ramesses II has been subjected to the harmful effects of variations in temperature and humidity levels as it was before the journey to Paris for a "treatment." This has been a serious (yet justified) criticism that has been leveled at the system of conservation and preservation designed by one of the officials at the Anthropology Museum in Paris.

# 20. Initial Egyptian Reactions

Even before the mummy of Ramesses II had arrived back in Egypt, and while the main part of the medical investigations was nearing completion, I returned to Cairo, although my stay there had nothing to do with Operation Ramesses II in Paris. While I was there, I saw for myself the extent to which those I met were affected by the French doctors' work: since 1975, the doctors had been studying the pharaoh's remains, and had set in motion the rescue operation. In particular, I should like to mention the appreciative comments made by Dr. Gamal Al Oteify, at that time Egyptian Minister of Culture and Information, who had taken the mummy under his wing.

I had hardly stepped off the plane on November 27, 1976, when to my surprise I found a short article on the front page of *Akhbar El Yom*, one of the two main Cairo daily newspapers, entitled *Ramesses II's Doctor Arrives in Cairo*. In it, I learned that I was to be received by the Minister of Culture—which was indeed news to me—and was reminded of the role I had played in the discoveries made on the mummy of Ramesses II and that of Merneptah.

The following day I met with the Minister. The conversation quickly turned to various aspects of the work done on the mummy in Paris, and the parts in which I had been involved. In order to facilitate the work being carried out in Paris, the Minister right then made two very important decisions that were immediately put into effect. The presence of the Head of Egyptian Antiquities at our meeting contributed to the speed with which the matter was dispatched. I was particularly eager for the Egyptian endoscopist who had collaborated with me earlier to come to Paris, for I wanted him to perform in Paris this special examination of the mummy, which had been initially planned with Professor Balout. In fact, several weeks later, Dr. Manialawiy was sent by his Government in order to explore the abdominal cavity of the mummy. Furthermore, I particularly wanted to bring back to Paris the embalmment resins dating from the period of Ramesses II. It would be a tremendous advantage to have a quantity of resins at our disposal for experimental atomic research. No sooner had I informed the Minister of the importance of such experiments then he ordered what I had requested, to ensure the successful radiosterilization treatment of the mummy.

The next morning I met the President of Egyptian Antiquities and the Head of the Egyptian Museum at the museum. A curator showed me several samples of resins taken from various periods, and I selected the ones that seemed to be of most use. Roughly one-third of Egypt's entire stock of resins from this period was donated to the research program planned by the Atomic Energy Commission at Grenoble prior to the gamma-ray irradiation of Ramesses II's mummy. There could be no doubt that Egypt's generosity in bestowing a large quantity of its last reserves of Nineteenth-Dynasty embalmment resins constituted, more than any speeches or declarations of intent, an act of confidence, a desire for helpful cooperation, and a mark of grateful acknowledgment that were deeply touching.

I was also moved by the satisfaction the Egyptians showed at the television program "A Man, an Event," broadcast eight days earlier on French television, to which I had been invited to present scientific documents relating to various pharaonic mummies including Ramesses II. Among them were the very same X rays of Ramesses II that the Minister of Information had agreed could be published a month earlier in the Egyptian review *Broadcasting and Television*. They also triggered an article that was greatly appreciated in Egypt. Documents dealing with Merneptah were also included in the French television broadcast.

After my departure from Cairo, several articles appeared in the Egyptian press, the most notable in the review *October*, which devoted considerable space—and even the cover story in one issue—to the work of the French and Egyptian doctors and their collaboration. The eminent Egyptian journalist Anis Mansour also praised the project in his article on May 4, 1977, which appeared in *Al Ahram*.

The Egyptian tributes mentioned above were directed toward the collaboration between ten Egyptian and French doctors and dentists. They stand in singular contrast to the sentiments expressed in the French press on the same subject. Apart from a few articles in weekly newspapers and reviews, which objectively presented the facts obtained from careful inquiry, mention was seldom made of the role the doctors played in setting the process in motion, leading to the arrival of Ramesses II in Paris. Nevertheless, it is very clear that the detection of the dangers facing the remains of a brilliant civilization—indeed, of a world heritage—was initially the result of the work of the doctors.

I will always remember how I was asked by the cultural section of the Egyptian Embassy in Paris, shortly before Ramesses II's mummy had been returned to Egypt, to give a public lecture on the contribution made by medicine to the study of pharaonic mummies. It was an extremely gracious tribute on the part of the Egyptians to all the doctors who had opened the way for Operation Ramesses II. This lecture was given on May 23, 1977, at the Guimet Museum at the initiative of Professor Atef Sedki, then Cultural Counsellor at the Embassy. (Today Professor Atef Sedki is Prime Minister of Egypt.)

May 1977 marked the completion of the rescue operation in Paris, which, to all appearances, had gone very smoothly. The reality was somewhat different, however, and a controversy between museum specialists was to ensue.

# Part VI

# UNSOLVED PROBLEMS CONCERNING THE MUMMY OF RAMESSES II

Few people were aware that the gamma-ray treatment, while not appearing to have damaged the mummy, had nevertheless impaired the transparency of the case in which the pharaoh was finally to rest. At first, little publicity was given to this fact, although Professor Balout did make a reference to it during a talk on June 16, 1977, at the Museum of Anthropology. The yellowing of the altuglass case following gamma-ray irradiation was treated as a matter of no great importance, even though the Egyptian authorities rightfully wished to display the mummy in its natural color and not through a tinted covering.

It was simply announced that all scientific documents concerning the rescue operation of Ramesses II in Paris would be published as soon as possible under the auspices of the Museum of Anthropology. During the years that followed this operation, the absence of scientific data had caused the Egyptian authorities much concern and distress because the specialists at the museum took complete charge of the techniques of conservation.

Serious differences of opinion developed between the Egyptian authorities and the French museum specialists concerning the condition of the case in which the pharaoh's body had been sent back to Cairo. Between June 1977 and the beginning of 1979, however, no information was forthcoming on those differences. Nevertheless, Christiane Desroches-Noblecourt and Professor Balout presented the results of the operation with obvious satisfaction, making no reference to the question of the case. Desroches-Noblecourt communicated the results to an audience of medical professionals, as did Professor Balout at a meeting of the French Egyptological Society in September 1978.

Desroches-Noblecourt gave one of the opening lectures at the "Entretiens de Bichat" (a medical convention in Paris) on October 1, 1978, before a professional audience. These cultural lectures usually attract a large audience because of their customary high standard. The subject for that day sounded promising: "Ramesses II, the Miracle-Making Pharaoh."

What a pity it was that the ideas expressed by Desroches-Noblecourt concerning the pharaoh's supernatural powers were, to put it mildly, to be regarded with caution. Her account of the events leading to the mummy's arrival in Paris and medical comments on the subject were totally unfounded.

In this instance a large number of untruths and rash statements were made before a public composed mainly of members of the medical profession. These statements included a correct diagnosis of arteriosclerosis, based on results obtained from an examination of the mummy, but asserted as having appeared when Ramesses II was roughly fifty-five years old. Also featured was the alleged presence of grains of pepper in the nose, discovered by X-ray analysis, although there was no definite confirmation of this. Tobacco was said to be present, stuck to the interior of the stomach, although this organ was in fact never found. This was the main reason I decided to publish a challenge to this account in a medical journal *Le Quotidien du Médecin*, October 17, 1978.

Desroches-Noblecourt presented the rescue operation in Paris under the most favorable light, investing it with her authority while completely ignoring the serious difficulties that had existed for over a year. Some idea of the difficulties was gained several months later when Egyptian discontent was made public.

Egyptian dissatisfaction was in fact reported in the press early in 1979, in particular in the account contained in an Associated Press dispatch:

### "RAMESSES II—WHO FOOTS THE BILL?"
#### By J. M. Garry

The sterile altuglass case in which Ramesses II is enclosed has yellowed and the pharaoh—on which so many French scientists had worked—is not fit to be seen. That is the truth of the matter and French scientific circles are beginning to acknowledge it.

Why did the envelope of this luxury incubator deteriorate? Nobody wants to say. According to some sources, the molecular structure of the material changed under the effects of the gamma rays and the tests to see how the altuglass would react were inadequate.

The company that produced the altuglass disclaims all responsibility; likewise the Atomic Energy Commission which notes that the choice of altuglass was not their decision but that of the Museum Administration (Direction des Musées). The laboratory in Grenoble had the sole task of sterilizing the mummy after the irradiations at Saclay. (These were the test irradiations.) The Egyptians, who had reluctantly parted up with the pharaoh, began to get impatient. Once again, the mummy is housed on the second floor of the Egyptian Museum, Cairo, waiting for a solution to be found. It has been over a year since the museum asked the French scientific team to intervene. This they did by sending a mission, but nothing has happened since.

Meanwhile, the people in charge have changed. Professor Lionel Balout, the head of the Museum of Anthropology who had led the scientific team, has gone into retirement, and in Cairo the official formerly responsible for the conservation of the mummies was appointed head of the museum.

Now as it happens, Mr. Ibrahim Nawawy is one of the Egyptian scientists who had come out against Ramesses II's "rejuvenation cure" in France. This may perhaps explain the impatience he has shown and the fact that the incident—which took place during the treatment—has reached the ears of the general public.

The French authorities are naturally embarrassed by the episode and the main problem is how to find funds to rectify this error. The Natural History Museum has none, nor has the Museum of Anthropology, and the private companies that had eagerly come forward to put their experts at the service of the French team of scientists—such as Xerox—were not disposed to commit themselves to rescue operations.

As there can be no question of transporting Ramesses II to France a second time, the operation will be performed in Cairo. The process envisioned for replacing the altuglass will be to envelop the bubble in a second, larger bubble, also containing a sterile atmosphere. It will be possible to work using airlocks. To perform this operation, however, experts will have to be sent, preliminary studies be made, permission obtained from the Egyptian authorities and—above all—funds provided.

According to the most recent news, as indicated by scientific sources, the nuclear power plant at Saclay is expected to finance the necessary operations.

Articles appearing early in 1979 in the Egyptian press pointed toward Desroches-Noblecourt, naming her as the person responsible for Operation Ramesses II, and toward Professor Balout, the former head of the Museum of Anthropology. The statements made by these specialists—such as the one that appeared in the French newsweekly *Le Point* on February 19, 1979—do not seem to have appeased the Egyptians.

The Egyptians complained that they could not put the mummy on display because of the deterioration of the case and, as they feared, of the mummy itself. That was how the Cairo magazine *Al Musawwar* reported the situation on February 2, 1979. The magazine stressed the fact that uncertainty was heightened by the refusal of the French authorities to provide them with the scientific documents on Operation Ramesses II in Paris.

In reply to such accusations, in the French press we find statements such as the following, made by Professor Balout: "They must be joking, there was never any question of bacteria . . . The whole thing is ludicrous."

# 21. The Mummy

As we shall see, the problems with the mummy are infinitely more complex than this discussion suggests. It would be a mistake to imagine that they can be reduced to a simple question of microbic pollution. Microbic agents obviously existed on the body of the mummy before it was sterilized, as they exist everywhere, and just as obviously they could return to it in the future (in spite of sterilization) if the systems protecting the mummy break down. In any case, a logical and reasonable course of thinking should be adopted, and not the simple or extreme suggestions made by laymen and, alas, so-called experts alike. Even at gatherings of supposed specialists, totally unfounded rumors are often spread. I myself witnessed this with regard to the mummy.

During the discussion following a report I read at an international meeting of experts, I was astonished to hear a very distinguished doctor claim that the fungal infection had recurred on the surface of the mummy. In fact, the mummy was still enclosed in its case, making it impossible, given these conditions, for samples to be taken from it. Only by taking them would one have been able to demonstrate that the infection had indeed recurred. Furthermore, there was no evidence whatsoever of damage of this kind on the exposed surfaces of the mummy. At present, there is nothing to indicate that the gamma-ray sterilization treatment was inadequate in achieving an effective preservation.

Was the treatment excessive? It is easy to suggest that it was—and people have not hesitated to say so—but, here again, the fact remains to be proven.

The first time this question seems to have been raised was at the Second International Congress of Egyptologists in Grenoble in September 1979—more than two years after the mummy had been returned to Cairo. Dr. Peter K. Lewin, known for his collaboration in studies on mummies in Canada and the United States, maintained that a link should be established between the deterioration that can be seen on the exposed parts of the mummy and gamma-ray irradiation. He kindly informed me of his opinion in a letter in which he made the following observation: "Those who have recently seen the royal mummy have, in addition to the opacity of the glass case, noticed obvious cracking in the skin of the mummy, which confirms that biological disintegration is continuing. (In simple language: The mummy was literally roasted.)"

Lewin explained this as the result of the corrosive action of gamma-ray irradiation. Owing to ionization, such action produces substances, among them certain acids, from the natron salts still present in the mummy. These changes result in the production of lime, calcium chloride, and hydrochloric acid, substances that destroy biological tissues.

Regarding these critical observations, I was fortunate to receive the opinion of two members of the French Atomic Energy Commission, Robert Cornuet and J. Laizier, who had devoted particular attention to these problems and to the mummy of Ramesses.

It is interesting, however, to recall the words of the specialists at the Atomic Energy Commission at a meeting of November 3, 1976, arranged by Professor Balout. On that occasion, the address was given by Robert Cornuet, the head of the department responsible for the application of irradiation techniques at the Grenoble Center for Nuclear Studies and his colleague Christian de Tassigny. I had raised the question of whether or not the gamma rays were likely to cause chemical changes in the irradiated material. Christian de Tassigny stated that the only changes likely to take place would be physical ones. He cited the example of a pair of ordinary eyeglasses exposed to gamma rays: In such a case, the glasses lose their transparency and become translucent, and can no longer be used as spectacles. The change is caused by alterations in the position of the electrons orbiting around the nuclei of atoms. To return the eyeglasses to their original state, all that is needed is to heat the lenses. The physical change disappears and their chemical composition remains unaltered.

As far as the mummy was concerned, therefore, the only changes that could take place were physical ones. For example changes in color. That is why it was imperative to perform irradiation trials on mummified tissues from mummies other than Ramesses II, and to experiment on mummification materials, resins in particular.

The atomic specialists' observations prompted me to suggest that the Egyptian authorities be asked to provide France with a sample of mummification resins for this purpose. I knew there was a stock kept in Cairo and as I happened to be going there myself several weeks later, I volunteered to explore the possibility of acquiring some resin. I mentioned earlier that the Egyptian authorities agreed to relinquish some of their tiny stock of mummification resins. What they gave me were samples from the Nineteenth Dynasty in which Ramesses II had lived. One month later, I brought the resins back to France. Experiments were performed on them, which proved that there was no immediate risk in using gamma-ray irradiation. It was at this point that I ceased my involvement with Operation Ramesses II.

Today it is interesting to hear the comments these same specialists at the Atomic Energy Commission make about Dr. Lewin's observations. Apart from the arguments described above, they insist that the irradiation of the mummy was preceded by trials on other mummies involving extremely stringent microscopic checks, both before and after irradiation. These tests were applied to various parts of the body, even the hair. No changes were discovered. It is important also to realize that *Nucléart*, the department of the Atomic Energy Commission responsible for the irradiation of many ancient artworks, had had considerable experience that indicated that the irradiation technique was without risk.

The fact remains, however, that irradiation in gradually increased amounts could, on reaching a certain stage, theoretically liberate ions that might then unite with other ions to form new substances. These might cause deterioration, particularly in fragile mummified tissues. At this point in our hypothesis, the notion of degree comes into play: how important would the formation of a molecule of hydrochloric acid (formed by the union of a chlorine and a hydrogen atom) be in the midst of a mass composed of billions and billions of intact molecules? The new molecule would be nothing more than an undetectable impurity.

It is well known how difficult it is to determine whether foodstuffs have been subjected to gamma-ray irradiation, even though, as in the case of meat, for example, gamma-ray doses are much higher than those used on Ramesses II. That is why the specialists at the Atomic Energy Commission did not regard the potential risk theoretically arising from the ionization effect a danger worthy of practical consideration.

Apart from the possible dangers of ionization, it was also suggested that gamma-ray irradiation could overheat the mummified body. In the sterilization process, the mummy could literally be roasted. In fact, however, the process had been calculated in detail by specialists at the Atomic Energy Commission. They knew perfectly well that mummified tissues, which are dehydrated and extremely brittle, are sensitive to variations in temperature. That is why the total dose of irradiation was spread out over two sessions of six hours and twenty minutes during which each section of the body was exposed to a calculated number of rads (units of ionizing radiations) equal to 100 ergs of energy per gram of matter. I have been told that the quantity of heat received by the mummy did not exceed four calories per gram. When compared with the total twelve hours and forty minutes of irradiation, "the amount of energy infused at a given moment was negligible . . . and in any case, out of all proportion to the variations in temperature (the mummy) had undergone in its display case, even in an air-conditioned museum" (Robert Cornuet and J. Laizier).

Some observers claim to have detected surface deterioration in the mummy. The first hypothesis is that the cracks visible on the exposed parts of the mummy were simply the result of bursting at the points where the mummy was crumbling and had been patched together.

Lesions of this kind may be present now and could appear in the future. This eventually must be anticipated and ought to be examined in the light of the particularly regrettable fact that the display case is not equipped with air conditioning.

# 22. The Display Case

For practical as well as technical reasons, the use of glass in the construction of the display case was ruled out in favor of altuglass, a form of plexiglass. This decision was made in spite of the fact that altuglass is known to yellow slightly after a while, although in the long term it is supposed to lose this tint. Yellowing occurs for complex reasons, among them irradiation, and is also caused by mechanical and chemical factors.

In order to ensure maximum airtightness, both then and in the future, the number of joints in the display case was kept to a minimum by the use of two shells, the upper one forming the side walls and ceiling of the case. The yellowing is most clearly visible in the upper shell of the case. It appears in orangish patches when the walls are viewed from a certain angle. Glistening internal fissures may also be observed.

Although these phenomena were totally predictable and are without danger, some critics immediately hailed them as a disaster—Ramesses II's display case was going to disintegrate because of the cracks in it. Critics also said that this would entail serious consequences for the mummy, which was supposed to remain isolated inside its case, protected from any contamination from the outside.

It was suggested that this phenomenon, particularly evident when seen from certain angles, was similar to that observed in airplane windows. There is no danger of the window disintegrating, even though the forces at work in an airplane are much greater than those applied to the walls of Ramesses II's display case.

I was informed by Robert Cornuet that before the display case was delivered to the atomic plant for irradiation, the upper altuglass shell had been wiped down with a cleaning product. Subsequently the altuglass had been attacked by the cleaning product so that the visible effects of the cracks which in reality were only a result of the incidence of light appeared to be much more serious than they would have if this cleaning agent had not been applied.

The apparent deterioration in the walls and ceiling of the case had no serious practical effect on Ramesses II, although it did impair viewing of the mummy. Experts in Cairo expected the phenomenon to abate, and eventually to disappear, but apparently the anticipated improvement did not occur quickly enough and they were unable to put the world-famous mummy on display. Nevertheless, in the closing months of 1979, the mummy was displayed at the Egyptian Museum in Cairo, following the official opening by President Anwar Sadat of the museum's War and Peace Room, in which the mummy was placed. Professor Ragay El Meligiy, a radiologist and colleague of mine, attended the opening ceremony. Afterward, he wrote telling me that he had not noticed any particular change in the display case.

It is difficult, therefore, to understand the reasons prompting certain French experts in museum conservation to recommend changing the case. The operation could have easily been performed in Cairo with the aid of an inflatable tent. Sterilizing gas would have been injected to decontaminate the entire exterior of the case and inside of the tent. Next the gas would have been extracted and a new case assembled by experts working through the sleeves in the side of the bubble. The operation would, however, have been extremely costly. The price quoted in the magazine *Science et Avenir* (No. 397, March 1980. p. 27) was close to 500,000 French francs. There was also the obvious risk of ending up back at square one—with a case that still looked damaged. In order to prevent this, it was suggested that a second case be placed over the altuglass case, once the latter had been changed.

All these highly costly schemes for perfecting the system seemed to be somewhat farfetched, especially when one realizes that the museum experts in Paris had not even taken the trouble to devise a suitable arrangement for correcting the other, infinitely more alarming, factors causing the mummy to deteriorate: those arising from changes in temperature and humidity levels inside the display case, since the ventilation system, which injects air into the display case, is not isolated from the surrounding atmosphere.

# 23. The Absence of
# Air Conditioning

Earlier, it was stated that variations in the temperature and humidity levels of the surrounding air are extremely harmful to the correct preservation of the mummy. Furthermore, long before the mummy of Ramesses II was transported to Paris, these aspects of museum conservation had been jointly examined by Professor Balout and myself at the Egyptian Museum in Cairo. On November 20, 1975, we both signed our names in a report on this very subject, intended for the Egyptian Government, which I personally submitted to President Sadat. The following was mentioned in the text: "The combined mummy and coffin (with the exception of the cover) will be placed in a transparent case made of altuglass, which is resistant to ultraviolet light. The case will be hermetically sealed and sterilized, and will contain monitoring and regulating devices. It is important that lighting, temperature and humidity levels remain perfectly constant, wherever the mummy is displayed."

These precautions for the museum conservation of the mummy were perfectly reasonable. Indeed, once the mummy was installed in an air-conditioned room at the Paris Museum of Anthropology, where temperature and humidity levels remained constant, the sourish odor emanating from the mummy disappeared after a few weeks. This observation would seem to indicate that the biological decay shown to be taking place was reduced simply by gradually lowering the temperature to 19°C, while maintaining an average humidity level of fifty-five percent.

I should like to point out that these observations were made on a mummy from which the pieces of cloth surrounding it had been removed. This material was left behind in Cairo, along with other pieces of decaying cloth, which until 1975 had filled the mummy's abdomen. These were removed and replaced with fresh cloth before the mummy was sent to Paris. I was present in November 1976 when the fresh pieces of cloth plugging the abdomen were removed. The beneficial effect of almost constant temperature and humidity levels was therefore noted on a mummy without wrappings, save for a few turns around the upper limbs. Contrary to whatever may have been said or written, the mummy never gave off an odor of putrefaction, not even in Cairo, and the link established between this supposed odor and the centers of bacterial activity in the decaying tissues surrounding it still had to be proven.

These considerations, which represent the fruit of experience gained in late 1976, provided ample justification for the imperative tone of the measures described in the report of November 20, 1975, signed by Lionel Balout and Maurice Bucaille. The plans for the mummy's display case were drawn up at the Paris Museum of Anthropology, but they did not contain any provisions to meet these imperative needs, in summary:

—It was advisable to protect the mummy from ultraviolet rays. This was done with the use of altuglass.
—It was vitally important to prevent secondary contamination of the mummy once it had been sterilized with gamma rays. Provided no serious defect developed in the airtight

sealing of the case, which would in any event be coun-
teracted by the slightly higher pressure inside, there was
little to fear in this area. Of course, special care had to be
exercised when the antibacterial filters are changed, to
make sure that the sterile atmosphere was preserved.

—It was also imperative to ensure that the mummy was preserved in a display case in which temperature and humidity
levels remained constant. This absolute necessity was not
respected—an omission that constitutes the most serious
criticism leveled at Operation Ramesses II by museum
conservationists.

It is heartbreaking to see a mummy exposed to the physical dangers inherent in variations in temperature and humidity levels,
especially when one thinks of all the goodwill and technical
expertise that came together to help save it. The installation of
mechanisms to correct such variations could today be performed
without difficulty. The absence of air conditioning left the
mummy prey to deterioration, even though such a system could
easily have been provided.

In view of this, it was hardly being pessimistic to wonder what
the next piece of bad news concerning the mummy was likely to
be. A question mark hung over the fate of the pharoah's mortal
remains, for we had not heard the last of Ramesses II.

# 24. A Survey Carried Out Nine Years Later

Nine years after the return of the mummy to Cairo, I carried out an inquiry into the condition of the mortal remains of the Pharaoh. This was not easy to do. At the time that the French edition of the present work was finished, in 1986, no document written by those who have had or still have the mummy in their care had been published, particularly concerning the result of the rescue operation in Paris. I cannot call a "document" the declarations made by French specialists in museology who used grandiose words to describe a success that was ultimately, in fact, a failure.

In Cairo those responsible for Egyptian Antiquities said nothing, as far as I am aware. Nevertheless, in Egypt several journalists have published unofficial articles concerning the condition of the mummy, such as the one in the review *Al Musawwar* (issue of 2.2.1979). After 1979, the Mummies Room of the Egyptian Museum, Cairo, was closed to tourists. The mummy of Ramesses II was not kept in this room. Many visitors to the museum told me that in a certain room, they saw a piece of thick fabric covering a catafalque-like exhibit with a notice saying that the mummy of Ramesses II lay underneath. No explanation of the deliberate concealment of the mummy was given.

What had happened beneath this cover? I knew something about the case originally constructed for the display of the mummy. The case had turned yellow, a change which Professor L. Balout predicted at a meeting of the French Society of Egyptology, on September 19, 1979: "This yellowing will disappear after one or two years." In fact, during my 1986 inquiry into the damage to the case, M. Claude Picard, the new director of the Society La Calhène which constructed the case, absolutely confirmed what R. Cornuet of the Nuclear Centre of Grenoble had told me several years before: the phenomenon of "stress cracking"—related to the unfortunate use of a cleaning product at the Paris Museum of Anthropology before the gamma ray irradiation—cannot be expected to disappear. Such changes in the plexiglass case were not compatible with the good conditions of display aimed at during the operation concerning the mummy in Paris. Fortunately, the precise purpose of the project planned by the Getty Conservation Institute is to create good conditions of display for all the Royal Mummies of the Egyptian Museum.

The validity of this project for the mummy of Ramesses II cannot be appreciated by those whose only source of information is the book, published in 1985, by the specialists in museology who directed the operation in Paris. In the 1985 book, *The Mummy of Ramesses II* (Editions Recherche sur les Civilisations, Paris), these specialists expressed their smug satisfaction at the success of the operation, so much so that any project to improve the condition of the mummy seemed totally unnecessary. If the operation were as successful as they claimed, then the Getty Conservation Institute project would not have been necessary at all.

In the French edition of the present work, I included a seventeen-page appendix containing comments on the many strange assertions made in *The Mummy of Ramesses II*. I discussed the inaccurate information on the background to President Sadat's decision to send the mummy to Paris, the mummy's stay at the Museum of Anthropology, and the questionable results of certain investigations. In view of the fact that scientific documents published prior to the arrival of the mummy in Paris had been ignored, I felt that I had to speak my mind. My arguments published in November 1987 censuring such misleading statements did not arouse the least protest from the authors involved. As far as the English edition of the present work is concerned, the author has decided to omit this appendix, in order to concentrate on matters pertaining to the future of the mummy and the Getty Conservation Institute Project.

From this point of view, the reason that the rescue operation in Paris failed was clearly the lack of scientific experts advising the specialists in museology who directed the enterprise. Such scientists—having competence for drawing conclusions from medical investigations in the fields of the application—would have been able to point out mistaken ideas. Several weeks after the arrival of the mummy in Paris, I thus realized that I was not in a position to correct decisions which contradicted my knowledge of the mummies based on my examinations of them as a medical doctor. I was therefore relieved when my already limited collaboration in the operation came to an end.

The program initially submitted to the Egyptian and French Presidents was cancelled. According to the initial plan, the display case was to have contained monitoring and regulating devices to maintain perfectly constant temperature and humidity levels. Official commitment to these ideas was formally confirmed in a letter from President Giscard d'Estaing to President Sadat, published in Paris in the newspaper Le Monde (May 9–10, 1976). The letter stated that, "It seems highly useful [to the mummy] to provide new conditions for its display that ensure perfect preservation, particularly concerning hygrometric levels."

In fact, when the mummy was returned to Cairo, the display

case did not contain a single regulator: Temperature and humidity were not controlled at all. The system actually constructed injected ambient air through a ventilation device using a recycling process which was not airtight and which was to be installed in a museum without air conditioning; the aim of this system was to allow the case to be pressurized at a level slightly above that of atmospheric pressure.

Immediately after the return of the mummy to Cairo, there was no danger of contamination by the ambient air introduced into the case, since antibacterial filters had been inserted into the ventilation circuit. The filters which remain effective for four and a half years at the most, should have been replaced every three years, as an extra precaution. In 1986, nine years after the mummy returned to Cairo, the constructor of the case, who was the only one capable of supplying the replacement filters, told me that he had never been asked to change the filters. This means that for years the mummy has been surrounded by humid air from outside the case, which undoubtedly contains microscopic agents of pollution. Such an enclosed atmosphere is highly favorable to the proliferation of fungi on the mummy. At the Paris Museum of Anthropology J. Mouchacca made a study of the fungi which had invaded the mummy and emphasized the seriousness of the poor conditions in Cairo which considerably fostered the proliferation of the fungi. Now that the filters are no longer effective, the contamination of the mummy by the ambient air is inevitable, despite the sterilization of the mummy by gamma rays in 1977.

Professor L. Balout who was responsible for the work carried out in his museum did not write a single word in *The Mummy of Ramesses II* on the serious danger to the future of the mummy, and more generally on the characteristics of the case, the failure to keep the promises made to Egypt, and the final result of the operation. In the book a description of the case is given by the director of the company that constructed it (but he nowhere refers to the severe damage to the plexiglass walls).

By the time I had finished my inquiry in 1986, I reluctantly had to reveal the truth, which meant giving a grim prognosis for the future of the mummy of Ramesses II. I was particularly sorry to note that Mrs. Desroches-Noblecourt, the author of a significant but misleading narrative concerning the mummy of Tutankhamun—described in Part Two of the present book—had dared to endorse an equally misleading statement on the mummy of Ramesses II.

Once the French edition of the present book was ready for publication, I wondered who, and in what country, would take an interest in the rescue of the mummy? Would the medical investigations I had reported be enough to convince people that the mummy was in great danger? Would my arguments stressing the threat be taken seriously, especially when the highly titled persons who directed the operation in Paris had triumphantly claimed that their enterprise had been successful?

# 25. Possible Resolutions Offered by the Getty Conservation Institute

My visit to the United States in spring 1987 gave me a chance to discuss the problems that were threatening the preservation of the mummy of Ramesses II. It was a long visit, encompassing many places in the United States and Canada, where I delivered lectures on several topics, including the medical investigations of mummies, and of course the case of Ramesses II. While in Los Angeles, I naturally thought of what the Getty Conservation Institute had done and was doing for the preservation of antiquities, and particularly for the restoration of the tomb of Nefertari, the favorite wife of Ramesses II. In Marina del Rey, California, in April 1987, I had the pleasure of visiting Dr. Frank Preuser, Director of the Scientific Research Program of the institute. We spoke of the danger threatening the mummies kept in the Egyptian Museum in Cairo, and the failure of Operation Ramesses in Paris. During my talk with Dr. Preuser, I emphasized the disastrous effect of the lack of control of temperature and humidity levels, and the injection of ambient air inside the case. I stressed the fact that formal promises had been made to Egypt by the Director of the Paris Museum of Anthropology, Professor L.

Balout, that monitoring and regulating devices would be joined to the case.

I also noted that, if for any unforeseeable reason this initial plan were not carried out, the use of inert gas and thermic regulation would be substituted. Such a plan would have avoided the need to use gamma-ray irradiation to destroy the biological polluting agents, since the inert gas would itself carry out the decontamination. (Since the discovery of the properties of nitrogen by the French chemist Antoine Laurent de Lavoisier, who died in 1794, the impossibility of life in a nitrogen atmosphere is a well-known phenomenon. For this reason Lavoisier, in French, called nitrogen *azote*, the Greek derivation meaning deprivation of life.)

Thirteen months after my visit to the Getty Conservation Institute in California, I was delighted to hear the official announcement of the measures they had taken after my visit. I learned of them from the newsletter of the Getty Conservation Institute and the reports on a seminar that took place on May 10, 1988. Attending the seminar were the Director General of the Egyptian Antiquities Organization, the Director of Scientific Research, and researchers of the Getty Conservation Institute. The documents reported that starting in September 1987, at the Getty laboratories in Marina del Rey, scientists of the institute and from Egypt conducted an extensive series of tests lasting six months and involving a three-thousand-year-old mummy on loan from the Egyptian Antiquities Organization. The objective was to experiment with the preservation of this mummy from cultures grown from different species of bacteria and fungi. It was shown that these growths of micro organisms were arrested by an atmosphere consisting of nitrogen filling the hermetically sealed case where the mummy was lying. Monitoring equipment registered a complete absence of biological activity inside the case. The scientists of the institute noted that similar results were obtained—in the fight against biological pollution—by the use of nitrogen and other inert gases such as helium, which were able to preserve organic material including the document on which the United States Constitution was originally written and the mummies in the British Museum in London. Moreover, they emphasized the usefulness of establishing a humidity level low enough to halt biological growth, but not so low as to embrittle organic material, and of ensuring a strict control of temperature. A scale prototype of a new type of display case was presented at the seminar, featuring a nitrogen atmosphere and a monitoring system that controlled temperature, relative humidity, and oxygen. The royal mummies housed in the Cairo Museum, which are due to go on display at a new exhibition sometime in the next few years, planned by Dr. Zahi Hawass, Director General of Egyptian Antiquities Organization, could benefit from this conservation procedure.

It is a source of great satisfaction to note how closely the project of the Getty Conservation Institute agrees with what I had previously suggested as an excellent method of preserving the mummy of Ramesses II. Not only the mummy of this pharaoh but all the royal mummies in Cairo are in great danger of deterioration. The Getty project offers a way of solving this problem, and is a program with which I wholly agree.

In May 1989, the Egyptian Museum, Cairo, received the first "Getty" display case. Recently a statement by the President of the Egyptian Antiquities Organization was reported in *Al Ahram*, June 17, 1990, concerning the reopening—programmed for next October—of the Mummies Room of the Egyptian Museum, Cairo. The first stage of the reopening will involve twelve Royal Mummies, among them that of Ramesses II. All of them will be set in a "Getty" display case. The wisdom of the Egyptian decision leads us to firmly hope that the misfortune of Ramesses II in Paris will be rectified.

*July 5, 1990*

# Index

# INDEX

# INDEX

Egyptian Museum, 5, 21, 31, 47, 61–
    64, 166–168, 199, 216, 218, 221–
    222
  environmental conditions in, 19–20
  Mummies Room of, ix–xiii, 4, 13,
    14, 17, 19–20, 26, 27, 64, 174,
    178, 221, 228
Eighteenth Dynasty, 11, 17, 27, 28
Elf Erap, 166
embalmment, 3–14, 85
  equipment for, 4, 5
  on left side of body, 120, 122
  in modern times, 13
  places for, 4
  techniques of, 4–14
  time period for, 7
  trepanations and, 118–120
Emery, W. Brian, 46–47
endoscopic investigations, 5, 59, 87–88,
    91, 108–114, 158, 174, 191
"Entretiens de Bichat," 206–207
epiphyseal ends, 33
"Era of Ramesses II," xviii, 163–164,
    175
*Escherichia Coli*, 80
Exodus, viii–ix, xii, xiii, xvii, 125–160
  in Bible, viii, xi, 106–107, 127, 130,
    139–145, 148–149, 156–157
  in chronology of the pharaohs, 139–
    155
  date of, 57, 139–140, 142–143, 150–
    151
  de Miceli's theory of, 57, 141–142
  de Vaux's theory of, 142–145
  *Habiru* and, 134–136
  hieroglyphic texts and, 130, 134–138
  *Israel* and, 130, 136–138
  Merneptah and, ix, xi, 57, 85, 86, 95,
    124, 127, 136–138, 144–145, 148–
    150, 156–160
  Montet's theory of, 138, 141, 144–145
  pharaoh's health requirements and,
    106–107
  in Qur'an, viii, 107, 127, 130, 133–
    134, 143, 156–157
  Ramesses II and, xii, xvii, 106–107,
    129, 142–152
  Ramesses II-Merneptah theory of,
    148–150
  reasoning methods and, 128–129
  recent discoveries strengthening
    author's theory of, 153–155

thirteenth century B.C. historical data
    and, 145–148
eyes, x, 5, 9–10

Fauré, Clément, 83, 88, 90, 91, 94, 185
Ferly-Thérizol, Madeleine, 79, 173,
    180, 188
fingernails, ix–x, 10
fixatives, 70, 72
food, dental decay and, 101, 103
forensic medicine, xii, 34
forgery, 83
Fouquet, M., 17–18
*France-Soir*, 181
Freed, Rita E., 154
French Egyptological Society (Société
    Française d'Egyptologie), 189, 206,
    222
French National Centre for Scientific
    Research, 176
French Society of Forensic Medicine,
    xiv, 115, 118, 173
French Society of Radiology, xiv, 83, 88,
    90, 173
"Full Story of Ramesses II's Mummy and
    Its Journey to Paris, The," 169–170

gamma-ray treatment, 63, 74, 192–196,
    205, 211–214, 227
Garry, J. M., 207–208
genetics, research in, 80–81
genital organs, 10, 55
Gessain, Robert, 172
Getty Conservation Institute project, ix,
    222, 223, 226–228
gilt shrines, 16
Giscard d'Estaing, Valéry, xiv–xv, xviii,
    169–173, 175, 181–182, 223
Giza pyramids, 15, 25
Goedicke, Hans, 49–50
Gray, P. H. K., 82–83
Grenoble Nuclear Center, 194, 207
Griffith Institute–Ashmolean Museum,
    39–45, 47, 49
Guillerm, Catherine, 92
Gustafson, G., 102

*Habiru*, 134–136
Haertig, Alain, 193
hair, 74, 194
Harris, J. R., 45
Harris, James, 84, 106

# INDEX

# INDEX

# INDEX